Chicano Literature

Twayne's United States Authors Series

Warren French, Editor

Indiana University

TUSAS 433

Chicano Literature

By Charles M. Tatum

New Mexico State University

Twayne Publishers • Boston

Chicano Literature

Charles M. Tatum

Copyright © 1982 by G.K. Hall & Company
All Rights Reserved
Published by Twayne Publishers
A Division of G. K. Hall & Company
70 Lincoln Street
Boston, Massachusetts 02111

Book Production by John Amburg

Book Design by Barbara Anderson

Printed on permanent/durable acid-free
paper and bound in the United States of
America.

**Library of Congress Cataloging in
Publication Data**

Tatum, Charles M.
Chicano Literature.

(Twayne's United States author series;
TUSAS 433)
Bibliography: p. 188
Includes index.
1. American Literature—Mexican Ameri-
can authors—History and criticism.
2. Mexican American literature
(Spanish)—History and criticism.
I. Title. II. Series.
PS173.M39T36 1982 810'.9'86872073 82-1059
ISBN 0-8057-7373-8

Contents

About the Author

Charles Tatum was born in El Paso, Texas, in 1943 and raised in Parral, Chihuahua, Mexico. His mother's family is from the state of Sonora. He graduated with honors from Notre Dame in 1965 and then spent a year on a Fulbright Fellowship at the University of Madrid. In 1968, he received the M.A. degree in Spanish from Stanford University and the Ph.D. from the University of New Mexico in 1971. He has held teaching positions at the University of Minnesota, Morris, and at Holy Cross College in Worcester, Massachusetts. Currently, he is associate professor of Spanish at New Mexico State University in Las Cruces.

Tatum has published scholarly works in the areas of contemporary Latin American literature, Chicano literature, and Mexican popular culture. In 1976, the first edition of his *Selected and Annotated Bibliography of Chicano Studies* appeared. It was revised and significantly expanded into a second edition in 1979. He is coeditor of a collection of essays, *Latin American Women Writers Today,* and editor for the 1977 special issue of the *Latin American Literary Review* devoted to Chicano literature. Since 1974, he has been editor of publications of the *Latin American Literary Review,* a journal of international circulation, which publishes scholarly articles, reviews of recent literature, and original literary works. Tatum is coauthoring a book on the Mexican comic book and is co-editor of a new journal, *Studies in Latin American Popular Culture.*

Preface

At the time I initiated this project there was no book-length study of Chicano literature available. It was with mixed feelings of apprehension and excitement that I approached the challenge of organizing and analyzing this body of literature. Apprehension, because the task had not been done before and there were no models to follow; excitement, because I anticipated making a contribution to the awareness and understanding of Chicano literature. As my study neared completion, both feelings intensified as I realized what I had accomplished and what yet needed to be done. It is now time to let go of my fears and to offer to you the results of my efforts. I introduce you to Chicano literature hoping that you will share my excitement of its vastness and richness and that you will see this study as a small part of the totality of literary scholarship that is burgeoning around this magnificent creative phenomenon.

A few words need to be addressed here to the question of terminology. Both Chicano and non-Chicano scholars have hotly debated which of several labels should be used to identify Americans of Mexican descent. Virtually every monographic study and textbook which deals with this ethnic minority discusses the appropriateness of terms such as Chicano, Mexican-American, Hispano, Mexican, Spanish-American, and Spanish-speaking. This critical history of Chicano literature is no exception, for it is important to establish at the outset the limits of the study and to clarify for the reader who is not familiar with the terminology why I have chosen to use "Chicano" throughout the text. This initial brief discussion will serve to lay the terminological question to rest so that I can move on to the literary focus of the study.

I have chosen the term "Chicano" for several reasons. First, it most accurately identifies the contemporary emphasis of the study and one of the major characteristics of this body of literature, namely, the preponderance of works whose theme is an outcry against the oppression of the rural farmworker and urban *barrio*-dweller. In the political arena, "Chicano" is of recent vintage. Until approximately twenty years ago it was used derogatorily to identify Mexican lower-class immigrants from rural areas and small towns, but with the dawning of the age of political militancy in the 1960s, it acquired a positive connotation. Political activists (and others) began using the term proudly to identify themselves with their Mexican Indian ancestry. Because of the close association between political activism and the practice of literature—many times those who were most aware and involved in political activities were the writers themselves—it is most appropriate to identify the literature I will examine in this study as "Chicano."

A second good reason for using the term is its general wide acceptance by academics as well as by the public. Increasingly, for example, the print and electronic media seem to prefer this term over others. Thus, because it is a term that many Americans of Mexican descent believe best characterizes their values and goals and because it is one that is likely to be recognized most readily by readers, I will use it exclusively in the pages that follow.

For practical purposes, it should be understood that "Mexican-American" is an interchangeable label and is also frequently used to identify this minority group and its literature. It is also important to note that in certain geographical areas individuals resent being called "Chicano," preferring a less politically and sociologically charged term. There is a complex of cultural and historical factors which influence these preferences but it is not in our interest to discuss them here.

Also deserving of a brief discussion are a few other important words which the reader will encounter frequently in the study: Aztlán, *barrio,* and *pachuco.* Aztlán is used to designate the cultural and spiritual homeland of the Chicano in the American Southwest. It derives from the belief that approximately eight hundred years ago the Chicano's Aztec ancestors, responding to the prophecy of one of their gods, left Aztlán to journey southward to establish a new homeland in Mexico's Valley of Anáhuac, the site of present-day Mexico City. The use of the term Aztlán by contemporary Chicano artists, writers, and militants is a recognition and an affirmation of their Indian cultural and racial roots. Further, it identifies the Chicano's sense of belonging to a southwestern culture with a unique history, traditions, and language distinct from those of the dominant Anglo culture. *Barrio* literally translated means urban neighborhood but, like the term Aztlán, carries a deeper emotional connotation evoking generally pleasant memories and images. The *barrio,* a collage of comforting sights, sounds, and smells, is a source of cultural and linguistic continuity for the Chicano who can return to its streets as a retreat from the alien Anglo world. The *pachuco* is a social rebel, a young Chicano male *barrio*-dweller who in the 1940s established his independence through flamboyant dress, language, and behavior. He is generally depicted in Chicano literature as a cultural hero, an individual who has refused to assimilate, defying social convention and challenging both Anglo and traditional Mexican values.

A few words need to be addressed here to the language of Chicano literature. As the reader will find in the following chapters, all the works written prior to about 1850 are in Spanish. From about that point through the first part of the twentieth century we find only a few examples in English. Then after the 1920s to the contemporary period the language of literary expression shifts decidedly to English, perhaps reflecting the loss of native first-language ability and the desire to reach a wider audience. Within the last twenty years, the language of Chicano literature falls into three general trends: (1) many Chicano writers, particularly novelists and short-story writers, write in standard literary English; (2) a significant number of writers use Spanish to express themselves; (3) a third group consists of writers, especially poets and playwrights, whose language is a natural blend of both English and Spanish. Known linguistically as code-switching, this language reflects the spoken idiom of millions of Chicanos. It is too early to discern a pronounced preference among contemporary Chicano writers for English, Spanish, or the unique mixture of the two.

Because of the burgeoning of Chicano literature during the last twenty years, the bulk of this study deals with contemporary literary expression. It is important, however, that the reader have an overview of the development of this literature; consequently Chapter 1 is a synthesis of the history of the Chicano people and Chapter 2 traces the evolution of Chicano literature from its origins in the sixteenth century through about 1960. Each subsequent chapter then focuses on a specific genre since then: Chapter 3, theater; Chapter 4, short story; Chapter 5, novel; and Chapter 6, poetry.

The Selected Bibliography has been especially devised for this book in order to provide the greatest amount of useful information within the limits of the series format. The bibliography is divided into two parts.

The first is a guide to the most useful sources for a general study of the Chicano people and culture; the second is a guide to the growing body of critical writing about Chicano literature, including unusually full annotations of important works using material from what had been conceived as a concluding chapter on the development of a Chicano literary criticism.

This study was made possible through a research fellowship from the National Endowment for the Humanities. I would like to thank the Endowment for its support. The Instituto de Estudios Chicano Latinamericanos and the Arts and Sciences Research Center at New Mexico State University provided funding for the early stages of research and for the typing of the manuscript. Rolando Hinojosa, Nicolás Kanellos, and Sergio Elizondo gave generously of their time to read and comment on portions of this study. I thank them for their many valuable suggestions. Finally I would like to express my appreciation to Gloria Lewis, who typed most of several versions of the manuscript.

Charles M. Tatum

New Mexico State University

Chronology

1542   Alvar Núñez Cabeza de Vaca, *Los naufragios* [The Shipwrecks] (diary).

1598   Gaspar Pérez de Villagrá, *Historia de la Nueva México* [History of New Mexico] (epic poetry). *Moros y cristianos* [Moors and Christians] (pageant-drama).

1822   *Los comanches* [The Comanches] (allegorical drama).

1831   Fray Gerónimo Boscana, *Chinigchinich* (diary).

1881   *Las aventuras de Joaquín Murieta* [The Adventures of Joaquín Murieta] (short fiction).

1910–1929   Benjamín Padilla, "Kaskabel" (humorous vignettes published in southwestern newspapers).

1924–1927   Julio G. Arce (Jorge Ulica), "Crónicas diabólicas" [Diabolical Chronicles] (short satire published in several southwestern newspapers).

1935   Miguel Antonio Otero, *My Life on the Frontier 1865–1882* (memoir).

1945   Josephina Niggli, *Mexican Village* (short stories).

1959   José Antonio Villarreal, *Pocho* (novel).

1963   John Rechy, *City of Night* (novel).

1965   Foundation of El Teatro Campesino.

1968   *El Grito, A Journal of Contemporary Mexican-American Thought* begins publication.

1969   Abelardo Delgado, *Chicano: 25 Pieces of a Chicano Mind* (poetry). *El Espejo. The Mirror* (literary anthology). Raymond Barrio, *The Plum Plum Pickers* (novel).

1970   Tomás Rivera, *". . . y no se lo tragó la tierra"* [. . . and the earth did not part] (novel). Richard Vásquez, *Chicano* (novel). Omar Salinas, *Crazy Gypsy* (poetry).

1971 Alurista, *Floricanto en Aztlán* [Flower and Song in Aztlán] (poetry). Miguel Méndez, *Petegrinos de Aztlán* [Pilgrims of Aztlán] (novel). Ricardo Sánchez, *Canto y grito mi liberación* [I Sing and Shout My Liberation] (poetry). Sabine Ulibarrí, *Tierra Amarilla: Stories of New Mexico. Cuentos de Nuevo México* (short story). Luis Valdez, *Actos. El Teatro Campesino* (collection of *actos* written between 1965 and 1971).

1972 Oscar "Zeta" Acosta, *The Autobiography of a Brown Buffalo* (novel). Rudolfo Anaya, *Bless Me, Ultima* (novel). Alurista, *Nationchild Plumaroja* (poetry). Sergio Elizondo, *Perros y antiperros* [Dogs and Antidogs] (poetry). Rodolfo "Corky" Gonzales, *I am Joaquín* (poetry). José Montoya, *El sol y los de abajo* [The Sun and the Underdogs] (poetry). Tino Villanueva, *Hay Otra Voz Poems* [There Is Another Voice Poems] (poetry).

1973 *El Teatro de la Esperanza. An Anthology of Chicano Drama.* Rolando Hinojosa, *Estampas del valle y otras obras* [Sketches of the Valley and Other Works] (novel). *Revista Chicano-Riqueña* begins publication (literary journal).

1974 Lin Romero, *Happy Songs Bleeding Hearts* (poetry). José Antonio Villarreal, *The Fifth Horseman* (novel).

1975 Ron Arias, *The Road to Tamazunchale* (novel). Angela de Hoyos, *Chicano Poems for the Barrio* (poetry).Estela Portillo, *Rain of Scorpions and Other Stories* (short story). Alejandro Morales, *Caras viejas y vino nuevo* [Old Faces and New Wine] (novel).

1976 Alurista, *Timespace Huracán* (poetry). Miriam Bornstein-Somoza, *Bajo cubierta* [Under Wraps] (poetry). Reyes Cárdenas, *Antibicleta haiku* [Antibicycle Haiku] (poetry). Rolando Hinojosa, *Klail City y sus alrededores* [Klail City and Its Environs] (novel). Ricardo Sánchez, *HechizoSpells* (poetry). Gary Soto, *The Elements of San Joaquín* (poetry). Bernice Zamora, *Restless Serpents* (poetry).

1977 Nash Candelaria, *Memories of the Alhambra* (novel). Sergio Elizondo, *Libro para vatos y chavalas chicanos* [A Book for Chicano Guys and Girls] (poetry). Rafael Jesús González, *El hacedor de imágenes/The Maker of Images* (poetry). Marina Rivera, *Sobra* (poetry).

1978 Gary Soto, *The Tale of Sunlight* (poetry). Luis Valdez, *Zoot Suit* (play).

1979 Angela de Hoyos, *Selected Poems. Selecciones* (poetry).

1980 Sergio Elizondo, *Rosa, la flauta* [Rosa, the Flute] (short story). Miguel Méndez, *Tata Casehua y otros cuentos* [Tata Casehua and Other Stories] (short story). Lucha Corpi, *Palabras de mediodía. Noon Words* (poetry). Nina Serrano, *Heart Songs* (poetry). Gary Soto, *Father Is a Pillow Tied to a Broom* (poetry).

1981 Jim Sagel, *Tunomas Honey* [Only You, Honey] (short story). Rolando Hinjosa, *Mi Querido Rafa* [My Dear Rafa] (novel). Max Martínez, *The Adventures of the Chicano Kid and Other Stories* (short story). Gary Soto, *Where Sparrows Work Hard* (poetry). Alurista, *Spik in Glyph?* (poetry).

Chapter One
Historical Background

While it is acknowledged that the Mexican-Indian tradition constitutes an important part of the cultural heritage of the Southwest, it is the Spanish component that has dominated and is today more clearly reflected in the language, traditions, customs, and values of Spanish-speaking peoples in Texas, New Mexico, Colorado, Arizona, and California as well as in other areas of the country. One of the reasons for this has to do with what Carey McWilliams has called a highly paradoxical aspect of Spanish influence in the New World in general and in the Southwest in particular; that is, although the Spaniards succeeded in transplanting their language, their religion, and many of their institutions, they did so through and at the expense of other groups.[1] Spanish culture was forced on native people who did not do well in the face of this onslaught of a technologically superior culture. Another reason for the dominance of Spanish culture in the Southwest and California is the result of the deemphasis, beginning in the mid-nineteenth century, of the Mexican-Indian cultural heritage by Spanish-speaking people themselves in order to be more acceptable to their Anglo-American conquerors, whose attitude on race was clearly prejudicial.

The history of Spanish culture in the Southwest begins with Alvar Núñez Cabeza de Vaca in 1528, when the expedition of his military superior, Pánfilo de Narváez, ended in disaster. By 1525, the Spaniards had thoroughly explored the southeastern coastline of the United States but they had not made significant inroads into the hinterland. Several explorers had perished trying, including Ponce de León and Lucas Vásquez de Ayllón. Narváez enjoyed little more success as he and his men encountered hordes of insects, disease, hostile Indians, and an uncompromising climate in the Florida Everglades. Discouraged by such odds, the expedition returned to where the ships were anchored

1

but to their great dismay they found they had disappeared. Narváez and his men resourcefully fashioned makeshift rafts using their weapons for tools. They set sail from the coast of Florida, but only Cabeza de Vaca's raft was not lost at sea. He and his men shipwrecked on an island near Galveston, Texas, and from this point he began an eight-year trek across Texas, Kansas, New Mexico, and finally to Mexico City. He lived among Indian tribes for the duration, sometimes as their slave and sometimes as a kind of priest held in high esteem because of his knowledge of medicine.

The much-exaggerated tales of gold that Cabeza de Vaca brought back to Viceroyalty at Mexico City in 1536 spawned many new attempts to explore the Southwest and California. Viceroy Mendoza immediately dispatched an expedition under the leadership of Fray Marcos de Niza, who was accompanied by Estevan, a Moorish slave. Other expeditions soon followed hot on the trail of the fabled Seven Cities of Cibola that Estevan purportedly sighted and reported back to the viceregal capital. Coronado set out in 1540 to seek the Seven Cities, only to find dilapidated little Indian villages. Even the Pueblo of Acoma, situated on a flat-topped mountain, was a far cry from the visions of streets paved with gold and jewel-laden natives that had inspired further exploration of the Southwest after Cabeza de Vaca. Undaunted, Coronado proceeded across the plains into Kansas in search of the Gran Quivira, another chimera that clouded the Spaniard's view of reality. Like the Seven Cities, the Quivira turned out to be a modest collection of Indian mud huts.

Meanwhile, while Coronado was pillaging Indian settlements and killing nonhostile natives in retribution for being led astray on his quest of treasure, Juan Rodríguez Cabrillo was exploring the west coast of Mexico. In 1542 he discovered the Bay of San Diego, and by 1602 much of the coast of California as far north as Monterey had been explored and charted by the Spanish.

Others who followed Coronado into the Southwest were Francisco de Ibarra, who in 1567 declared the land traversed by the Río Grande to be "a new Mexico"; Francisco del Cano, Francisco Sánchez Chamuscado, and Antonio de Espejo continued further explorations in 1583. In 1598, the Viceroy of New Spain commissioned Juan de Oñate to claim the land to the north in the name of the Spanish crown. He successfully settled most of what is today New Mexico and opened up much of the rest of the Southwest for exploration and eventual settlement.

The Indians in the Upper Rio Grande Valley did not welcome the alien culture and religion and expressed their great displeasure in 1680 by rising against the Spanish invaders, driving them back to El Paso. The Pueblo Revolt succeeded in keeping the Spanish out of Indian lands for twelve years; in 1692 Diego de Vargas once again pacified the pueblo peoples and established settlements along the river valley from southern Colorado to El Paso.

In southern Arizona and northern Sonora, Father Eusebio Francisco Kino founded the mission of San Xavier del Bac in 1700 and set about the task of converting the Indians and charting the Colorado River from the mouth of the Gila to the Gulf of California. Almost three-quarters of a century later, Juan Bautista de Anza led an expedition from northern Sonora across the desert to what is today San Gabriel, California. He later went on to Monterey and San Francisco, where he founded the presidio.

By the end of the eighteenth century, the Spanish had established a string of missions the length of the coast of California from San Diego to San Francisco, had founded many settlements in New Mexico, and had begun important pueblos in Texas and Arizona. But no sooner had the Spanish crown consolidated its gains in the Southwest and California than it lost them. In 1810, Mexico began its long and bloody road to independence which culminated in 1821 with the coronation of Agustín de Iturbide as Emperor. Administratively, the former Spanish colonies became official territories of the new Mexican government. One important change that occurred was the desire on the part of Spanish-speaking Californians, New Mexicans, and Texans for more power and influence in the affairs and policies of the Mexican government that affected the northern territories.[2] Sectionalism and bitter political fights developed, particularly in California, where politicians spoke ominously of separation from Mexico. Distance from the Mexican capital and indifference on the part of Mexican officials exacerbated the alienation which had already begun to fester during the later years of Spanish rule. The territories had not been prepared for self-government, however, nor did they form a cohesive power base to separate successfully from Mexico. Dissension was rampant among the northern Mexicans, a situation which greatly facilitated the American occupation during the next twenty-five years.

Chicano historian Rodolfo Acuña characterizes the period from 1820 to 1850 as the conquest of the Southwest by Anglo-Americans.[3] In taking Mexico's northwestern territory, the United States committed many acts of violence against Mexico including the murdering of her people, the raping of her land, and the plundering of her possessions. This period in the history of American foreign relations is a sad one for it reflects the most extreme forms of expansionist philosophy and left a legacy of hatred and deep suspicion that remains strong today among the Chicano population in this country and among Mexicans to the south.

Beginning with the founding of the first settlement of San Felipe de Austin in Texas in 1821, Anglos steadily flowed into Mexican lands for the next quarter of a century. Texans, under the leadership of Stephen F. Austin, pressed the Mexican government for autonomy and then independence. After the Mexican victories at the Alamo in San Antonio and Goliad, Texans won an impressive battle at San Jacinto in 1836, and later that year Sam Houston was elected president of the newly formed Republic of Texas.

Events in Texas generated much anti-Mexican sentiment throughout the United States and prepared many Americans to accept their country's expansionist war against Mexico of the mid-1840s. On 13 May 1846, Congress declared war on Mexico, which ended two years later with the defeat of the Mexican forces and the proclamation of the Treaty of Guadalupe Hidalgo in 1848. In this treaty, Mexico accepted the Río Grande as the Texas border and ceded to the United States the present-day states of Arizona, California, New Mexico, Utah, Nevada, and parts of Colorado in return for $15 million. Four years later, in 1852, Mexico sold part of New Mexico and southern Arizona to the United States under military threat.[4] The occupation of the Southwest and California was now complete.

The rights of Mexican citizens in the newly acquired territories were supposedly protected under the provisions of the Treaty of Guadalupe Hidalgo, but in fact these protections were substantially ignored by the American government. For example, Article IX guaranteed Mexicans who elected to stay in the United States "the enjoyment of all the rights of citizens of the United States according to the principles of the Constitution; and in the meantime shall be maintained and protected in the free enjoyment of their liberty and property, and secured in the free exercise of their religion without restriction."[5] Rodolfo Acuña, Carey McWilliams, and others have made a convincing argument that, with the exception of the free exercise of religion, Mexicans' constitutional rights and guarantees were systematically violated during the next hundred years.[6] The practice of language and customs were denied, properties in the form of land grants were taken away through legal and illegal means, discrimination in education, housing, and employment is a matter of public record, etc. Specific cases of cultural eradication through lynchings, and other forms of racism against Chicanos are amply documented elsewhere.

A few examples will serve to illustrate this tragic history of abuse. In their book on the Texas Rangers, Julián Samora, Joe Bernal, and Albert Peña assess the popular myths and legends that grew up around this impressive constabulary. They show how the Texas Rangers evolved into a conservative and elite group charged with carrying out repressive state policies against the Chicano population. Originally established in 1823 as a paramilitary force to rid the Texas territory of both warring and peaceful Indians, they concentrated their efforts in the 1840s and 1850s on harassing Mexican inhabitants. The authors observe:

The Texas Revolution and the Mexican-American War provided justification for Ranger zeal in ridding the Texas territory of thousands of Mexicans and for terrorizing into submission those who survived. Once Texas earned statehood in 1845, all those "citizens"—so called Mexican-Americans—residing within the new state boundaries were doomed to an existence of inequality, poverty, maltreatment by Ranger lawmen, and a judicial system that had no justice for the Mexican-American. The "crime" of these people was simply that they had been born Mexican and lived north of the Río Grande; for many the punishment was instant, often whimsical killing at the hands of the Texas Ranger.

The seeds of Mexican-American distrust, bitterness, and fear of the Texas Ranger lawmen were planted in the fertile region along the border between Texas and Mexico. Those seeds have been nourished by the Texas Rangers in their treatment of Mexican-Americans for over 120 years.[7]

In New Mexico, the Anglo-Americans' systematic theft of land grants from Mexican owners constitutes a sad page in that state's history. Acuña describes the methods used to carry out the massive transferral of land:

1. The superimposition of Anglo-American laws and administrative rules upon the Spanish-speaking majority. Many of these laws and rules were antithetical to the Mexicans' traditions and therefore were not understood.
2. Anglo-Americans taxed the Mexicans' land heavily. Many Mexicans who did not have the capital to pay these taxes saw their land sold at auction.
3. The new Anglo-American system made access to capital imperative, but because Anglos also owned most of the lending institutions, Mexicans were denied access to the source of capital or were charged excessive interest rates.
4. The lands and natural grasses of New Mexico were destroyed by overgrazing, a practice of large cattle ranchers and speculators. The small Mexican rancher soon began to disappear.
5. The U.S. government made large tracts of land available to corporate agriculturalists which drove the small Mexican farmer out of business. Also under reclamation projects, the communal villages no longer had priority in water usage as they had under Mexican law.[8]

A more recent example of Anglo-American racial discrimination against Chicanos is the famous Sleepy Lagoon case in Los Angeles in 1942. The local press had sensationalized the activities of a Chicano gang and the police consistently violated their rights during the gang's protracted trial for the alleged murder of another Chicano. Harsh sentences were passed against the defendants but they were later overturned by the unanimous decision of the Second District Court of Appeals. A related incident involved servicemen on furlough in the Los Angeles area in 1943. After a period of increased tensions between soldiers and Chicanos, one evening sailors went on a rampage in the Chicano community, destroying property and wantonly assaulting Chicano youth. The Los Angeles police did little to abate the situation.[9]

It would be false to view the invasion and occupation of the Southwest and California as a process that Mexicans and Chicanos did not resist. A close examination of the historical events from the 1850s through the 1960s clearly shows that the Anglo conquest was not bloodless and that the resident Spanish-speaking population did not stand by passively as the foreign culture was superimposed upon its own. Notable foci of resistance are the so-called Chicano bandits who spearheaded guerrilla warfare activity against the Anglos throughout the latter half of the nineteenth and the early twentieth century.[10] In Texas, Juan N. Cortina, popularly known as the "Red Robber of the Rio Grande," led a band of men with a definite ideology and organization. They made many successful raids against Anglo military and quasi-military forces from about 1859 to 1875. Gregorio Cortez was another social rebel who was a thorn in the side of Texas authorities for almost a quarter of a century after the demise of Cortina. In New Mexico, Elfego Baca became a defender of his people during the last part of the nineteenth century. At first operating outside of the law, Baca eventually became a United States marshal and later a lawyer. Two figures stand out in California history as symbols of anti-Anglo resistance: Tiburcio Vásquez and Joaquín Murieta. The first is commonly portrayed as a criminal by Anglo folklorists and historians, but Chicanos even today consider him a hero. From about 1859 to 1874, Vásquez robbed stages, attacked trains, and held up wealthy Anglos. While he was pursued by authorities from Los Angeles to Santa Barbara, the Mexican population protected and adored him. Joaquín Murieta is also seen as a legendary hero who defended his people against exploitation and other forms of abuse.

In addition to the activities of the five Chicano rebels discussed above, there are a number of other outstanding examples of resistance to Anglo oppression. Rodolfo Acuña identifies the 1878 El Paso Salt War as a people's revolt that was clearly racial and caused by extreme economic exploitation.[11] Early on in the occupation of New Mexico, influential New Mexican patriots such as Tomás Ortiz, Colonel Diego Archuleta, and the controversial Catholic priest Padre José Antonio Martínez conspired to drive the Anglos out of the Mexican province. An ill-fated revolt stimulated by these rebels occurred in northern New Mexico in 1846. Although it was easily crushed by the occupying army, it did serve as a source of inspiration for future resistance in this area.[12] Later in the century, Spanish-speaking New Mexicans again resisted in the form of Las Gorras Blancas [The White Hats], a paramilitary and political organization which operated in San Miguel County in northeastern New Mexico. The defense against Anglo oppression manifested itself in the journalistic protests which issued forth from the many Spanish-language newspapers published throughout California and the Southwest. One example is *El clamor público* [The Public Outcry], published in Los Angeles. Under the aggressive editorship of a young Chicano, Francisco P. Ramírez, the newspaper condemned Anglo injustice and called for the full participation of Californios in governmental processes.[13]

Most of the Mexicans who immigrated to the United States in the late-nineteenth century and the first quarter of the twentieth century worked in mines, on the railroads, and in agriculture. It was in these areas that the Spanish-speaking working population was most dramatically able to express its resistance to economic exploitation.[14] In large part, these efforts were initiated by Ricardo Flores Magón, a Mexican intellectual who in 1906 crossed over to the United States, where he continued publishing his radical newspaper *La regeneración* [Regeneration]. Although he was eventually jailed and mysteriously died in his prison cell in 1922, his impact on the struggle for justice within the labor movement was deeply felt. As a result of his efforts and those of other activists, Mexican and Chicano agricultural workers organized a number of unions and initated strikes on several occasions during the turbulent years of the Depression and afterwards. Examples of work stoppages are the berry strike of 1933 in El Monte, California, the San Antonio pecan sheller's strike of 1938, and the DiGiorgio strike at Arvin, California, in 1947.

The founding of economic, educational, and political associations by Mexican immigrants and the resident Chicano population was an effective way of combating the alienation and isolation and of fulfilling the social needs of Spanish-speaking communities.[15] The early form of these associations was the *mutualista*, which usually arose spontaneously and provided a particular social service. While early organizations sought to promote good will with Anglos and to improve the Mexicans' image, later associations were established to protect them against injustices such as deportation. La Liga Protectiva Mexicana (The Mexican Protective League) and La Orden de Hijos de América (The Order of

Sons of America) are examples and predecessors of later more outspoken organizations such as LULAC (League of United Latin American Citizens) formed in 1928 and the American GI Forum, established after the Second World War for the benefit of Chicano veterans who experienced discrimination in employment.

During the decade of the 1960s, the resistance against Anglo exploitation and discrimination became more militant and more focused due to the general atmosphere of discontent in this country combined with the cumulative frustration of both urban and rural Chicanos because of decades of treatment as second-class citizens. The Chicano population had become progressively more urbanized forming a large segment of the blue-collar working class competing for jobs in industry. In addition to experiencing discrimination in this area and in the trade union movement, urbanized Chicanos were also becoming more acutely aware of the inadequacy of the educational system to deal with their particular cultural and linguistic needs and were progressively more disillusioned with their efforts to gain fair treatment in housing. One perceptive social critic summarizes this complex of feelings and circumstances in the following way: "Anguished by the lack of social mobility, frustrated by insensitive economic terms which festered discrimination and racism, and exploited in economic terms, the Chicano community engaged in a total evaluation of its relationship to the dominant society."[16] This evaluation process coincided with the discontent among much of the general population which was reflected in growing opposition to the Vietnam War, the outbreak of mass urban violence and rioting, the growth of the New Left, and the rise of Black Power.

In addition to the impact of these events on the formation of a new Chicano political consciousness, several others took place in the mid- and late 1960s which led to the coalescence of a Chicano Movement. On 15 September 1965, the National Farm Workers Association voted to support the Filipinos in the Agricultural Workers Organizing Committee in their strike against the grape growers of the Delano area.[17] This was the first step in the long and successful César Chávez–led campaign to organize Chicano farmworkers in California and the Southwest. In October 1967, Chicano activists boycotted and picketed the hearings of the Mexican-American Affairs Cabinet Conference (that President Johnson had initiated) at El Paso—Chicano leaders such as César

Chávez, Reies López Tijerina, and Rodolfo "Corky" Gonzales had not been invited. In March 1968, Chicano students, protesting racism and discrimination in public education, walked out of five Los Angeles high schools. In 1967, the Brown Berets and other militant *barrio* groups began to be formed in cities throughout the Southwest and California, and student organizations such as the Mexican American Youth Organization (MAYO) and the Chicano Student Movement of Aztlán (MECHA) were established on college campuses. In New Mexico, Tijerina gained national prominence in 1966 and again in 1967, when his Alianza Federal de Mercedes (Federal Alliance of Land Grants) organization occupied parts of the National Forest lands in order to bring to public attention the legitimate land grant claims of Chicanos. In 1970, José Angel Gutiérrez (one of the founders of MAYO) and others established La Raza Unida party (LRUP) as a vehicle to achieve political self-determination independent of the two major political parties.[18] In the same year, the LRUP won municipal elections in several communities in south Texas. In 1966, Rodolfo "Corky" Gonzales had founded an urban-based militant organization, the Crusade for Justice, in Denver, and in 1969 held the First Annual Chicano Youth Conference, which brought together Chicanos from all over the country for a frank exchange of ideas on liberation and political activism. El Plan Espiritual de Aztlán (The Spiritual Plan of Aztlán) emerged from this historical meeting. In this document, the participants at the conference affirmed the importance of cultural nationalism and placed great emphasis on spiritual regeneration. They saw Chicano unification in terms of culture rather than within the Marxist framework of class struggle.[19] The artist was seen as playing a vital role in extending the political consciousness of his audience and in heightening its awareness of the world.

Along with the political activities of the various activists and organizations, a number of important cultural and artistic events were also taking place during the decade of the sixties. While no well-defined group of intellectuals or artists had organized into a movement or school with a discernible identity, there was significant activity in various areas of the Chicano world.

Of paramount importance were the many Spanish-language newspapers—fifty at one point—that carried news of a social and political nature as well as creative literature and occasional short reviews.[20] These newspapers were distributed in *barrios* and rural areas throughout the Southwest and California and served to create a cultural consciousness among average Chicano readers, perhaps never before achieved.

Parallel to these popular publications was the establishment of literary journals and informal associations of writers. Tomás Ybarra Frausto points out that the "earliest and most historically significant group which functioned as purveyor of the new Chicano aesthetic was 'El Grupo Quinto Sol' established in Berkeley, California, in 1967."[21] *El Grito: A Journal of Contemporary Mexican American Thought* was launched in the same year. It published creative literature and important evaluative studies in the social sciences, all from a Chicano perspective. In 1969, some of the same writers and intellectuals—Octavio Romano, Nick Vaca, and Herminio Ríos—who had founded the journal established Quinto Sol Publishers and published *El Espejo/The Mirror,* the first comprehensive anthology of contemporary Chicano literature. Other literary journals that were important in developing a Chicano artistic consciousness were *Con Safos* and *El Pocho Che.* The first adopted a defiant tone, establishing itself as an alternative publication, an outlet for writers who had a positive vision of urban *barrio* life. The second expressed the views of a San Francisco Bay-area militant art group which was "formed out of political struggle, was nurtured by the spirit of urban barrio life and sustained an ongoing dialectic between artistic and political praxis."[22] It is important to note that Chicano writers played an essential role in the creation and development of the sociopolitical and cultural consciousness that formed the base of the Chicano Movement during the 1960s and 1970s. This has not always been the case, as we shall see in our discussion of the origins and evolution of Chicano literature in the pages that follow.

Chapter Two

The Origins and Evolution of Chicano Literature from the Sixteenth Century through the 1950s

Introduction

It is generally accepted that the origins of both American and Latin American literatures are found in writers who are not, strictly speaking, American or Latin American. A cursory examination of the standard histories of American literature reveals that its beginnings include English-born writers such as John Smith, William Bradford, and Nathaniel Ward. Regarding Latin American literature, both histories and anthologies almost always encompass the Spanish chroniclers of the New World as well as indigenous Aztec, Mayan, and Incan writings. In a similar way, our discussion of Chicano literature will reach back to the sixteenth century, well beyond 1848, which is generally considered to be the beginning of Chicano history. We will discover rich literary oral and written traditions in each of the major genres that reflect the vitality and tenacity of the Spanish-speaking population of the Southwest and California. These traditions have endured and prospered for over four hundred years to form the broad base of contemporary Chicano literature that will be discussed in subsequent chapters.

Drama and Theater

While there is no evidence of professional theater—that is, works presented by professional acting companies to a regular theatergoing audience—until the late eighteenth century, the Hispanic Southwest does have a long tradition of folk drama—nonprofessional community theater—that can be traced to the sixteenth century.[1] The first record of folk drama is found in Gaspar Pérez de Villagrá's long epic poem, *Historia de la Nueva México* [History of New Mexico], in which he recounts the history of the founding of New Mexico. He describes how on 30 April 1598 Don Juan de Oñate and his men paused among the trees on the banks of the Rio Grande somewhere near the present site of El Paso to witness the performance of a play written by Captain Farfán, one of the members of the expedition.[2] Villagrá's account of the play is sketchy; all that can be ascertained is that the soldiers themselves were the actors. We know nothing of the dramatist himself or of the content of the work, but it is safe to surmise that it probably took the form of a religious thanksgiving.

We know more about the second dramatic production in the Spanish Southwest which was performed on either 10 July or 8 September 1598 in the plaza of San Juan de los Caballeros, the first Spanish capital in New Mexico. Villagrá records the festivities surrounding the dedication of the church, including the performance of the age-old Spanish pageant-drama *Moros y cristianos* [Moors and Christians].[3] Perhaps the Spaniards wanted to warn the Indians who witnessed the dramatic proceedings of the consequences of resistance, for the play is a reenactment of the routing of the Moorish infidels by Christian knights. Performed on horseback, it must have been all the more impressive.

Mary Austin, one of the first scholars to explore Spanish folk drama in the Southwest, maintains that in addition to *Moros y cristianos,* many other plays made the journey from Mexico to the northern territories.[4] She claims that already in circulation were numerous versions of Spanish medieval mystery plays and some of biblical derivation. Perhaps the oldest is a version of *Los reyes magos* [The Three Kings], which is a part of the Mystery of the Magian Kings dating from the thirteenth century. The conquering Spanish used this and many other religious plays, or *autos* as they were known in Spain, to aid in the process of converting the Indians all over the New World, including the Southwest. In the absence of a common language, pantomime and mimicry were utilized as the missionaries adapted the *autos* to their

particular needs.[5] Thus the Spaniards had their own presentations in
addition to the religious plays directed to their Indian audience, and
both circulated widely throughout all of Mexico and the Southwest.
Not all Spanish-language folk drama written and performed in the
Southwest and California was religious. During the latter part of the
eighteenth century and during the nineteenth century, there are excellent examples of secular folk plays. These include *Los comanches* [The
Comanches], an allegorical drama staged in New Mexico in 1822 to
celebrate Mexican Independence, and *Los tejanos* [The Texans]. In
addition, there are records of theater troupes who traveled throughout
the Southwest and California during this period.

Los comanches is a heroic drama of the last quarter of the eighteenth
century—written after 1777 and before 1800—based on a campaign
against the Comanche Indians between 1777 and 1779.[6] Up to 1777,
the Comanches had raided Spanish settlements as well as other Indian
tribes in the Southwest. In New Mexico, Galisteo, Taos, and Tomé
were the sites of particularly bloody massacres, and it was after the last
that an expedition under the command of Don Carlos Fernández set out
to end these attacks. The sound defeat of the Indian forces forms the
base of the play. A later defeat in 1779 of another band of Comanches by
Juan Bautista de Anza is also referred to. Although it is difficult to
assign authorship of the play, it may have been written by Don Pedro
Pino of Santa Fe, one of the members of the first expedition, along with
Don Carlos Fernández, the leader, and Juan de Padilla.[7] The language
is the simple, direct Spanish of the eighteenth century without much
adornment or eloquence. The versification consists of 515 octosyllabic
verses and the rhyme scheme is mostly irregular assonance and blank
verse. Don Carlos Fernández and Cuerno Verde, the Indian leader who
was killed in 1779 by de Anza, are the main characters although other
Spanish and Indian figures make briefer appearances. Cuerno Verde is
characterized unsympathetically as an arrogant, boorish man who
terrorizes the land with his band of renegades. Don Carlos, on the other
hand, firmly opposes this "uncivilized heathen" with the best Spanish
qualities of faith in a Christian God and a keen sense of justice.
Dialogues tend to be too long and grandiloquent, yet the play has a
dramatic force in its simplicity.

Another New Mexican dramatic composition is *Los tejanos,* believed
to have been written between 1841 and 1846.[8] Like *Los comanches,* it,

too, is based on a historical event, the defeat and capture of the Texan expedition to New Mexico in 1841 by the soldiers of General Manuel Armijo. General Hugh McLeod commanded what is well known as the Texas–Santa Fe Expedition. The play focuses on the capture of McLeod, but many of the events which took place before are also included. The dramatic work is not historically accurate in all instances; however, enough background is given to make it an interesting historical document as well as a literary piece. It is possible that the author was trying to present in a patriotic way a composite picture of the New Mexican victory over the Texans, who were considered foreign invaders and a definite threat to the autonomy of Spanish-speaking New Mexico. It is no coincidence that the aggressors are Anglo-Americans and that the defenders are Mexican, a fact that reflects the fear that the latter had of their expansionist neighbors. After all, the Texas-Mexican War had just ended, and the Battle of San Jacinto was certainly fresh in the minds of the New Mexicans. Like *Los comanches,* the meter of the 497 lines of *Los tejanos* is the popular assonanced octosyllabic verse.

The earliest reference to Spanish-language professional theater dates from 1789 in California, but, as Nicolás Kanellos has documented, it is not until the 1840s that we can be sure that such theater existed.[9] By 1860 the professional theater was so firmly established in San Francisco that Mexican theater companies began to make regular visits to that city. One of these companies was the Compañía Española de la Familia Estrella (The Spanish Company of the Estrella Family), whose cast consisted of Mexican and Spanish actors. This professional troupe would appear on Sundays during a three- or four-month season to a group of regular theater subscribers. Romantic melodramas by Spanish playwrights were of greatest popularity, but the company would occasionally perform Mexican and Cuban works as well as a variety of other shorter dramatic pieces with musical and humorous content. Gerardo López del Castillo, a Mexican actor with a solid reputation in Mexico and other Latin American countries, was the troupe's central figure and later its director.

Los Angeles was another West Coast center of theater activity.[10] The existence of professional theater companies can be traced to as early as the 1860s; by the 1870s the Spanish-language community of this city already had its own theaters. Two companies regularly gave dramatic performances in these theaters, and between 1873 and 1882 both of them toured the Southwest from Los Angeles to Tucson and even appeared in some northern Mexican cities.

There is also evidence of professional theater activity in other Southwestern cities, especially in Texas, late in the nineteenth and early in the twentieth centuries.[11] After 1900, perhaps as many as twenty-five professional Mexican troupes could be found touring in Texas. During the Mexican Revolution from 1910 to 1920, many companies left Mexico to set up permanent residence in the Southwest. They became active in San Antonio, Houston, Victoria, and other Chicano population centers in Texas and, to a lesser degree, in New Mexico and Arizona.

Theater outside of the Southwest and California is another example of the vitality of Chicano literary expression prior to the 1960s. Nicolás Kanellos has made a valuable contribution in this area with his studies of Mexican theater in the Midwest. One such study focuses on the theatrical activities of the Chicano community in East Chicago, Indiana, during the 1920s.[12] This urban center experienced a rapid influx in the 1920s and the 1930s of Mexican immigrants and Chicanos from the Southwest, both groups drawn to the area by the promise of employment in the booming steel industry. At the same time, intellectuals and professionals, many of them refugees from the Mexican Revolution, were instrumental in founding societies for the preservation of their cultural identity. One in particular, the Círculo de Obreros Católicos "San José" (The "San José" Circle of Catholic Workers), created a drama group, El Cuadro Dramático (The Dramatic Group), which produced plays for entertainment and education of the community during the 1920s. Records show that the community participated actively in the dramatic productions as actors, prompters, scenographers, musicians, ushers, etc. In addition to amateurs, professional Mexican actors were also common. The Cuadro Dramático produced both European and Latin American plays. Contrary to popular belief, it was not the arrival of motion pictures which brought the activities of this group to a close, but the financial disaster of the Depression and the mass repatriation of Mexicans.[13] Not until the 1940s and the 1950s did East Chicago exprience a resurgence of Spanish-speaking theater.

Other theater groups that enjoyed success in this area as well as in Gary, Indiana, were the Cuadro de Aficionados de Gary (The Gary

Theater Devotees), the Arcos family, and the Cuadro of the Cruz Azul Mexicana Benefit Society.[14] Both Gary and East Chicago were also toured by professional companies presenting a variety of different dramatic forms. The evolution of Chicano drama and theater from the sixteenth century through the middle of the twentieth century does not follow a neat pattern but instead includes a wide variety of sources, themes, and styles: secular and religious folk drama, allegorical and historical plays, community and professional theater. This rich combination is a strong manifestation of the richness and vitality of Hispanic literary expression in the Southwest, California, and elsewhere throughout four and a half centuries.

Prose—Folk Tales

Like theater, Chicano prose has a rich folk tradition rooted in the traditional Spanish and (later) Mexican tales that were passed on orally from generation to generation from the arrival of the Spanish in the sixteenth century up to today. Folklorists such as Aurelio E. Espinosa, Juan B. Rael, Aurora Lucero-White Lea, and Elaine Miller have collected and analyzed these tales, many of which are still a part of a thriving storytelling tradition in rural areas such as northern New Mexico and southern Colorado.[15] Although most of the tales that have survived have undergone many changes, their similarity to original Peninsular Spanish versions of the sixteenth century and earlier attest to the continuous Hispanic presence in the Southwest and California throughout these many years.

Rael has put together the most complete collection of Spanish tales (*Cuentos Populares de Colorado y Nuevo Mexico,* 1977) gathered over a period of many years in his native north central New Mexico and south central Colorado. He comments on the fidelity with which this and other Spanish traditions have been retained on this Spanish frontier while they have been lost in many other parts of Spanish America. Although a few of the five hundred stories in his collection are local, he has convincingly argued that they are often of indisputable Old World origin. Rael believes that this phenomenon "can be explained by a desire among some narrators to make their stories more realistic and dramatic."[16] He classifies his tales in the following way: (1) riddle stories in which the hero or heroine has to provide the correct answer for a riddle in order to obtain a reward such as marriage to a desired person; (2) human stories which are divided into those that follow the style of the *fabliaux* of medieval French literature, the Italian master Boccaccio, and others, and those that are short anecdotes; (3) tales of a didactic nature; (4) stories of enchantment such as the traditional folk tale of the enchanted prince; (5) stories of a picaresque nature in which a rogue, such as the stock Spanish character, Pedro de Urdemales, goes about playing his pranks; and (6) animal stories, many of which are very close to the Aesopian fable.

The Los Angeles area has provided a rich source of both Spanish and Mexican folk tales. Elaine Miller has collected an impressive array of eighty-two narratives (*Mexican Folk Narrative from the Los Angeles Area,* 1973) which, like those in Rael's collection, have their roots in the Spanish oral tradition of storytelling. She divides her collection into legendary narratives and traditional tales, including in the first category narratives having to do with religion, the devil, return of the dead, buried treasures, and supernatural beings. In the second category are animal, magic, religious, romantic, and the stupid ogre tales.

Prose Chronicles of the Spanish Occupation

With the rooting and flowering of the Spanish oral tradition there also developed a written tradition in the form of the chronicles, reports, logs, correspondence, and diaries of the hundreds of Spanish explorers, soldiers, and missionaries who visited and settled the Southwest and California from the sixteenth century to the middle of the nineteenth century. Many of these documents contain highly imaginative, literary elements which compare to the writings of Columbus, Hernán Cortés, and Bernal Díaz del Castillo. They are characterized by the wonder of discovery of exotic flora and fauna, reports of epic struggles against nature and hostile Indian tribes, and the spirit of adventure in quest of fabled cities of gold, as well as the reporting of daily travails and tragedies.

Alvar Núñez Cabeza de Vaca's account of his eight-year trek through the wilds of parts of Texas and New Mexico is recorded in his *Los naufragios* [The Shipwrecks]. It contains not only much ethnographic information of the Indian tribes with which he came into contact but also a thrilling adventure story of human endurance and survival. He is one of the Spanish chroniclers who is most adept at storytelling and seems to keep the reader in mind. As he unravels his tale he evokes both the harrowing and rewarding aspects of his journey. The effect of his account is very similar to that of a captivating adventure novel which succeeds in maintaining a high level of suspense while creating a rich texture of details and leaving much to the reader's imagination. Another important literary value of *Los naufragios* is Cabeza de Vaca's ability to retain its epic quality by keeping himself as the focus of the narrative. While never exaggerating his role in his own survival and that of his men, he does manage to hold before us in an unpretentious way his resilience and resourcefulness throughout the ordeal. His style flows easily and naturally from page to page, a characteristic not found in many early chronicles.

Fray Marcos de Niza's *Relación del descubrimiento de las siete ciudades* [Relation of the Discovery of the Seven Cities] is a good example of the opportunities the Southwest provided for the literary embellishment of reality.[17] While he is generally careful in the account of his expedition into New Mexico to distinguish between observation and hearsay, he seems to lose his good judgment as news of the fabled cities of Cibola becomes more intense. While the whole narrative is of interest as a piece of imaginative writing, it is Niza's description of his supposed sighting of one of the cities of Cibola that particularly stands out:

> With these and with my own Indians and interpreters, I continued my journey till I came within sight of Cibola. It is situated on a level stretch on the brow of a roundish hill. It appears to be a very beautiful city, the best that I have seen in these parts; the houses are of the type that the Indians described to me, all of stone with their storeys and terraces, as it appeared to me from a hill whence I could see it. The town is bigger than the city of Mexico. . . . When I said to the chiefs who were with me how beautiful Cibola appeared to me, they told me that it was the least of the seven cities, and that Totonteac is much bigger and better than all the seven, and that it has so many houses and people that there is no end to it. (218–19)

Carried away by his desire to find truth in the hundreds of rumors of gold and precious jewels that had accumulated around Cibola, the author apparently created what he imagined to be in that place, and what he had in fact sighted was a simple Zuñi village. If not of documentary and historical value, this section of Niza's work does illustrate the propensity on the part of the early Spanish to pepper their accounts of discovery and exploration with gems of literary creativity. His description compares to that of Cortés who only twenty years before had come upon the Aztec capital of Tenochtitlán.

The accounts of the Coronado as well as later expeditions into New Mexico also make fascinating reading.[18] The Chamuscado-Rodríguez expedition of 1581, the Espejo expedition of 1582, the Castaño de Sosa expedition of 1590, and the Morlete expedition of 1591 all are amply documented with diaries, memoirs, and correspondence.[19]

During the last half of the eighteenth century, during the period of intense Spanish exploration and settlement of California, it was the practice to record, sometimes in careful detail, the events and impressions of the expeditions. We are fortunate that so many of the diaries, logs, memoirs, biographies, and correspondence of missionaries and explorers have been preserved. Of greatest interest for their imaginative elements are the writings of Fray Junípero Serra, Francisco Palou, Gaspar de Portolá, Miguel Costansó, Juan Bautista de Anza, Fray Francisco Garcés, Fray Juan Díaz, and Fray Gerónimo Boscana. A longer list might also include Joaquín de Moraga and Fray Francisco Palou's accounts of the founding of San Francisco, Fray Thomas Eixarch's diary of his winter on the Colorado, Fray Pedro Font's diary of the second de Anza expedition, and José Antonio Navarro's memoirs.

The correspondence of Fray Junípero Serra from 1765 to 1784 to three Spanish viceroys—Marquis de Croix, Don Antonio María Bucareli, and Don Martín De Mayorga—and to others not only is a good source of early California history but also provides a good example of the spirit of adventure combined with missionary zeal that motivated many clergy to risk their lives and limbs for God and Crown.[20] His letters reveal his unfaltering optimism and complete dedication as he set about the task of teaching California's coastal Indians what he believed to be a reasonable balance of religion, work, and recreation. The letters also give us an insight into what was considered to be his difficult personality. He believed that eschewing many of life's pleasures was a means of achieving a higher level of spirituality and closeness with his supreme being.

Fray Francisco Palou's contemporary biography of Serra (1787) confirms this view and is in itself a fine work both stylistically and psychologically.[21] Palou, a fellow Franciscan, had been Serra's student in philosophy at the Lullian University on the Island of Mallorca, and his admiration for his master is clear. His highly laudatory work chronicles Serra's missionary efforts along the coast of California, especially between San Diego and Monterey. What emerges is the picture of the missionary as a tireless and intrepid explorer who foresaw the importance of creating missions as a means of colonizing the coast in God's name.

Gaspar de Portolá's diary covers the period from 1769 to 1770 while he was in command of the Spanish expedition from San Diego to Monterey.[22] He focuses on his encounters with different Indian tribes, some hospitable and some hostile, and the extreme hardships of going for days with little water and no food. Perhaps more captivating than Portolá's account of the expedition is Miguel Costansó's narrative, which is a remarkably articulate account of the founding of Alta, California. His translator describes him in the following way: "The mind which made possible the *Narrative* belonged to a man of broad intellectual background, of intense perception, whose ability for detail was matched by an amazing capacity to view the broad spectrum of events and give those events meaning."[23] Costansó not only takes notice of the climate, geography, ecology, and natives of the area the expedition passed through, but conveys a sense of almost childlike amazement at what he is observing and recording.

The accounts of the two de Anza expeditions—1774 and 1775–76—are a rich source of literary creativity from the latter half of the eighteenth century. Foremost are de Anza's own diaries, in which he faithfully records the long marches and operations from the Royal Presidio of Tubac (in the present-day Mexican state of Sonora) to California.[24] He gives landmarks, detailed directions, and the names of rivers and mountains, and describes different Indian groups encountered along the trek. De Anza clearly communicates his keen admiration for the Yuma Indian tribes, particularly how they worked their land and managed their governmental affairs. His poetic descriptions of the natural beauty of the mountain valleys and rivers are moving examples of the lyrical quality of much of his prose. De Anza becomes even more confident in his expression in the second diary, in which there emerges the self-portrait of a gentle and sensitive commander aware of the needs and limits of endurance of both the men and women who accompanied him. Finally, his assessment of a site on which to found the presidio of San Francisco is a flight into fantasy as he describes the incredible beauty of the bay from the heights of the peninsula (3:123ff.).

While not as rich in literary expression as de Anza's diaries, the Fray Juan Díaz's and Fray Francisco Garcés's accounts of the first expedition are of interest. Fray Juan Díaz is much less tolerant than the Spanish commander of the Indians, especially the Pápagos: "They care nothing for the conveniences of life which civilized men so much love. . . . They lack almost completely a sense of honor and shame, which is so fundamental in civilized life. They are ignorant of eternal truths, those who are Christians only in name."[25] The greatest value of Fray Francisco Gracés's record is found in his descriptions of the treacherous natural obstacles, such as whirling rivers, encountered along the way. These descriptions read like good fiction. He shares with Fray Juan Díaz a low opinion of the Indians, conjuring up for the reader the pleasures of a veritable missionary's paradise: "Oh, what a vast heathdom! Oh! What lands suitable for missions!"[26]

A more favorable view of the Indians is found in Fray Gerónimo Boscana's *Chinigchinich* (1831), an account of the origin, customs, and traditions of the Indians at the mission of San Juan Capistrano.[27] This account was found among the priest's personal effects when he died in 1831. Besides the considerable ethnographic detail, Boscana's description includes a wonderfully imaginative summary of this Indian tribe's story of the creation of the world. The title of his work comes from the superdeity who, looking favorably upon the Indians, gave them rain, agriculture, and other gifts and then commanded them to build a temple in his honor. Boscana focuses on the importance of astral bodies and the seasons in their mythology. Rather than an objective third-person account of the Indian's religion, the missionary tries to re-create the creation story with all its charm and fantasy. This part of *Chinigchinich* reads like the Greek account of the Gods on Mount Olympus.

Lorenzo de Zavala's 1834 work, *Viaje a los Estados Unidos del Norte de America* [Voyage to the United States of North America], is an account of the Mexican author's experiences in the United States. It is of interest for presenting a favorable view of the American character and a harsh criticism of the Mexican. Zavala eventually emigrated to the United States settling in Texas where he became an advocate of Texan independence from Mexico.[28]

Spanish-Language Newspapers

Along with the rapid pace of historical events in the mid-nineteenth century—the Texas-Mexican War, the Mexican-American War, the Treaty of Guadalupe Hidalgo, and the Gadsden Treaty—profound sociopolitical changes occurred in Spanish-speaking communities across the Southwest and California. This population found itself threatened for the first time in its 350-year history by a technologically and militarily superior culture, and, as we have discussed earlier, this new relationship with Anglo-Americans had a lasting impact on many facets of its culture.

One clear sign of the will to survive culturally in the face of the Anglo-American occupation is the proliferation of Spanish-language newspapers throughout the Southwest and California from the mid-nineteenth century on. One preliminary survey indicates that almost four hundred such publications appeared between 1848 and 1958, providing indisputable proof that Chicano culture during this much-neglected historical period was experiencing tremendous growth and vitality.[29]

These newspapers are a rich source of Chicano literary expression. While some dailies and weeklies published only an occasional literary piece, others like *El Cronista del Valle* from Brownsville and *Hispano América* and *La Crónica,* published in San Francisco, ran poetry or short narrative pieces in almost every issue. [30] Although examples of prose abound throughout the hundred-year period, we will focus on a few of the more widely published writers whose works appear after the turn of the century. It is important to note that few of these writers offer us a perspective of the sociohistorical circumstances of their era, and social commentary is noticeably lacking in their works.

An exception to this is the late-nineteenth-century anonymous account—it appeared in serialized form in a Santa Barbara newspaper, *La Gaceta*—of the adventures of the legendary Chicano social rebel

Joaquín Murieta.[31] This fictionalized version relates Murieta's boyhood in Sonora, his journey to California as a young man in 1850, the assassination of his brother by authorities, his first encounters with the law, and his life as a fugitive from justice. Specific incidents from Murieta's long period of encounters with authorities form the basis for this serialized account, which depicts the bandit as a victim of hapless circumstances and outright prejudice: his relationship with Three-Fingered Jack, the knifing of a law officer near San José in 1851, the 1852 shooting of a Mr. Clark by Murieta, the flight to Mount Shasta after a shoot-out with R. B. Buchanan, sheriff of Yuba County, etc. Murieta emerges as a fierce and brave defender of his people, a leader much admired by his band of men.

One writer whose work was widely published in newspapers from Texas to California is Benjamín Padilla, who is best known by his pseudonym "Kaskabel." Padilla writes short humorous pieces satirizing human foibles. He often concludes his pieces with a lighthearted message that is more entertaining than didactic. A few examples of his work will serve to illustrate both his skill as a writer and perceptiveness as an observer of his fellow-man. In "Los celos de Don Crispín" [Don Crispín's Jealousy], an innocent and simple young man falls in love with a beautiful blond with seductive eyes and a voluptuous body.[32] Obviously mismatched, Crispín's jealousy and possessiveness intensify as their wedding nears. He devises a plan to entrap his future bride but it backfires when he discovers that a hat left in Leonila's parlor is really his own. He promises never again to suspect his fiancée. Kaskabel warns young women to beware of these promises, for they only last as long as the first occasion to be jealous. In "Los ricos sin cuartilla" [Rich People without a Shred], he pokes fun at the pretentions of the supposedly wealthy who strut about in public places putting on airs and lording it over others only to return at night to their miserable huts in the poorest sections of the city.[33] With a mixture of sympathy and scorn, the writer describes one such person who has sacrificed everything to buy his formal attire. In order to maintain appearances he has forced his family to go through much pain. "Los ricos pobres" [The Poor Rich] and "Las peladas ricas" [Poor Rich Women] deal with essentially the same theme.[34] In "Memento Homo," Padilla turns his satirical pen on the time-honored Ash Wednesday custom of receiving ashes on the forehead. Young women, when they receive their ashes, are thinking thoughts other than "returning to dust" as they seek out the church where the prettiest ash cross is made. Old women, on the other hand, are concerned with how long their smudges will remain visible. They go to great lengths—putting a cup over the ashes at night and not washing—to preserve this outward sign of their piety. Padilla comments wryly: *La influencia de la humana coquetería se deja ver hasta en estas prácticas serias y tristes* ("The influence of human coquetry enters into even these sad and serious practices"). He takes a humorous jab at doctors in "Los médicos" [Doctors], identifying them as individuals who after ten years of study acquire the prerogative of killing Christians without being prosecuted for their crimes.[35] He warns us to avoid all doctors. One of Padilla's most hilarious pieces is his essay on lies, "Las mentiras," in which he cautions the reader to resort to them sparingly lest he be trapped in his own dishonesty.[36] Although he concedes that lies may be used in a conjugal situation, he gives the example of a man who was unoriginal and thereby suffered the consequences. The message is clear: be judicious and creative when lying.

Padilla effectively employs a correspondence format in some of his prose pieces. "Cartas de una casada" [Letters from a Married Woman] consists of two letters from a married woman to her girl friend.[37] The first is positive, even idyllic, communicating her joy and happy expectations in the marriage. The second, six years later, is decidedly negative, describing the realities of her relationship. She ends on a philosophical note: *Esta es la verdadera vida del matrimonio, María. Primero vienen las ilusiones, luego los desencantos y más tarde la paz y la tranquilidad que son los precursores de la dulce vejez* ("This is the true life of the married couple, María. First come the illusions, then the displeasures and later peace and quiet which precede the sweetness of old age"). "Carta de una muchacha tapatía a su Santidad Pío J . . ." [A Letter from a Girl from Jalisco to His Holiness Pius J . . .] is written in a familiar tone to the Pope imploring him to intercede on the behalf of the letter writer and her boyfriend Chencho so that they can get married. It seems that the financial arrangements at the local parish are too high.[38]

"Jorge Ulica" (Julio G. Arce)

Like Benjamin Padilla, Julio G. Arce, known by the pseudonym
Jorge Ulica, was widely published in southwestern and California
newspapers during the 1920s. Appearing beneath the rubric "Crónicas
Diabólicas" [Diabolical Chronicles], his short satirical prose pieces are
more biting than Padilla's yet as mild in their criticism of Anglos. As
Clara Lomas has pointed out in her study of a few of Ulica's works, he
takes an ambivalent position in the cultural battle that was being waged
between Chicanos and Anglo-Americans. While he is critical of the
excesses of certain American institutions and customs, he also tends to
take an elitist, distant stance regarding fellow Mexicans and
Chicanos.[39] He is reluctant to identify himself with his compatriots
lest he, too, become the victim of Anglo racism. Although there is little
biographical information available on Ulica, we can surmise from his
crónicas that he was a well-established journalist. Thus, he had much to
lose by taking a hard stand against the dominant culture.

Among the aspects of Yankee culture of which he is mildly critical
are football games, dance halls, elections, Prohibition, and a worsening
economic situation. In "Touchdown extraordinario" [Extraordinary
Touchdown], Ulica refers to the common myth that in the United
States there is a philanthropist on every corner.[40] He receives a free
football ticket from a woman whose husband died tragically five years
before. During the course of the game he learns that she kicked him to
death for not cheering for the right team, and threatens the narrator
with the same fate. Ulica thus satirizes the Anglo-American propensity
to become obsessively involved in competitive sports. He pans another
American pastime in "Sanatorios para bailadores" [Hospitals for
Dancers]. He gives a long, humorous description of the elaborate,
well-equipped hospitals and their well-trained professional staff set up
to receive dance-hall victims such as a poor young man who received
eleven kicks from an angry mother whose daughter he had become too
friendly with on the dance floor; a woman suffering from bite wounds
on her shoulder; poison victims who, rejected by their dance partners,
have tried to take their own lives, and those who have forgotten to spit
after kissing—the red in the lipstick has a poisonous chemical compound.[41] "No voté pero me botaron" [I Didn't Vote But They Threw

Me Out] is a satire of the American political process.[42] A bewildered Mexican national is visited by a strange array of political pressure groups who try to convince him to vote for or against a proposition he does not fully understand. In "¿Quién arrebató mi paleto?" [Who Stole My Overcoat?], Ulica focuses on the fanaticism of police agents during Prohibition.[43] The narrator is stripped and searched at a dance merely because someone has spilled whiskey on his coat. Later he is threatened with a fine and imprisonment because his overcoat, which he had lost, is found stuffed with liquor bottles. In "Con la toilette moscovita" [With the Moscovite's Dress Shop], the writer warns foreigners not to come to the United States because of the financial upheaval that is taking place.[44]

Ulica's view of the Spanish-speaking residents of the southwest and California is no more favorable than that of Anglo-Americans. He is critical of their aping American ways and yet attacks their failure to adapt to the culture of their new country. For example, in "No estamos bastante aptos" [We Aren't Competent Enough], he satirizes Mexicans who are inadequately prepared to become United States citizens.[45] The examination of a Mexican musician who wishes to become naturalized becomes a comedy of errors as he gives all the wrong answers. Ulica comments: *Siempre he creído que muchos de nuestros amados hermanos de raza no están enteramente aptos para la democracia químicamente pura . . .* ("I have always believed that many of our compatriots are not competent enough for a chemically pure democracy . . ."). In "Por no hablar inglés" [Because She Doesn't Speak English], "No hay que hablar en pocho" [You Shouldn't Speak in *Pocho*], and "La estenógrafa" [The Stenographer], he takes Spanish speakers to task for not learning how to speak proper English.[46] The second story is a sharp criticism of Mexicans who misuse Spanish. In "La estenógrafa," the author's secretary types in a letter *AJOTAR* ("to engage in homosexual activity") instead of *AGOTAR* ("to be exhausted"), a mistake which proves to be highly embarrassing to Ulica. "Como hacer surprise parties" [How to Give Surprise Parties] is directed at Mexicans who reject their own culture to adopt the negative aspects of American life.[47] Dolores Flores, who has changed her name to Pains Flowers (a literal translation), tries to convince her daughters to have their Anglo boyfriends throw her a surprise party. "Buscando al quinto" [Looking for the Right Person] and "Esposas y suegras 'standard'" [Standard Wives and Mothers-in-law] provide other examples of Ulica's negative characterization of the Mexican who stumbles in his clumsy attempts to become acculturated.[48]

Several of Ulica's stories are enjoyable purely for their humor. They have little to do with the satirization of either Anglo-American or Mexican culture as in the works referred to above. "El recurso del aullido" [Recourse to the Howl] is a hilarious tale of how the author devises an ingenious way of extracting himself from a difficult situation.[49] He attends a car show, and returns very late at night from a long ride with a salesman. In order to slip into his house undetected by neighbors, he pretends to be a cat howling in the alley; however, he is arrested for disturbing the peace. In court, the judge drops charges against him and the prosecuting attorney requests howling lessons so that he, too, might slip in his house late at night.

Other Newspaper Writers

The works of Benjamin Padilla and Jorge Ulica are humorous and satirical. In contrast, Eusebio Falcón's short stories deal with legends, the supernatural, and psychic phenomena. Also in contrast with the aforementioned writers, Falcón creates more fully developed stories with a central narrative focus with greater attention to detail. His "Leyenda maya Lol-ha" [The Mayan Legend of Lol-ha], in which he traces the origin of the legend of the flower of the water Lol-ha, is a good illustration of his qualities as a storyteller.[50] A god descends from the heavens to share with the Mayan Pixán Tunich the secrets of a plant which in the hands of a woman has the power to bewitch a man. Suhuy Lol, the man's evil daughter, forces her father to share the secret which she uses to seduce and then kill many unsuspecting Mayan warriors. Suhuy Lol's excesses finally result in her own death, however, when she seduces and kills a handsome brave who is to be married to the daughter of a powerful king. As a punishment she is thrown with heavy weights tied to her body into the same well in which her victims had perished. A deadly poisonous flower—Lol-ha—grows in the place where she dies. "Apariciones" [Apparitions], which falls in the realm of the supernatural, is an eerie tale of an employee of a large hacienda who is followed one night by a white phantom whose coldness suggests the presence of death itself.[51] "Leyendo a Flammarion" [Reading Flammarion] deals with a different aspect of the supernatural: the life of the soul after the death of the body.[52] The narrator, who has recently read an essay on disembodied souls by the French astronomer Flammarion, is run over and killed by a streetcar. He experiences picking himself up off the street, dusting off his clothes, and going about his normal day. He soon discovers, however, that he is invisible to his office mates and his family, who are mourning his death. Most of Falcón's other stories, which explore social themes, are less successful artistically than those just discussed.

Two women stand out among the most interesting writers to be published in Spanish-language newspapers: María Esperanza Pardo and Laura de Pereda. They are representative of a significant number of Chicana writers whose prose and poetry works appear over a hundred-year period in these publications (another notable female writer is Maria Enriqueta Betanza). It is important to note that this group defies the popular stereotype of the illiterate or semi-literate subservient woman whose primary duty is to her family. On the contrary, these women's literary output is impressive both qualitatively and quantitatively.

The works of Laura de Pereda are illustrative of the vitality of this group of Chicana writers. Her stories contain elements of mid-nineteenth-century romantic sentimentality but they are not marred by the melodramatism or excessive fatalism associated with this literary movement. The author captures the reader's imagination with her evocative prose style as she explores different facets of human emotions. "Bucólica" [Bucolic] is perhaps her best work, a beautifully rendered, gentle tale about a shepherd's discovery of his love for another.[53] Juanillo falls in love with the fairy described in a story his friend Rosalinda reads to him while his sheep graze peacefully in the mountain meadows. Rosalinda, who loves Juanillo and wishes he would reciprocate, becomes angry with him when he expresses his longing for the fictional creature. Juanillo searches in vain for the illusory creature, finally recognizing that Rosalinda has all the qualities of the fairy. "Más muerto que la muerte" [More Dead Than Death] is an allegory of the triumph of life over death.[54] Death offers a young woman a deal: to return her lover in exchange for another's life. She is tempted but then refuses, knowing that for her the spirit of the living is more precious even than her own tragedy. The same struggle is presented in "Víctimas del deber" [Victims of Duty], in which Roberto, a switchman, must choose between the lives of his young wife and son and those of a trainload of people.[55] He opts for the latter knowing that in either case he must live with his sadness. Other stories, such as "Ideas fuerzas" [The Power of Suggestion], "Una arma siempre invencible" [An Always Invincible Arm], and "Imposible venganza" [Impossible Vengeance], deal with the power of love.[56] In the first, a gentle old man overcomes his godson's recalcitrance through persistent demonstrations of affection and acts of love; in the second, a king learns that respect and generosity are more powerful than force; and, in the third, a vengeful lover finds that forgiveness allows him to become reconciled with life.

Unlike the optimism and joy of life that pervades de Pereda's stories, those by María Esperanza Pardo are tinged with sadness. Most of the protagonists are women who have suffered some form of personal disaster with which they are not able to cope. For example, "El perfume de la otra" [Another's Woman's Perfume] describes a young woman who has lost the will to live.[57] She attempts to overcome her depression, succeeds momentarily, but then lapses deeper into her previous state. Most of Pardo's female characters are victims in their relationships with men.

Early Novels and Memoirs

Together with the impressive number of authors who published their prose pieces in southwestern and California Spanish-language newspapers in the late nineteenth and the first part of the twentieth century, there are several notable writers whose works were published in book form. Five stand out in this group: Manuel M. Salazar, Eusebio Chacón, Felipe Maximiliano Chacón, Miguel Otero, and Andrew García, (whose book was not discovered until 1948).

Manuel M. Salazar was a New Mexican known mainly for his poetry but he was also a prose writer who wrote what is perhaps the earliest published Chicano novel, *La historia de un caminante, o sea Gervacio y Aurora* [A Traveler's History, or Gervacio and Aurora].[58] Written in 1881 when Salazar was twenty-seven years old, the novel traces the amorous adventures of Gervacio who skips from affair to affair in the best Don Juan tradition. The work contains many romantic bucolic elements that leave us with the impression that the New Mexico of Salazar's time was a utopia that enjoyed an unequaled pastoral life.

Eusebio Chacón is best known for a pair of short novels in Spanish which appeared in 1892: *El hijo de la tempestad* [Son of the Tempest] and *Tras la tormenta la calma* [Calm after the Storm]. They are important for being among the first novels to be published (1892) by a Chicano author.[59] The first revolves around a bandit chieftain who, with his band, terrorizes the populace. In the end, he and his men are justly punished for their misdeeds. The work is marred by the author's attempt to incorporate many disparate elements into the narrative. The second novel also suffers from too much nonessential material and too little attention given to characterization and plot development. We are given a heavy dose of Chacón's erudition—he discusses literary works and figures—but it is not enough to sustain his lack of talent as a novelist.

Born in Santa Fe in 1873, Felipe Maximiliano Chacón was a professional journalist who edited Spanish-language newspapers in various New Mexico cities.[60] Among his prose publications is a thirty-page novela, *Eustacio y Carlita* (n.d.), cut in the mold of nineteenth-century Romanticism. Just as they are about to consummate their marriage, the protagonists discover they are brother and sister.

Miguel Antonio Otero, who was governor of the Territory of New Mexico from 1897 to 1906, is the most prolific of nineteenth- and twentieth-century Chicano writers. Although his memoirs were written earlier, they were not published until the 1930s and 1940s. In them he paints, with an energetic and self-assured style in English, a vivid picture of life on the frontier during the last half of the nineteenth century. The two-volume work, *My Life on the Frontier 1865–1882*, focuses on his experiences as a boy and as a young man in Kansas, Colorado, and New Mexico. Otero's account of his years in boarding school under the tutelage of stern schoolmasters reminds us of Dickens's *Oliver Twist*. Descriptions of Hays, Kansas, and other wild frontier outposts convey the ebullience of that period of our lawless West. He recalls how the main street was almost a solid row of saloons, dance halls, restaurants, barber shops, and houses of prostitution kept by such notorious individuals as "Calamity Jane," "Lousy Liz," "Stink Foot

Mag," and "Steamboat," a rogues' gallery of legendary Western characters.[61] Otero devotes a chapter to Wild Bill Hickok and also an entire
book to Billy the Kid. The latter, which is an excellent personal
biography of one of the West's most famous outlaws, is filled with both
the excitement and tragedy surrounding Billy's life.[62] The author
sympathetically depicts him as an intelligent, misunderstood boy
whose life of violence began through an unfortunate set of circumstances over which Billy had no control. Mistreated by a cruel and
tyrannical stepfather, he was predisposed to the violence that was to fall
into his path in later years.

Besides having considerable literary merit, Otero's epic work is an
abundant source of historical information on the building of the West,
including the Indian Wars, the spanning of the great railroads, and the
political intrigue that plagued territorial governments. As a member of
one of New Mexico's leading Spanish-speaking families, the author was
appointed governor of the territory by President William McKinley in
1897. His exciting account of the nine years he held this office provide
us with a valuable insight into the struggles between Anglo-Americans
and New Mexicans during a troubled period of the state's history.[63] For
example, he relates how Thomas Catron, a ring-leader of a famous
land-grabbing Santa Fe cartel, tried to have him assassinated. For their
energetic style and rich texture. Otero's works hold a distinguished
position in the evolution of Chicano prose.

Like Otero's three works, Andrew García's *Tough Trip through
Paradise, 1878–1879* (not published until 1967) stands out as a vivid
account of the "shoot-'em-up" days of the Wild West. Raised in Texas,
in 1876 García came north to Montana, where he settled among the
Nez Percé Indians. His writings, which span his life among these
Montana natives from 1878–1879, were not discovered until 1948
packed away in dynamite boxes. García nostalgically recalls his days of
reckless abandon in unexplored territory where Indians and Anglo-
Americans sometimes peacefully coexisted and other times fought
bitterly. Having served in the frontier army and having been married to
a Nez Percé woman, the author's loyalties are divided between his
pleasant recollections of life among the troops and his implied criticism
of the government's treatment of the Indians. The work is also infused
with García's moral dilemma of choosing between his often disreputa-
ble behavior as a hard-drinkng, brawling, whoring young man and his
Mexican Catholic background.

Chicano Local-Color Writers

During the last three decades of our overview of Chicano prose fiction, writers, all of whom write in English, fall into two main groups: those who emphasize the folkloric aspect of the Spanish-speaking experience and those who begin to strive for greater psychological depth and artistic completeness in their works.[64] While, thematically, the writers in the first group narrow their focus to concentrate on regional and local cultural aspects such as legends, superstitions, customs, character types, and dialectical speech, they are also excellent storytellers who know how to hold our interest. Writers in the second group seem more aware of their role as practitioners of their literary craft, which is reflected in more fully developed works with more attention given to style, characterization, and structure.

The works of the following writers fall decidedly within the first type of prose: María Cristina Mena, Nina Otero, Josefina Escajeda, Jovita González, Juan A. A. Sedillo, Mario Suárez, and Fray Angélico Chávez.

Maria Cristina Mena is a fine writer whose short stories and sketches appeared early in this century in the *Century* and *American* magazines. Unfortunately, her talents are undermined by her tendency to create obsequious Mexican characters who fit comfortably within the American reader's expectations. This results in trivial and condescending stories.[65]

In "Count la Cerda's Treasure," Nina Otero describes the history of the Estancia Plains, the supposed site of the Gran Quivira in New Mexico. The slightly insane narrator tells how she came to Gran Quivira with a band of Brazilian gypsies to search for buried treasure.[66]

Josefina Escajeda's sketches are of San Elizario, a once-prominent town south of El Paso.[67] Most of her brief tales emphasize the superstitious nature of the town's residents, their belief in the evil powers of *brujas* and *brujos* (men and women with magical powers) and the opposing forces of God, the Virgin Mary, and the angels.

Jovita González's vignettes, titled "Among My People," are affectionate portraits of the rural people along the Texas-Mexican border. In "Shelling Corn by Midnight," she captures the sweetness of the change from hot, humid summer days to balmy nights when ranch folk gather to shell corn and swap tales of *brujas* and buried treasure.[68] González skillfully manipulates sensorial elements in this and other works. Several of her stories have to do with local characters: Pedro the hunter who went "north" to Houston to see the world; Tío Esteban the mail carrier, the community's "weather-beaten, brown-faced, black-eyed Cupid," who loans stamp money, writes love letters for the unlettered, sings ballads, and gossips; Carlos who made love to two generations of local women; and Don Tomás, the stern believer in patriarchal justice who comes in conflict with the Anglo legal system.

Juan A. A. Sedillo also deals indirectly with the conflict of cultures in his "Gentlemen of Río en Medio."[69] An old New Mexican whose family has owned land on the Río Grande for hundreds of years is forced to sell to the Anglos. He wisely offers them a low price in exchange for their agreeing to allow his grandchildren to play in the trees which he planted when each of them was born.

Mario Suárez's stories also contain much local color and are quaint pictures of the Chicano community. El Hoyo, an area of Tucson, is such a place described in his story by the same name.[70] Its Chicano population raises hell on Saturday nights, listens to Padre Estanislao's sermons on Sunday morning, and raises hell again on Sunday night. Joy, vitality, generosity, and caring characterize Suárez's view of this *barrio,* a place for down-and-outers, thieves, and the unfortunate. Señor Garza, in another story by the same name, is one of the *barrio*'s sustaining members.[71] Philosopher, counselor, banker, and expert on world affairs, Señor Garza draws a parade of community characters to his place of business. The author describes him affectionately as the owner of the barber shop which will never own him.

Fray Angélico Chávez, a Franciscan priest from New Mexico, is a recent writer who emphasizes folklore and local color. His stories deal, in the main, with religious themes. The following titles, taken from his collection *From an Altar Screen, El Retablo: Tales from New Mexico,* are indicative of his predilection for local legends: "The Bell That Sang Again," "The Fiddler and the Angelito," "The Ardent Commandment," "The Black Ewe," "Wake for Don Corsinio," "The Lean Years," and "The Colonel and the Santo." "Hunchback Madonna" from his *New Mexico Triptych* is Chávez's best-known story.[72] An old hunchback woman, La Mana Seda, gathers flowers for the yearly May celebration in which young girls pay homage to the Virgin. One year she goes deeper than usual into the forest in search of flowers, is caught by a rainstorm, and takes refuge in a young man's cabin. He inadvertently transfers the old woman's hunchbacked image onto a *retablo* he is painting for the town church.[73] She dies soon after and is buried in the graveyard next to the church.

Fiction—Beyond Local Color

Among the writers in the second group are Josephina Niggli, Robert Hernán Torres, and Robert Félix Salazar. Their works reflect a greater familiarity with contemporary narrative techniques and an interest in a wider variety of themes than the writers of the first group.

Josephina Niggli is an accomplished novelist and short-story writer. All of her prose works are set in Mexico, most of them in the northern states of Nuevo León and Coahuila. Her novel *Step Down, Elder Brother* (1917) takes place in Monterrey in the years following the Mexican Revolution and its plot is linked to some of its important figures. We find Domingo Vásquez de Anda, the son of a wealthy Monterrey family, disillusioned and cynical after the sudden end of a torrid love affair with an American woman. He is intrigued by and then falls in love with Márgara, a sensual, mysterious woman whose father was associated with one of the Revolution's most brutal torturers. The novel is also structured around the love affairs of Domingo's two sisters, Sofía and Brunhilda, as well as other less important subplots. A period piece, the work is rich in local details and historical references. Niggli's *Mexican Village* (1945) consists of ten stories centered around the town of Hildago in Nuevo León. The long cast of characters appears and reappears throughout the collection as the author puts together her tapestry of simple village life. As a gifted writer, Niggli succeeds in maintaining a high level of suspense and tension throughout the collection and at the same time creates multi-dimensional and credible characters who fit within their local ambience without being stereotypically drawn.

Robert Hernán Torres's stories, several published in *Esquire,* are also set in Mexico and deal with the senselessness of war. In "Mutiny in Jalisco," a group of revolutionary soldiers refuse to obey their officer's orders to attack a machine gun emplacement.[74] Having lost his perspective on human life, the officer is willing to sacrifice his men in order to redeem himself in the eyes of his superior. In "The Brothers

Jimínez," a similar aberration is operative as a brother denies he is related to a captured federal officer who faces certain execution. He, in turn, is shot by Pancho Villa for lying about his relationship. In both stories, a first-person narrator, a non-Mexican, observes how the violence of the revolution has compromised the rules of human decency. He speculates on the many new reasons "men had found lately for killing each other."[75]

Roberto Félix Salazar also touches upon the same theme in "Nobody Laughs in Yldes," a story about a traveler who comes upon an isolated European village whose inhabitants seem afflicted by a deep sadness.[76] He learns from an old man the reason for their misery: the children defending the town were slaughtered by attacking Germans. The author captures the town's profound tragedy in the final scene, in which the old man shows the narrator the field where the children are buried. Bayonets, which the narrator had mistaken for cornstalks, mark their graves.

With its roots planted deeply in the varied non-fiction works of Spanish soldiers and missionaries who explored and settled the Southwest and California, Chicano prose has slowly developed over the last four centuries to become an interesting blend of works, some emphasizing the idealized folkloric aspects of reality and others focusing on the grimmer side of existence. What many of the works discussed in this section lack in multi-dimensionality and psychological insight they make up for in the richness of their cultural backdrops and historical detail.

Poetry—The Oral Tradition

As in the case of drama and prose, poetry has a dual tradition: oral and written. Regarding the oral tradition, folk poetry is as old as the arrival of Spaniards in the Southwest and California in the sixteenth century. The Peninsular folksong had taken firm root in the Spanish settlements in Mexico by the early 1600s, and it made a successful journey north to the mountain and river valleys of New Mexico later in the century. The most common forms found along the Río Grande and in other areas of heavy Spanish settling are the *romance,* the *corrido,* the *décima,* and the *canción.*[77]

The *romance* is a ballad form with lines varying between seven and sixteen syllables.[78] It was sung by troubadours who visited homes and taverns, bringing news from neighboring towns or singing of someone's singular achievement or tragedy. It is a type of poetic composition that evolved from the Spanish epics of the eleventh century. Those still found in New Mexico and elsewhere which are descended from sixteenth century *romances* are (1) those of a religious nature, which are found in the folk-drama tradition discussed earlier in this chapter; (2) those that fall into the nursery-rhyme pattern and which are still sung and told to children; and (3) those sung ballads of an episodic nature with a universal tragic theme.[79]

The *corrido*—a popular form in Mexico as well as in today's Southwest and California—is often confused with the *romance,* probably because it evolved from it just the way the *romance* grew out of epic poetry.[80] This fast-paced narrative ballad, usually with a theme of struggle, adventure, or catastrophe, flourished in the lower borderlands of Texas.[81] The animosity between Anglos and Mexicans in this as well as in other areas of the Southwest is consistently reflected in *corridos,* which are usually composed immediately after the incident on which they are based. For example, ballads sprung up after the Texas social rebel Juan Cortina shot the Anglo marshal of Brownsville for pistol-whipping a fellow-Mexican. Early in the twentieth century, Gregorio Cortez, another "bandit," was also immortalized in *corridos.*[82] Raymond Paredes believes that better than any other art form, *corridos* celebrate and validate the experience of first the Mexican and then the Chicano in the Southwest.[83]

The *décima,* a form of folksong popular in New Mexico during the nineteenth century, is a forty-four-line poem composed of an introductory four-verse *copla* (stanza) followed by four ten-line stanzas that incorporate the *copla* lines in the last verse of each stanza.[84] Like the *romance,* the *décima* is of Spanish origin. The metrical structure is probably too confining to have allowed this form to become very popular. In the nineteenth century, troubadours sang both religious and amorous *décimas* whereas today they appear in published form as political diatribes.

The *canción,* which is a very versatile form of folksong, may appear in any verse form its composer prefers. While it is generally lyrical, it can also be used to treat a wide variety of subjects. Arthur Campa has observed that its subjective quality "reveals more readily the fine nuances of folk sensibility in outpourings of the lovelorn, in candid denunciations of unrequited lovers, in sincere expressions of undying affection, and in melancholy murmurings of the introvert."[85]

In his study of Spanish folk poetry in New Mexico, Campa mentions several widely known troubadours of the nineteenth century whose reputations ranged wide and far: El Viejo Vilmas, Chiloria, and El Pelón.[86] These bards sang old Spanish *romances, corridos, décimas,* and *canciones,* as well as composing their own. El Pelón's real name was Jesús Gonzales, born close to Santa Fe in 1844. One of his manuscripts, written on rawhide, was discovered in a cave in 1934. Little is known about Chiloria and what information we have about El Viejo Vilmas comes from his *trovos* or the long series of verses that he composed.[87]

The first written poetry recorded is Gaspar Pérez de Villagrá's epic history of New Mexico, *Historia de la Nuevo México,* published in Spain in 1610.[88] Pérez de Villagrá accompanied Oñate on his expedition to New Mexico and soon after composed his work. It focuses, in large part, on the heroic qualities and accomplishments of his leader. The poem's thirty-three cantos narrate how the Spanish entered and conquered New Mexico, the infamy and loneliness of the commanders and their soldiers, the choosing of Juan de Oñate as their leader, his discretion and prudence, the tribulations of the first part of the trip, the discovery and taking possession of "Río del Norte," the founding of the first Spanish settlement at San Juan de los Caballeros, the exploration of lands bordering on the Río Grande including the mountain city of Acoma, and the siege of Acoma. Throughout, the Indians are depicted as treacherous and marauding while the Spaniards' positive qualities are emphasized. Villagrá's style is simple and natural.

Other examples of early recorded poetry are by two Californians, Joaquín Buelna and Guillermo Zúñiga. Buelna composed a long poem in praise of the Virgin, *Loa a la Virgen del Refugio* [In Praise of the Virgin of Refuge], and Zúñiga, a military man, put in verse the rebellion of the Tulare Indians against the Spanish colonists of Santa Barbara. His work is *La batalla de los Tulares* [The Battle of the Tulares].[89]

Spanish-Language Newspaper Poetry

As in the case of prose, the bulk of Chicano poetry published between 1848 and the 1950s is found in the many Spanish-language newspapers which spring up in virtually every important urban center in the Southwest and California. Much of the early poetry in the 1850s and 1860s is anonymous, but by the 1870s, several names began to appear with increasing frequency in these newspapers. While it is well beyond the scope of this study to discuss the hundreds of poets and thousands of poems that were published in over a century of vigorous literary activity, we have chosen a few of the most important poets and we have also made an outline of the major themes found in the poetry of this period. It must be emphasized that much research and analysis in this area still needs to be done.

The most common types of poetry published in Spanish-language newspapers are about love and nature; religious, spiritual, and moralistic; patriotic; cultural pride; social protest; and commemorative and eulogistic. The poets who appear most frequently in these publications are Julio Flores, María Enriqueta Betanza, Felipe Maximiliano Chacón, Antonio Plaza, Moisés, Dantés, José Escobar, Fernando Celada, Manuel Arellano, Fray Sinreb, Miguel Godoy, and Carlo de Medina. Of greatest popularity are the sonnet and other traditional forms such as the twelve-, eleven-, and eight-syllable quatrains, octaves, and ten-line stanzas. The rhyme is both assonant and consonant.

Love poetry: virtually every newspaper that published literature carried love poetry in its pages. Poetry praising the beloved and poetry of unrequited love constitute the two most popular themes. The earliest examples are found in mid-nineteenth-century anonymous poetry. For example, in "A mi amada," [To My Beloved], the anguished lover is consumed in the presence of his beloved, a sensuous lass who is described with traditional imagery: she has cherry-red lips, undulating hair, and a snow-white bosom.[90] Another beguiled lover would give a thousand lives for a glimpse of his beloved's seductive eyes and sweet smile just as monarchs give treasures in trade for their desired objects.[91] One poet wishes he were as inspired as Dante, Tasso, and Petrarch, who dedicated lovely words to their women. In the typically exaggerated fashion of his day, the poet would trade his future for a kiss.[92] Other early poets protest the cruelty and insensitivity of the women they love or once loved. E. Montalván in his poem "Para ti" ["For You"], protests his lover's rejection of him; like the volcano that pours its lava over the peasant's home and orchard, her eyes burn lava into his heart.[93] He takes refuge in the total beauty of his native San Antonio, which becomes his source of hope. Another poet realizes how deceitful his beloved's charm and grace have been. Now that the veil of illusion has been lifted from his eyes, he can be indifferent to what before had blinded him.[94] Other poems depict the lover as the tormented victim who regrets having bound himself to love, see love as a blinding force that drives a wedge between two good male friends, or characterize the lover as engaging in a battle between anguish and joy.

Several of the better-known poets deal with the theme of love. Julio Flores compares his lover's disdain for him as "My Black Flowers" that blossom forth out of bitter memories.[95] Flores, whose love poetry is highly lyrical, uses natural imagery to evoke his longing for contact with his absent lover.

Felipe Maximiliano Chacón, one of the most prolific writers of the first part of the twentieth century, devotes several poems to the theme of love, both fulfilled and unrequited. He complains bitterly in "Desengaños" [Deceptions] that the woman he loves rejected his offer when they were both young, innocent, and pure. Now, years later, when no one else will accept her, he confesses that his affection for her has persisted.[96] This poet views love as the source of pain and joy, capable of felling its young, unsuspecting victims like a cold autumn wind or able to sustain the dream of someday realizing a fulfilling relationship. "A mi Elvira" [To My Elvira] is a poem that emphasizes the latter sentiment.[97] His lover's eyes are like two stars in his soul that light the way, giving him joy and hope. "Celos y amor" [Jealousy and Love], a light, rhythmical poem replete with nature imagery, identifies the love relationship as a source of both sorrow and childlike lightheartedness.[98]

Much of the love poetry can best be described by its penchant for the exaggerated powers of love. The male—and it is almost always a man—sees a beautiful woman from a distance, at a dance, in a window, etc., and falls madly in love with her. Two poems by the popular bard

Dantés exemplify this. "A una desconocida" [To an Unknown Woman] is in praise of the beauty of the woman the poet does not know but who is the source of his ecstasy.[99] "A Laura" begins with a bucolic scene: the sunrise, dew glistening on the flowers, a serene, beautiful sky, birds singing their melodious songs, a small stream pleasantly winding its way through the meadow. All this is an extended metaphor to describe the woman the poet has seen at her window. She is nature's most perfect creation.

Religious Poetry: poetry devoted to Christ and the Virgin Mary constitutes the most common type of religious poetry, but a few poets deal with theological questions as well. J. J. Pesado, a mid-nineteenth-century poet, directs his poem "El dolor" [Pain] to a God who, while seeming to be beneficent, has also created pain in the world: the old man suffering on his deathbed, the young mother grieving the loss of her child, war, pestilence, hunger, disaster. Perplexed, the poet at first cannot explain how this God can allow this seeming evil to exist among so much good. Then he hits upon the answer to his paradox: God, just in his wisdom, created pain as a kind of regulator, a reminder of our sins. The poem concludes: "Sólo se llega a la vida/Por la senda del dolor" (You only arrive at life's door/On the path of pain).[100] In the same vein is Manuel Caballero's long poem "Entrevistando a Cristo" [Interviewing Christ], in which an old soldier asks Christ to manifest himself so that he may understand the hardships and misery in his own difficult life. Christ speaks to the soldier, who determines to face his problems with newfound faith.[101]

Although his works did not appear in Spanish-language newspapers, the best-known Chicano religious poet is Fray Angélico Chávez, who has published several volumes of poetry in this vein: *Clothed with the Son* (1939), *Eleven Lady-Lyrics and Other Poems* (1945), and *Selected Poems with an Apologia* (1969). The poems devoted to the Virgin are his most successful.

Social Poetry: conscious of their status as second-rate citizens, Chicanos used newspapers from 1848 through the 1950s to protest the gross abuses of their rights, the denigration of their culture, and the questioning of their patriotism.[102] Poets stand in the forefront of this effort to defend *la raza* against the Anglo-American-dominated governmental and economic system in the Southwest and California. The social poetry of this period falls into three different categories: (1) poetry that addresses specific political issues or historical occurrences; (2) poetry that affirms the positive cultural aspects of Hispanics in general and Chicanos in particular; and (3) patriotic poetry that attempts to combat the negative stereotyping of Chicanos as cowardly or more concerned about Mexico than the United States.

As early as 1856, an anonymous poem published in the Los Angeles newspaper *El clamor público* protests the double standard of the United States Supreme Court in its treatment of Anglo-Americans and others:

> Allá en la Corte Suprema
> Donde reina la intergridad
> Veo que no hay igualidad
> Por llevar otro sistema.
> ¡Quién es el que no se queja
> Al mirar que el tribunal
> No nos considera igual
> Ni en su última providencia.
> Dándole la preferencia
> A don fulano de tal.[103]

> (There in the Supreme Court
> Where integrity reigns
> I see that there is no equality
> For he who abides by another system.
> What person does not complain
> When he sees that the Court
> Does not consider us equal
> Not even in its final ruling.
> It gives preference
> To any Tom, Dick, or Harry.)

The poet observes that the Supreme Court is part of a hierarchical system which is far too arbitrary and powerful.

In 1886, two New Mexico newspapers, *El Guía de Santa Fe* and *El Tiempo,* carried anonymous poems critical of a J. W. Dwyer who was a candidate for territorial delegate to Congress. "Oración de Dwyer" [Dwyer's Prayer] is a highly satirical piece in which Dwyer invokes the powers of the heavens to aid him in his political quest.[104] In his "Our

Father," he tells God that because all Texans—apparently Dwyer was an out-of-stater so feared and hated by New Mexicans—are good Christians, his request should be granted. In his credo, Dwyer affirms his faith in money and banks. In "Saludo a Dwyer" [A Greeting to Dwyer], the poet chides the politician for his ambition and in the poem's last stanza he predicts that, if elected, Dwyer will use the state's natural resources for his own financial gain.[105] The most scathing attack on Dwyer is contained in "Que entienda Dwyer que los neo-mejicanos no se venden ni los necesitamos para nada" [May Dwyer Understand That New Mexicans Are Not for Sale Nor Do We Need Him for Anything][106]. This long, sixteen-stanza poem questions Dwyer and his cohorts' condescending attitude toward Chicanos and their mistaken assumption that Spanish-speaking voters would be easily manipulated. The poet urges his fellow-Chicanos to reject this traitorous Texan—it would be better to elect a pig.

A few other examples of specific historical occurrences that are addressed in social protest poetry are the assassination of one Faustín Ortiz, whose assassin, an Anglo, was never brought to justice;[107] the New Mexico county Democratic convention—the poet is critical of the Anglos who were elected;[108] and the bad faith of Anglo-Americans who have repeatedly broken their promises to support New Mexico statehood. In this last case, the poet blames the delay on the secondary status of Spanish-speaking New Mexicans and he urges Congress to recant:

> La esperanza es el consuelo
> De las almas afligidas,
> Que al sentirse doloridas
> Dirigen su vista al cielo;
> No se logró nuestro anhelo
> En el caso ya pasado
> Pero se verá logrado
> Y tendrá nueva atención
> Eso está que sin razón
> El Congreso ha rechazado.[109]

> (Hope is the consolation
> Of afflicted souls

Who feeling pained,
Direct their sight to heaven;
Our desire was not achieved
In the term just passed
But it will be successful
And will get new attention
This case which without reason
Has been rejected by Congress.)

Poetry that expresses cultural pride is common. López Ayllón's short poem "Mi raza" [My Race] is typical of the efforts of Chicano poets to combat the racist attacks upon Chicanos in the press and elsewhere.

Mi raza es una raza de espíritu guerrero
valiente hasta la audacia, tenaz hasta morir,
de nobles sentimientos, de genio aventurero
que supo un nuevo mundo llegar a descubrir.

Es una raza fuerte que lucha con firmeza
por conseguir los fines que tiene su ideal . . .
Antes buscaba guerras, por su ansia de grandeza
y ahora tan sólo anhela la paz universal.

Es una raza noble que vive de ideales
y lleva enarbolada, en sus marchas triunfales,
un bandera blanca que es símbolo de unión . . .

Y en su escudo de guerra ostenta como mote
"el espíritu noble que tuvo don Quijote
y el ansia de conquista de Cristóbal Colón."[110]

(My race is one with a warlike spirit
valiant even unto daring, tenacious unto death,
of noble feelings, of an adventuresome nature
a race which knew how to go about making discoveries.

It is a strong race which struggles firmly
to obtain its ideals' goals . . .
while before it sought war in order to enhance its greatness,
now it only desires universal peace.

It is a noble race that lives according to its ideals
and carries on high on its triumphant marches
a white flag that is a symbol of unity . . .

> And on its shield of war it brandishes as its emblem
> "the noble spirit that Don Quixote possessed
> and the eagerness of conquest of Christopher Columbus.")

The poem is quoted here in its entirety in order to illustrate the determination with which this and other literate Chicanos respond to negative stereotyping. Another good example is a poem in praise of the Spanish language, "Composición poética en loor del idioma castellano" [A Poetic Composition in Praise of the Spanish Language], in which the entire literary history of Spain and Spanish America is given in order to instill pride in Chicanos of their Hispanic culture.[111] The poet comments in the last stanzas that some misguided individuals—it is implied that they are Anglo-Americans—treat Chicanos as a stupid people while holding themselves up as wise. The poet urges his people to prefer the language of Cervantes over English.

Social societies, predecessors of today's American GI Forum and the League of United Latin American Citizens (LULAC), were founded in many Chicano communities in the late nineteenth century and early twentieth century. One of their purposes was to give the Spanish-speaking a sense of social and cultural cohesiveness in order that the language and traditions would not be lost. An example of the poetry devoted to the societies is M. Padilla Mondragón's "Salutación a la Sociedad Hispano-Americana" [A Salutation to the Hispanic American Society], in which he praises the society as a refuge in times of difficulty.[112]

In response to accusations by Anglo-Americans that Chicanos, because of their Mexican ancestry, were aliens and cowardly, poets wrote patriotic poetry affirming their loyalty to the United States. An anonymous poem, "The Voice of the Hispano," published in 1898 on the eve of the Spanish-American War, epitomizes this defense:

> Muchas son las opinones
> En contra del pueblo hispano,
> Y le acusan de traidor
> Al gobierno americano
>
> Haciendo un experimento,
> Quedarán desengañados,
> Que nuestros bravos nativos
> No rehusan ser soldados,

No importa lo que se diga
Y difame de su fama,
Pero pelearán gustosos
Por el águila americana,

A nuestro pueblo nativo
Le acusan de ser canalla,
Pero no ha demostrado serlo,
En el campo de batalla. . . .

Como buenos compatriotas
Y fieles americanos,
Libraremos de ese yugo
A los humildes cubanos . . .[113]

(Many are the opinions
Against the Hispanic people
And they accuse them of betraying
The American government.

Making an experiment,
They will be disillusioned,
Our brave native men
Do not refuse to be soldiers.

It matters not what is said
Or how our fame is insulted,
As they will fight with pleasure
For the American eagle.

They accuse our native people
Of being rabble,
But they have not proven to be so
On the battlefield.

Like good countrymen
And faithful Americans,
We will free from that yoke
The humble Cubans.)

In the same year, another New Mexican poet, Eleuterio Baca, devotes a long laudatory poem to the American Union on the occasion of the United States victory over Spain in the Caribbean.[114] Tragically, the poet must turn on his own Hispanic culture to defend his country's history and present policies.

The First World War was the occasion for the outpouring of patriotic sentiments on the part of many Chicano poets. Typical is the poem "Patria querida" [Beloved Country], by Alfredo Lobato, who bids farewell to the United States as he sails off to fight the Germans:

> Oh América querida,
> por ti vamos a pelear
> por no verte sumergida
> que otro venga a gobernar,
> por ti, tus hijos se
>   arriesgan
> hasta sus vidas dejar.[115]

> (Oh, beloved America,
> for you we are going to fight
> in order not to see you defeated
> so that others might govern you,
> for you, your sons risk themselves
> even to the point of giving up
>   their lives.)

Occasional poetry: Other than love, religious, and social themes, the most common type of Chicano poetry during this period is commemorative and elegiac. Poetry is devoted to newspapers, states, cities, famous people, months of the year, birthdays, etc. Moving elegies abound, most written on the occasion of the death of a close friend or relative. The New Mexican poets excel at both types of poetry, particularly the second.[116] José Manuel Arellano's poignant elegy to his young son is an excellent example:

Juan Cristóbal

> Se acabó de esta casa la alegría
> Con la ausencia de nuestro hijo muerto
> Juan Cristóbal Arrelano sin mancilla

> ¡Oh! hermosura sin igual en esta vida
> ¡Oh! delicia de tus padres y hermanitos

Nos dejaste lamentando tu partida
Afligidos, angustiados y solitos.

¡Oh! qué cruel separación hemos sufrido
Con la muerte de Juanito nuestro encanto
Nos dejaste prenda amada hechos un llanto
Lamentando amargamente sin sentido.[117]

Juan Cristobal

(Joy in this house has ended
With the absence of our dead son
Juan Cristobal Arellano without sin
has flown quickly to heaven where he will be happy.

Oh! Beauty without equal in this life
Oh! The delight of your parents and family
Your parting left us crying
Afflicted, anguished, and alone.

Oh! What a cruel separation we have suffered
With the death of little John our delight
Precious thing, you left us crying
Deeply lamenting your departure.)

Chicano poetry, with its strong oral and written traditions, is a rich source of literary expression. Both oral and written poetry have served as vehicles to transmit and keep alive Hispanic cultural values brought to the Southwest and California from Spain and Mexico, to cultivate refined themes, and to express the discontent of an oppressed people. Local bards sang of the feats of legendary heroes and recounted the mundane occurrences of daily life in the mountains and the valleys, and Spanish-language newspapers appeared and prospered.

Conclusion

The early seeds of Chicano literature took root in the rich soil of the Spanish Southwest in the sixteenth century and tenaciously grew during the next four hundred years. Continuing the long tradition of Hispanic literature, theater, prose, and poetry prospered in both oral and written forms. Then, with the rapid and profound changes that accompanied Mexican independence and the loss of the vast northern territories to the United States in the nineteenth century, Chicano literature began a hundred-year struggle to survive. From about 1850 to the post–Second World War period, works in the different genres appeared in Spanish-language newspapers, were independently published, and were even passed on from generation to generation by word of mouth. Like the Chicano people themselves, the literature has withstood the onslaught of a technologically superior Anglo culture to emerge, in the decade of the 1950s healthy, vital, and ready to burst into full bloom in the next twenty years. Contemporary Chicano writers thus draw on a literary tradition that is several centuries old, and they will mold and shape it to fit the artistic and social needs of the new age.

Chapter Three
Contemporary Chicano Theater

There is little continuity between Mexican and Chicano theater activity of the first half of the twentieth century and the last fifteen years, which comprise the period of contemporary Chicano theater. The reasons for this are found in the fortuitous combination of the sociohistorical circumstances of the mid-1960s and the impact of Luis Valdez, a dynamic and original artist, on the theater scene. The impetus for much of Chicano performing theater since 1965 can be traced to his efforts. In this chapter, we will discuss the evolution of his creation, El Teatro Campesino (The Workers' Theater), the development of other important theater groups and organizations, and the works of playwrights who have experimented with different dramatic forms.

El Teatro Campesino

Contemporary Chicano theater had its beginnings in 1965 when Valdez, with a fresh undergraduate degree in drama from San Jose State University and a stint with the San Francisco Mime Troupe behind him, founded El Teatro Campesino to support the César Chávez–led strike against the grape growers in the San Joaquin Valley. Valdez has continued to play a key role in the development of Chicano theater during the last fifteen years through his efforts on behalf of farmworkers as well as through his own evolution as a playwright, director, and producer.

His background is similar to that of many Chicano writers. He grew up in the small valley towns of central California where picking cotton, fruit, and vegetables has been the livelihood for generations of Chicano families.[1] Valdez remembers his first contact with theater when he got a part as a monkey in an elementary-school play. His family moved before the first performance, but he was never to lose his keen interest in the stage. He began organizing his own plays at school and would set up puppet shows in his garage. Based on his participation in drama productions in high school, Valdez was awarded a scholarship to San Jose State University, where he excelled as an actor and won a school prize for a one-act play called *The Theft.* He soon discovered the San Francisco Mime Troupe and about the same time began reflecting on what kind of theater might be developed to reach the farmworkers who had recently organized themselves into the National Farmworkers Association. After a few months with the Mime Troupe, enough to cut his teeth on their open, lively, and bawdy commedia dell'arte style, Valdez went to Delano, the center of union activity, to organize a theater group to carry the message of the strike to the workers in the field. This was the beginning of El Teatro Campesino and the *acto,* the dramatic form that has been central to this and other Chicano theater groups' repertory. Valdez relates how the *acto* spontaneously grew out of his ideas combined with the dynamics of the farmworkers' meeting held to organize a theater:

The second meeting started out very slow. We got about twelve people. About four or five were, again, student volunteers, and I was a little disappointed because I wanted farmworkers. And with another five—some were very serious. It seemed dismal. I talked for about ten minutes, and then realized that talking wasn't going to accomplish anything. The thing to do was do it, so I called three of them over, and on two hung *Huelguista* signs. Then I handed one an *Esquirol* sign, and told him to stand up there and act like an *Esquirol*—a scab. He didn't want to at first, because it was a dirty word at that time, but he did it in good spirits. Then the two *huelguistas* started shouting at him, and everybody started cracking up. All of a sudden, people started coming into the pink house from I don't know where; they filled up the whole kitchen. We started changing signs around and people started volunteering, "Let me play so and so," "Look this is what I did," imitating all kinds of things. We ran for about two hours just doing that. By the time we had finished, there were people packing the place. They were in the doorways, the living room, and they were outside at the windows peeking in, . . . and I think it got the message across—that you can do a lot by acting out things. That was the beginning. The effects we achieved that night were fantastic, because people were acting out real things. Then I got together an original group of about five, and we started working on skits—this was all done after picketing hours, by the way. Sometimes we wouldn't get started until eight or nine, but we went on every night for about three weeks. We gave our first presentation in Filipino Hall.[2]

Valdez preferred to call this dramatic form an *acto* rather than a skit because it would make more sense to his Spanish-speaking audiences.[3] Simply defined, the *acto* is a short—ten- to fifteen-minute— improvisational piece designed, in Valdez's words, to inspire the audience to social action, illuminate specific points about social problems, satirize the opposition, show or hint at a solution, and express what people are feeling.[4] While it is not a new form—it can be traced to commedia dell'arte, the Mexican *carpa* or tent presentations, the San Francisco Mime Troupe, and other radical guerrilla theater groups such as New York's Bread and Puppet Theater—what makes it characteristically Chicano is its bilingualism, the fact that it deals solely with Chicano experiences and addresses itself to the particular needs of the Chicano.[5] Valdez affirms that because Chicanismo calls for a revolutionary turn in the arts as well as in society, "Chicano theater must be revolutionary in technique as well as in content. It must be popular, subject to no other critics except the *pueblo* itself; but it must also educate the *pueblo* toward an appreciation of social change, on and off the stage."[6] He believes it is particularly important that Chicano theater draw a distinction between what is theater and what is reality, a concept that is close to Brecht's differentiation between epic theater and realistic theater. In fact, Valdez has acknowledged his debt to Brecht.[7]

The reality that El Teatro Campesino has effectively dramatized over the years is the farmworker's plight. This dramatization has been carried out through the simple device of the archetypal or stereotypical characters very familiar to El Teatro's audiences. Just as the commedia dell'arte had its stock characters—Arlecchino, Colombina, Pantalone, and Pulcinella—the *actos* have developed their own: "Super Sam," the arrogant white cop, who represents the various repressive establishment law enforcement agencies; the *Patrón* ("Grower"), who exploits his workers while pretending to be their friend; the *Vendidos* ("Sell-outs"), who have rejected their Mexican-Chicano cultural identity and are threatened by those who haven't; the *Coyote* ("Labor Contractor"), who cynically exploits his fellow-Chicanos for profit; the *Esquirol* ("Scab"), who is imported from Mexico to break the backs of the strikers by working for lower wages or by crossing union picket lines; the *Huelguistas* ("Strikers"), who man the picket lines and are committed to improving their working conditions in the agricultural fields of California and the Southwest; *Juanito Raza* (also known as *Johnny Pachuco* or *Juan Corazón*), whose *machista* behavior and drug addiction are depicted as harmful to the Chicano cause; the *Campesinos* ("Farmworkers"), who are characterized as poor and humble victims of exploitation. Other abstract characters such as Death, Churches, General Defense, Union, and Winter are also represented.[8]

Another unique feature of the *acto* is that it is the result of the collective creative effort of Valdez, the farmworkers-actors, and other interested participants. This is in keeping with the revolutionary ideology of the group and its commitment to social change; the creative process is collective and therefore revolutionary in itself. Valdez is aware that his audience would not respond to the individual introspective process that characterizes the theater of playwrights such as Tennessee Williams and Arthur Miller.[9]

Like other guerrilla theater groups, El Teatro Campesino uses no sets, few props, and few devices except for signs hung around the actors' necks identifying them as *Campesinos, Vendidos, Huelguistas*, etc., masks, an old pair of pants, a pair of sunglasses, and other easily transferable items. As Francisco Jiménez has observed, "The advantage in this scarcity of materials is that performances can be staged anywhere—in the streets, the fields, the back of the truck."[10]

Valdez's early *actos*, which were performed in the union hall and in the fields around Delano, were concerned exclusively with the farmworker and union struggle against the growers.[11] *Las dos caras del patroncito* [The Two-Faced Boss] focuses on the hypocrisy of the grape grower and the innocence and vulnerability of the *Mojado* ("Wetback"), imported illegally from Mexico to help break the California grape strike. The play was first performed in Delano in 1965. The farmworker from Mexico who speaks broken English communicates his plight as a desperately poor person who is being used to benefit the grower. Appropriately, the grower appears on stage with a yellow pig-face mask pantomiming driving his big car. Charlie the "rent-a-fuzz" or hired guard behaves like an ape, an obvious jibe at the local law-enforcement officers who solidly backed the growers throughout the early years of strife.[12] Midway through the *acto,* the grower exchanges roles with the farmworker as a way of enticing him to be a loyal Mexican rather than a "commie striker." This reversal serves to point out the contrast between the farmworker's poor living and working conditions and the grower's decadent life of luxury as well as to illustrate that beneath their masks—in the case of growers, the mask of money and power—the Mexican farmworker and the Patroncito are equal. In recognizing this, the audience's fear of the grower is reduced and at the same time the *acto* exhorts them not to desire his materialism.

La quinta temporada [The Fifth Season], created by El Teatro Campesino in 1966, deals with the hated figure of the *Coyote,* the labor contractor who delivers Chicanos and Mexican nationals to the growers in exchange for lucrative commissions.[13] The Fifth Season refers to the improved working and living conditions offered by the United Farmworkers Union. The allegorical figures of Winter, Summer, Fall, and Spring, which here are introduced into the *actos,* illustrate El Teatro's ability to translate ideas into visual experiences.[14] Summer's shirt is covered with money, a representation of its monetary importance to the farmworker, who must take advantage of this season in order to survive throughout the rest of the year. Winter, which in the *acto* takes on monstrous proportions, often brings starvation and disease. At the end of the *acto,* the three other seasons become Churches, the Union, and La Raza, thus holding out the hope for farmworkers that, in the future, Winter will not present such an ominous face.

The focus of El Teatro Campesino broadened in 1967 when it left Delano for Del Rey, California, where it founded El Centro Campesino Cultural (The Workers' Cultural Center). *Actos* now began dealing with problems the Chicano faced other than those related to the farmworker. *Los vendidos* [The Sell-Outs], one of El Teatro's most popular *actos,* reflects this shift from the fields to the urban centers where the majority of Chicanos live and work. The play deals humorously with the serious problem of the Chicano who leaves behind his language and culture as he climbs the social ladder in a society dominated by alien Anglo-American values. Honest Sancho's Used Mexican Lot and Mexican Curio Shop is the setting for this farce in which Miss Jiménez comes looking for an acceptable Mexican for Governor Reagan's office. Sancho, the astute storekeeper, shows her several models: the Farmworker, Johnny Pachuco, the *Revolucionario* ("Revolutionary"), and the Mexican-American, "a clean-shaven middle class type in a business suit, with glasses." The first three are immediately objectionable because they show various degrees of uncouthness or militancy. Only the last model seems acceptable until he, too, begins spouting La Raza slogans. The *acto* points the finger at the sell-out, which is a Chicano problem, and at tokenism, which is the Anglo practice of only accepting Chicanos who have completely assimilated the values of the dominant culture.

La conquista de México [The Conquest of Mexico], a puppet show, reflects El Teatro's desire to deal with larger social and historical questions. A farce that reenacts the Spanish conquest of the Aztecs, this *acto* heralds the solidarity among Chicanos to oppose oppression. It demonstrates the parallels between the sixteenth-century conquest and Anglo-American domination of the Mexican in the nineteenth and of the Chicano in the twentieth century.

El Teatro Campesino moved again in 1969. Their reputation had spread beyond the United States, and they were invited to the Seventh World Theatre Festival in France, where they were well received by enthusiastic audiences.[15] Later in 1969 they performed in Los Angeles at the Inner City Cultural Center, where, again, audiences enthusiastically applauded them. Dan Sullivan, the *Los Angeles Times* drama critic, commented favorably on their "rambunctious sketches" and their "ability to delight and instruct." He called them "superior farceurs."[16]

El Teatro Campesino continued dealing with the larger Chicano perspective. *No saco nada de la escuela* [I'm Not Getting Anything Out of School] is a three-part *acto* which takes Chicano students from elementary through high school to college, presenting the problems they confront at every level: insensitive, racist teachers and bewilderment in an English-speaking classroom. At every turn in the educational system, Chicanos face attempts to deprive them of a sense of cultural pride. So ashamed is she of admitting her Mexican roots that at one point a Chicana student in the play declares that her parents are Hawaiian. The *acto* ends with an affirmation of Chicano values and a call to organize in the best interests of La Raza. In *The Militants,* a brief *acto,* both the proverbial bleeding heart Anglo liberal and the young Chicano militant are satirized for their lack of effective action to bring about social change.

In 1970, El Teatro turned its attention to the Vietnam War with the production of *Vietnam campesino* [Vietnam Farmworker], a longer five-scene *acto* that focuses on the collusion between the growers and the Pentagon to exploit the Chicano farmworker both at home and in Vietnam. It calls for Chicanos to recognize that they have more in common with their Vietnamese brothers than with Anglos in their own country. The "Military Agricultural Complex," the title of the first scene, is represented by Butt Anglo and General Defense, two archetypal characters. The second scene deals with the dangerous practice of exposing humans to cancer-causing defoliants. The third scene introduces the allegorical figure of The Draft, a tall figure dressed in a mask and an American flag, who clearly symbolizes the fate of the farmworker, who is being inducted into the army. In the fourth scene, the stage is split; on one side are two Vietnamese farmworkers and on the the other are two Chicano *campesinos*. The device is highly effective as two culturally diverse worlds are juxtaposed to illustrate their sameness. Despite their common enemy, the United States military, Chicano and Vietnamese brothers turn on and kill each other. The *acto* ends with a call for solidarity among Chicanos and a resolve to fight the real war in Aztlán, not Vietnam.

Soldado razo [The Chicano GI], first performed in 1971 at the Chicano Moratorium on the War in Vietnam in Fresno, like *Vietnam campesino,* makes an antiwar statement from a Chicano perspective. It centers around a father and son's false concept of *machismo* and the military. It has been called "the exemplary *acto,* a slice of Chicano history which universalizes the Chicano war experience."[17] *La muerte* ("Death") plays a key role in this *acto* as a moralizing agent constantly reminding the audience of the stupidity of the son and his father's idea that going off to Vietnam will turn Johnny into a man. While Johnny's death does not come as a surprise—it is foreshadowed throughout the *acto*—the last scene serves as a poignant reminder to the audience of how useless the spending of a young Chicano life is.

The year 1971 signaled a major change in the evolution of El Teatro Campesino. Luis Valdez and his troupe of actors moved to San Juan Bautista, California, and began experimenting with another form, the *mito,* which differs significantly from the *acto*. Simply defined, the *mito* attempts to explore the content of Chicano culture while the *acto* concentrates on political issues expressed in the cultural terms of the Chicano audience.[18] El Teatro thus began deemphasizing sociopolitical content to focus more clearly on legends, myths, and religion. Valdez defines the *mito* as a "more mystical dramatic form" yet he does not disparage the *acto*. He calls the two forms dramatic twins (*cuates*) "that complement and balance each other as day goes into night, el sol la sombra, la vida la muerte, el pájaro, el serpiente. Our rejection of white western European (*gavacho*) proscenium theater makes the birth of new Chicano forms necessary—thus, *los actos y los mitos*; one through the eyes of man; the other, through the eyes of God."[19]

The first public experimentation with the *mito* was El Teatro Campesino's production of *La gran carpa de los rascuachis* [The Tent of the Underdogs], performed in 1973 in Santa Cruz, California. The work is divided into three parts: two *mitos* and a middle part, an *acto*, which tells the story of Jesús Pelado Rascuachi, a Mexican national, who with his family crosses the border to the United States in search of a better life. As a farmworker he is exploited and suffers discrimination. At the end of this middle section, the Rascuachi family breaks up. In the two *mitos*, Christian as well as native Mexican Indian figures are introduced: Jesus Christ, Quetzalcoatl, and the Virgin of Guadalupe.

La gran carpa has both its critics and its defenders. For example, Raúl Ruíz believes that the two *mitos* detract from the impact of the *acto* by eliminating the possibility of arriving at a human socio-economic solution. The *mitos* have the effect of raising the whole work to a supernatural plane.[20] When *La gran carpa* was performed in Mexico City in 1974 it drew further criticism from two Latin American dramatists, the Brazilian Agusto Boal and the Colombian Enrique Buenaventura. The former was critical of Valdez's idealized view of the indigenous past and the latter questioned whether El Teatro Campesino had strayed from its original purpose and was dwelling too much on its own identity.[21] Another critic, Yarbro-Bejarano, points out, in defense of the El Teatro, that the group was willing to incorporate criticisms into later performances of the work and to seek an artistic reconciliation between the *acto* and the *mito*. She believes that the 1977 airing of *La gran carpa* on public television "seems to respond even more earnestly to the urgings of Boal and others to place cultural and mythical content in the social and historical context of the Chicano today."[22]

Bernabé: A Drama of Modern Chicano Mythology is a *mito* in which historical and mythological elements are combined in a more harmonious way than in *La gran carpa*.[23] Valdez draws a parallel between the sacred Aztec ritual of offering a gift of the human heart to Huit-zilopochtli, the Sun God, and the *campesinos* of the Southwest who toil under the blazing heat of the sun. In both cases, "the sun retains that power of life and death, wonder and terror."[24] In the *mito*, the Sun God reappears in a golden feathered headdress as El Sol within the setting of a farm town in the San Joaquin Valley. Bernabé, the hero, is the village idiot possessed of the "divinity of madness." He symbolizes man's lost love for the Earth, and, in order to restore harmony with the Sun God, he must be sacrificed just as human sacrifices were offered in Aztec rituals. Bernabé asks the Sun for the body of his daughter, the Earth. He is taunted and then tempted by the Moon, who, in the drama, appears as a *pachuco* to protect his sister, the Earth. When the Moon asks the Sun to give his sister to Bernabé, the Sun makes the Earth a virgin again through the sacrifice of Bernabé. After the sacrifice, Bernabé and the Earth are joined in marriage. Bernabé thus fulfills his sacrificial role as the Earth and is once again able to provide sustenance and favor to those who, like Bernabé, love and honor her. The Earth appears dressed as a *soldadera* ("woman soldier") with cartridge belts draped across her chest, the figure of Adelita of the Mexican Revolu-tion. The Earth thus has a dual historical function as the spirit of life in Aztec religion and the spirit of freedom. Through his union with the Earth, Bernabé embraces the best of the Chicano's Mexican-Indian heritage.

In *The Dark Root of a Scream*, a parallel is again drawn between the Aztecs and the Chicanos.[25] As the Indian priests created strife and promoted human sacrifice, the Catholic Church is shown in this *mito* to be an instrument of destruction which sends young Chicanos to their deaths in wars. A young Chicano soldier killed in Vietnam is depicted as the modern reincarnation of the Aztec god-leader, Quetzalcoatl. Of special interest in this work is the stage set which is made in the form of a pyramid with two scenes at the base: Chicano youth on a *barrio* street corner on one side and a wake on the other. Above, there are images of modern civilization and, at the peak of the pyramid, there are ancient Indian images. Unlike *La gran carpa* and *Bernabé*, this work does not idealize Aztec culture but is quite critical of the ritual of human sacrifice. Perhaps Valdez had reassessed and moderated his romantic idealization of indigenous culture as a result of criticism received by Boal and others.

"El fin del mundo" [The End of the World] is another *mito* El Teatro Campesino worked with during the mid-1970s. Luis Valdez summarizes the plot and intent of this unpublished play in a long interview in 1973 with Francoise Kourilsky:

The *mito* we are working on now is called *El fin del Mundo*. It comes from a very popular myth about the end of the world, and it involves one central character, a Chicano, and his family. He runs into the angel Gabriel, who tells him that the world is about to end. There are three trumpet blasts, each one signifying a different level of reality. First, is the level of everyday life. Civilization comes apart, the Chicano's daily reality comes apart. Everything that is inconceivable and horrible in life happens to him; his sons become involved with drugs, his daughter is raped, his wife is murdered in the kitchen. . . . We are trying to make basic points about everyday life, about injustice, about human suffering, and yet we also see the humorous side to it all. Level two is the supernatural, where the devils appear, the dead arise, because at the end of the world the dead are supposed to arise. So the dead people this man has known come back and bring with them guilts, suspicions, things left undone, revenge, and so on. There is the cosmic phase, where the Chicano starts to come apart; and he eventually breaks down into earth, air, fire, and water. His breath leaves him, his body heat leaves him, his body and soul separate. He dies and the world ends. But the last scene shows the man lying in bed, surrounded by his family, and he simply dies. So it's not really the end of the world. In the events we are trying to explore the most elemental impressions our people have of reality. On the first level, for instance, we deal with sex. What do the Chicanos really feel about sex, and where do these feelings come from? They come from a basic concept of the nature of man and woman, of society. The use of drugs, the feelings of racial inferiority, all these take place on the first level, which is conscious. The second level is conscious too, but supernatural, and deals with man's suspicions, the things he fears and is unsure of. Where does *La Calavera* come from? *La Calavera* is the skeleton figure that for the Mexican designates human mortality and also the inner spirit that permits movement.[26]

The most recent dramatic endeavor of Luis Valdez's theater group is the unpublished "Zoot Suit," which focuses on the Sleepy Lagoon murder of 1942.[27] In the play, four young Chicanos represent the seventeen *pachucos* indicted and found guilty of murdering a youth and of lesser charges. They were sentenced to long prison terms. The play is the story of their release. "Zoot Suit" was first presented for fourteen performances in Los Angeles as part of the Mark Taper Forum's Theatre for Now Series in April 1978. It was then revised and reopened in August as the first play of the 1978–79 season at the Forum. Its California run was then extended at the Aquarius Theater in Hollywood, and in 1979 it moved to the Winter Garden Theater on Broadway in New York City. While it received generally good reviews on the West Coast, East Coast critics treated it harshly. [28]

Henry Reyna, the leader of the *pachucos* on trial, is the play's main character. We follow him from the moment he intends to enlist in the navy, through the gang fight at the Sleepy Lagoon, the arrest, and the next few years of trial, conviction, appeal, and victory. Valdez also focuses on Alice Bloomfield, head of the defense committee for the convicted Chicano youths. She is portrayed sympathetically, as is the defense lawyer. Valdez successfully condenses into a few short scenes the hundreds of pages of the courtroom proceedings as well as the long, painful deliberations that took place among the incarcerated Chicanos, their families, and the members of the Defense Committee.

"Zoot Suit" represents an important step forward for Chicano theater because, for the first time, a contemporary play by a Chicano has successfully made the transition from the *barrio* and the academic setting to commercial theater. With this dramatized social document, Valdez carries his message to a wider audience while not abandoning the simplicity and directness of his earlier *actos*.

TENAZ and Annual Theater Festivals

El Teatro Campesino was the major force in the late 1960s and the early 1970s that led to the formation of other Chicano theater groups, the founding of TENAZ (El Teatro Nacional de Aztlán [The National Theater of Aztlán]), and the holding of annual theater festivals. In 1970, El Teatro Campesino hosted the first national Festival de los Teatros Chicanos, attended by sixteen groups from all over the United States. Some of the *teatros* who participated were El Teatro del Piojo from Seattle, El Teatro Mestizo from San Diego, Grupo Mascarones from Mexico City, El Teatro Aztlán from San Fernanco, California, and

El Teatro Bilingüe from El Paso.[29] The success of this first festival led to a second, a year later, held in Santa Cruz, California, and again hosted by El Teatro Campesino.

Due to the increased number of participating theater groups and the perceived need to provide direction and training for directors and actors, TENAZ was founded in 1971. This coalition of Chicano theater directors assumed responsibility for coordinating national and regional festivals, publications, communications between groups, and establishing summer workshops for theater representatives. The first issue of its publication, *Chicano Theater One,* appeared in 1973. The first TENAZ summer workshop took place in the summer of 1971 in San Juan Bautista sponsored by El Teatro Campesino. Luis Valdez, his brother Danny, and other members of El Teatro worked closely with participants from various other groups.

The Third Annual Festival of Chicano Theatres was held in the spring of 1972 in San Jose, hosted by El Teatro de la Gente. It was a rousing success, with over twenty-five groups in attendance. Later that year, the second TENAZ summer workshop took place at El Teatro Campesino center in San Juan Bautista. Once again, members of El Teatro conducted classes and provided guidance for the many members of the Chicano theater groups who participated.

The Fourth Annual Festival de los Teatros Chicanos in 1973 in San Jose, California, saw the participation of several theater groups from Mexico as well as an increased number of Chicano groups. Valdez's remarks at the festival reflected the changing emphasis of El Teatro Campesino during this period and served to remind others of the importance of different currents in the contemporary theater. He cited improvisation, commedia dell'arte, Naturalism, Symbolism, Old Comedy, the choral work of the Mexican group, Los Mascarones, and the theories and practice of playwrights such as Artaud, Brecht, the Bread and Puppet Theatre, the Open Theatre, the Living Theatre, Grotowski, and the agit-prop drama of the 1930s.[30] In addition to the *acto* and the *mito* forms which dominated the festival, there were performances of children's theater designed to celebrate the pride young Chicanos feel in their culture. El Teatro de las Chicanas, a women's group, gave a performance challenging old sexist stereotypes that have proved so harmful to the equality of men and women in the Chicano struggle. Another kind of theater represented at the festival emphasized nostalgic scenes such as Saturday night in a Chicano dance hall complete with the songs of one of Mexico's favorite singers, Agustín Lara.

The performance-criticism format, which had been introduced into earlier festivals, became a focusing activity in San Jose. The morning after an evening's performances was devoted to extensive discussions by panelists and theater group members of ways in which different *teatros* might improve the quality and impact of their works. These critiques, which were generally carried out with a spirit of constructive criticism, gave groups with very diverse backgrounds and training the opportunity to exchange candid points of view. For example, El Teatro Campesino members were able to interchange ideas with their Mexican counterparts from Los Mascarones, a group with extensive theater experience ideologically committed to radical social change in Latin America. One festival observer remarks that Chicano groups were impressed not only with the skill and style of Los Mascarones but were aware that their own political nature had not manifested itself as clearly as that of the Mexican group.[31]

Mexico City, the site of the 1974 Fifth Annual Festival, saw the great strides that Chicano theater had made collectively during the short decade of intense activity and change. The oldest and the most recently created groups could comfortably participate in a festival which also featured student and professional groups from all over Latin America. Although some Chicano *teatros* had had previous international exposure, it was the first time that most of them would be performing before a foreign audience under the scrutiny of some of Latin America's most discerning drama critics. One critic who attended the festival has called it "the milestone that marked the beginnings of a maturity that hopefully would allow Chicano theater to survive and continue to grow even after many of its primary issues are solved."[32]

The Mexico City Festival, cosponsored by TENAZ and Mexico's CLETA (Centro Libre de Experimentación Teatral y Artistíca [The Autonomous Center for Theatrical and Artistic Experimentation]), was marked by frank and often biting criticism of Chicano theater groups for "taking refuge in cultural nationalism and for being philosophically retarded."[33] Several Latin American critics felt that although Chicano theater had perfected its style and technique, it had not entered into the mainstream of international protest theater due to its lack of ideological sophistication. Specifically, the predominance of performances that emphasized and tended to idealize the indigenous past were seen as politically naive.

The diversity of the groups and participants was impressive. The seven hundred participants from at least twelve countries of the Western Hemisphere ranged in education from illiterate workers to university professors and distinguished critics. The over sixty performances included dances and ceremonies from ancient American cultures, a recreation of an Indian dramatization of Mayan myths, newly created works—*mitos*—incorporating myths from the Mayas and the Aztecs, pieces performed by proletarian Indian workers, and documentary analysis detailing the working-class struggle against exploitation and oppression. The United States was consistently depicted as an imperialist monster.[34]

The Sixth Annual Festival, which was held in San Antonio in 1975, marked the tenth anniversary of contemporary Chicano theater. The festival theme, *el encuentro con el barrio* ("encounter with the barrio"), was an appropriate recognition of the social nature of Luis Valdez's original *actos* created at Delano a decade before. Participants were eager to heal the wounds opened by the ideological battles of the previous year's encounter in Mexico City.[35] This was accomplished, in large measure, by concentrating on both the political and aesthetic goals of presenting socially relevant material through a uniquely Chicano art form. Reports of the festival were overwhelmingly positive. Returning the site of the annual celebration to the *barrio* apparently succeeded in giving direction and cohesiveness to Chicano theater.

The 1976 Seventh Annual Festival was expanded from one to four sites by TENAZ in order to give the Chicano community increased exposure to this important artistic endeavor.[36] While not all of the forty theaters which participated were able to appear in all four cities—Seattle, Denver, San Jose, and Los Angeles—during the three-month traveling spectacle, TENAZ generally succeeded in its aim to return Chicano theater to the *barrio*. Although the Seattle segment of the festival was poorly attended and poorly organized, the second stop, in Denver, was characterized by the energetic participation of many young groups as well as three older ones. The San Jose segment, timed to coincide with a local cannery workers' strike, also went off well. Of special note was a collective cantata production by several veteran groups and a contingent of cannery workers which dramatized the 1907 Chilean massacre of 3,600 striking salt-mine workers, their wives, and children. The Los Angeles part of the festival was attended by some of the Mexican theater groups who had been present at the Fifth Festival in Mexico City in 1974.

San Diego was the sight of the 1977 Eighth Annual Festival. It was hosted by the Teatro Mesitzo and El Centro Cultural de la Raza.[37] No festival was held in 1978. Instead, a seminar workshop was organized for that year in Mill Valley, California, to discuss several questions of importance to the evolution of Chicano theater, including the significance of the theater, its audience, contradictions, aesthetic principles, politics, and future.[38] The 1979 Tenth Annual Festival in Santa Barbara was keenly anticipated and well attended, due, in large part, to there being no festival the previous year. Older experienced theaters as well as newer ones performed. In the opinion of Jorge Huerta, a veteran critic of other festivals, the performances were disappointing.[39] Far more successful were the critique panels made up of distinguished Latin American and American theater critics including Emilio Carballido, Enrique Buenaventura, Paulo Carbalho-Neto, and Tomás Ybarra-Frausto. No theater festival was planned for 1980.

TENAZ has a current membership of over forty Chicano theater groups, most of them affiliated with academic institutions or with urban community organizations. Unlike El Teatro Campesino, none is able to generate enough income from performances and other activities—workshops, television and movie rights, etc.—to be self-sufficient, nor are any as active as Luis Valdez's troupe. Yet, since the creation of TENAZ in 1971, several *teatros* have survived tenaciously and even prospered. A discussion of some of these groups will illustrate that Chicano theater is thriving today on college campuses, in the *barrios,* at festivals, and even on the international scene.

El Teatro de la Esperanza

After El Teatro Campesino, El Teatro de la Esperanza (The Theater of Hope) is probably the most vital Chicano theater group today. Formed in 1971 by Jorge Huerta and other students at the University of California, Santa Barbara, El Teatro de la Esperanza quickly established a solid reputation in the Santa Barbara area.[40] Working out of La Casa de la Raza, a Chicano community center, the group held its first workshop during the summer of its formation and performed songs and *actos* of El Teatro Campesino. Soom the group began to tour surrounding communities, performing in gyms, halls, auditoriums, and other community centers to enthusiastic audiences. A large room at La Casa was remodeled into a small auditorium and other support and money was given by a campus student group, local carpenters, architects, electricians, etc. The group began writing, producing, and staging its own works in 1972 and continued holding workshops. Within a couple of years of its formation, El Teatro de la Esperanza was being invited to theater festivals and other cities to perform its original *actos* and plays. In 1973, it published a collection of these works written collectively or by individual members of the group.

Like the early *actos* of El Teatro Campesino, the short skits of El Teatro de la Esperanza contained archetypal and allegorical characters who represent different components of the Chicano community and their oppressors, and as in the *mitos,* Aztec mythological characters also make their appearance as symbolic representations of important ideas in the Chicano movement. In keeping with the group's character as an urban theater, most of the settings are in the *barrio* rather than in the fields and most of the dramatic situations revolve around conflicts and problems encountered by Chicano city-dwellers.

Juan Epitaph is a short *acto* written by Joey García, the group musician, in response to the 1970 Chicano Moratorium in Los Angeles, with music and lyrics by the author. Combining ballet, music, and pantomime, the work dramatizes the killing of a Chicano by Anglo policemen during the Moratorium march. Frank Verdugo's *La trampa sin salida* [Trap with No Exit] is a hard-hitting *acto* which takes place in a *barrio* on a street whose name—La trampa sin salida—is symbolic of the utter despair experienced by the Chicanos who live on it. Its language is perhaps too strong for general audiences, yet it is in keeping with the scenes of frustration and bitterness arising from unemployment, discrimination, and exploitation. The group learned a valuable lesson from the first performances of this *acto*: it was useless to sacrifice the essential message of social injustice for the strong language which was alienating its audiences. Alterations were quickly made stripping the *acto* of its vulgarities.[41]

Pánfila la curandera [Pánfila the Healer], a collective creation of El Teatro de la Esperanza, focuses on the folk-medicine tradition of the *curandera,* whose cures are seen as more effective than those of the educated Anglo doctor. *La bolsa negra* [The Black Bag] by Frank Ramírez is an allegorical *acto* which portrays the effect greed has on a friendship among a group of young Chicanos who overcome its temptations to band together in a spirit of solidarity. *El Espíritu del Deseoso* [The Spirit of the Greedy One] floats in and out of the action, daring the young Chicanos to accept his inviting but destructive gift. *Los pelados* [The Downtrodden] by Felipe Castro is another *acto* with strong allegorical elements in which we are called upon to eliminate the division among Spanish-speaking peoples in the United States and to recognize the common enemy in oppressive capitalist institutions. The work, which deals specifically with the Kennedy-Rodino and Dixon-Arnett bills of the early 1970s, is seen as an urban version of Luis Valdez's *La quinta temporada.*[42] It urges Chicanos and Mexican nationals to examine their often unproductive relationship in order to unify their efforts on behalf of both groups. The allegorical figure *La Historia* ("History") provides the socioeconomic background of this relationship.

El renacimiento de Huitzilopochtli [The Rebirth of Huitzilopochtli] by Jorge Huerta, the director of El Teatro de la Esperanza, is a farce based on the legend of the birth of the Aztec God. The author contemporizes the mythological-historical figures to focus on the rivalry and petty jealousy among various factions in the Chicano movement. He makes a plea to abandon personal interest and to join together in unity. Huerta effectively employs the Brechtian *verfremdungseffekt* or estrangement technique to illustrate the alternatives open to the characters to continue squabbling among themselves or to organize.

Brujerías [Witchcraft] by Rodrigo Duarte-Clark is perhaps El Teatro de la Esperanza's best-known play. Written in 1972, it was republished in a revised version in an anthology of Chicano and Puerto Rican drama in late 1979.[43] It was also produced as a thirty-minute motion picture in 1973 and performed many times at festivals and on other occasions. It remains as one of the foundations of the group's repertoire. Representing its first departure from the *acto,* this comedy focuses on the superstitions and fears rampant in the Chicano community. The playwright takes a swipe at the Catholic Church, which he views as deceitful and manipulative in its historical relationship with Chicanos. One critic has commented that "unlike the typical *acto,* which demands a strong delineation between Good versus Evil, this play gives us two basically good people [Doña Petra and Don Rafael] who find themselves confronted with metaphysical opponents rather than an evil grower, brutal police, or the like."[44] Their superstitious nature is reinforced by their simplistic Catholic faith, and therein lies the play's social commentary; rather than addressing the deplorable social conditions that Chicanos live under, the Catholic Church preaches passivity and acceptance.

Guadalupe, a 1974 collective creation of El Teatro de la Esperanza, is another play that has enjoyed wide success with Chicano audiences. Like *Brujerías,* this work was also filmed. After a tour of California and Mexico in 1974, it was videotaped for channel 13 in Mexico City and was aired nationally in a ninety-minute special later that year.[45] It is a drama-documentary based on a report by the California State Advisory Committee to the United States Commission on Civil Rights in which cases of institutional racism in the small California town of Guadalupe are amply documented. Using the report, *The Schools of Guadalupe . . . A Legacy of Educational Oppression,* as a starting point, members of the group made many visits to the town for further research. They then improvised situations described in the document and verified firsthand in much the same way as El Teatro Campesino created *actos* from real-life situations in the agricultural fields. Lyrics and music were created and adapted to the improvised stage scenes. The characters were largely based on the figures who had organized the Chicano community to have its schools investigated. For example, the major figures in the play were the parents involved in El Comité de Padres (The Parents' Committee). The action on stage closely parallels the discussion and events that took place in Guadalupe up to the arrest of some of the most active adults. As in other *actos,* scenery was scanty. The importance of the play as a social document is based on its presentation of the complex interrelationship of oppression and apathy that exists in any Chicano community. The group succeeded in dramatizing the actual town as a microcosm whose problems have no easy solutions.

El Teatro de le Esperanza has continued the practice, initiated with *Guadalupe,* of creating plays with a broadened perspective of Chicano reality. For example, a 1979 production, *Hijos, Once a Family,* seeks to present through a family history the historical process of Chicanos within an alien capitalist society.[46] With the death of the mother, the family disintegrates: the father turns to drinking rather than face his failure to provide for the family; the oldest son drops out of school, becomes a drug addict, and ends up in jail; the daughter runs away with her lover; only the younger son, a university student, seems capable of withstanding the pressures of family breakdown. The question of who or what is to blame is repeatedly asked of the audience, which is invited to examine the socioeconomic context in which the disintegration occurs.

Other Theater Groups

El Teatro de la Gente (Bilingual Peoples' Theater) was formed in 1970 by a group of students from San Jose State University and San Jose City College. Most of the group's works—*actos*, puppet shows, *corridos*, and *mitos*—were collectively created. The troupe has established a solid reputation for itself in the Bay Area and has traveled extensively across the state and the country since its creation. It has given workshops in local schools and actively encouraged the formation of other *teatros*.[47] In 1973, El Teatro de la Gente hosted the Fourth Annual Festival de los Teatros Chicanos. Its *El corrido de Juan Endrogado* [The Ballad of Drugged John] deals with the addiction of poor people to the material symbols of success. The unity of the Chicano family is seen as the most effective way of combating this evil.[48]

El Teatro Aztlán was formed in the same year as El Teatro de la Gente by students at California State University, Northridge. Its repertoire consists mainly of *actos* based on current events such as the shooting in 1970 of the distinguished Chicano journalist Rubén Salazar. Other *actos* are more introspective. For example, the 1972 production *La casa de los locos* [The Insane Asylum] examines the commitment of the individual Chicano to changing himself. The group's philosophy is to educate its audiences about poverty, exploitation, and suffering in the *barrios* and elsewhere.[49] In the words of Esteban Oropeza, the group's spokesman, *La casa de los locos* deals "with us, and with the many times we criticize other people and organizations, but fail individually to look at ourselves so that we may see if we are coming from the best direction we are able."[50] In this self-critical view of La Raza, various stereotyped figures of the Chicano community are examined, including the *macho* and the *super-macha,* the women's liberationist. Mistrust and greed characterize many *barrio* relationships and in their place the *acto* presents the alternative of a truly united people with a revolutionary consciousness.[51]

El Teatro Urbano (The Urban Theater) is a community-based group formed in 1972 in East Los Angeles. It describes itself as producing guerrilla theater whose purpose it is "to educate and inform our Raza of problems that exist in the *barrios,* such as drugs, socioeconomic conditions, politics, etc."[52] Its *Anti-Bicentennial Special* mocks the empty promises of prominent Americans such as George Washington, Betsy Ross, Benjamin Franklin, Abraham Lincoln, and George Armstrong Custer.[53] Los Topes (The Dolts) Theatre Troup is another California community group. Established in 1971 in the San Francisco East Bay Area, it is also dedicated to sociopolitical change in the Chicano community. Its vehicle is laughter as it combines "a touch of Vaudeville . . . with Mexican music."[54] The group uses no scripts, relying entirely on improvisation.

In 1975, a group of Tucson farmworkers, activists, students, and laborers came together to form El Teatro Libertad (The Liberty Theater).[55] It had evolved from an earlier version, El Teatro del Pueblo (The People's Theater), which had performed El Teatro del Campesino *actos* adapted to the local situation. The new group created its own *actos:* a skit supporting the boycott of Gallo Wine; *Los peregrinos* [The Pilgrims], an episodic play stressing the unity of the Chicano family; *El Vacil de '76,* a comedy/drama that focuses on the common bonds of different oppressed groups in the United States; *Los cabrones* [The Bastards], a farcical look at the mistreatment of undocumented workers focusing on cultural value clashes; and *Los pelados* [The Downtrodden], an exploration into the lives of an urban working-class Chicano family.

Other Chicano theater groups that deserve mention are El Teatro Desengaño del Pueblo (The People's Theater of Disillusion) from Gary, Indiana; El Teatro Chicano de Austin; Carnales del Espíritu (Soul Brothers) from Austin; El Teatro de Ustedes (Your Theater) from Denver; El Teatro de la Revolución (The Theater of the Revolution)

from Greeley, Colorado; El Teatro del Piojo (The Louse's Theater) from
Seattle; El Teatro de los Barrios (The Theater of the Barrios) from San
Antonio; El Teatro Mestizo of San Diego; El Teatro de los Niños (The
Children's Theater) from Pasadena; and Teatro Causa de los Pobres (The
Poor Peoples' Cause Theater) from Denver.

Chicano Playwright: Carlos Morton

In addition to many Chicano theater groups associated with TENAZ
and modeled upon El Teatro Campesino, several playwrights have
distinguished themselves for their original and varied dramatic works.
While some of their plays can loosely be described as *actos* or *mitos* and
have been performed by the theater groups referred to in the previous
sections, they are sufficiently different to merit a separate discussion.

Most prolific is Carlos Morton, whose published plays are written in
a highly farcical style bordering on slapstick comedy. His first play, *El
Jardín* [The Garden], which resembles the *acto* in its use of Chicano
Spanish and stock *barrio* figures, is a hilarious parody of the fall of
man.[56] The traditional biblical figures of Adam, Eve, God, and the
serpent dominate the action, but Morton has thrown in a few extra
characters whom his Chicano audience will readily identify: *Matón*
("Killer"), *Ladrón* ("Thief"), *Nixón,* and *Cabrón* ("Bastard"). Eve is
aptly described as a *ruca* (pachuco for "chick") who is *media coquetona*
("halfway flirtatious") while the Serpent is a dissipated *barrio* type *lleno
de mota y vino* ("full of dope and wine"). The play is laced with other
references meant to enhance communication with the audience: Eve
complains that the traditional Mexican diet of beans, rice, and tortillas
is ruining her figure; Adam mentions Farah slacks; God's divine plan
includes having Adam and Eve join the Angel Mariachi Band; the
Serpent calls Eve his "little enchilada." Once having established a close
identification between the actors and the audience, Morton uses the
biblical tale to suggest that the real tragedy of the fall is that man has
lost touch with his spirit, the basis for racial and cultural pride. Adam
falls in with a group of violent militants whose tactics are characterized
as self-destructive and damaging to Chicanos. Through his play,
Morton preaches racial harmony as he urges fellow-Chicanos to assume
a role of peace-loving arbitrators between all races. His vision closely

resembles Mexican thinker José Vasconcelos's concept of the Cosmic race:

> And so ends this scene of El Jardín
> A Chicano version of the fall of man
> This mixed breed of New World Man
> Seeing visions of their own
> Which will melt with the drama of all men
> To form a unique conception of Cosmic People.[57]

El corrido de Pancho Diablo [The Ballad of Pancho Devil] is also a farcical Chicano version of a loosely based biblical story in which the devil quits his job in Hell to return to earth.[58] He soon finds that conditions on earth are as bad as they were where he came from. He laments:

> How sad is man's condition
> He lives on earth a mere rendition
> Of what befalls him when he dies
> and lands in the pit of woes and lies.[59]

He finds that Chicanos are mistreated by the police and the Texas Rangers while the Catholic Church, an exploitative landlord, preaches acceptance and nonviolence in the *barrio*. Chicano *vendidos* ("sell-outs") forsake their heritage and communities to get rich. The United States Immigration Service harasses brown brothers on city streets and the Teamsters and the Growers conspire against the United Farm Workers. As in *El jardín,* the devil tries to foment discontent and racial strife. But God appears on earth just in time in the figure of the Mexican revolutionary Emiliano Zapata. He neutralizes the devil's influence by preaching justice and reform of human institutions. Once again, Morton advocates nonviolence and racial unity as solutions to the Chicano's predicament.

Las muchas muertes de Richard Morales [The Many Deaths of Richard Morales] is the playwright's only experimentation with social realism.[60] The play, a docudrama based on the assassination of a young Chicano by the Anglo police chief of the Texas town of Castroville in

1976, focuses on the double standard of justice that still is applied to ethnic minorities in the Southwest. Part of the testimony given during the trial of the accused assassin, Hank Frayes, is used in order to heighten the sense of outrage experienced by the prosecuting attorney and the members of the Morales family.

Morton's latest work, *Rancho Hollywood,* is a return to the farcical humor of his early plays.[61] The playwright indicts the Hollywood film industry for its distortion of history and the creation of racial stereotypes. Using the device of rapidly changing scenes that parallel historic events, he manges to highlight the disparities between the official records and Hollywood's version of them. The main characters are Governor Río Rico, the last Mexican governor of California; Doña Victoria Rico, his wife; Ramona Rico, their daughter; and Jedediah Goldbanger Smith, "a Yankee trader-trapper-goldminer-soldier-capitalist with a vision." During the course of the play, Río Rico becomes transformed from an upper-class Mexican who denies his racially mixed anceestry to an assertive Chicano proud of what he is. His daughter Ramona, who also becomes more militant with the passing years, communicates the play's essential message: that Chicanos need to be acquainted with the truth of their history in order to counter false views of it promoted by Hollywood and other Anglo institutions.

In addition to the plays discussed above, Morton has also published two short pieces which are more dramatic sketches than fully developed works: the *Racist Rag* and *Buzzardville.*[62]

Other Chicano Playwrights

In his important three-act play *El corrido de California* [The Ballad of California] (1979), Fausto Avendaño uses a historical setting to dramatize the facts surrounding the Anglo military invasion of California in 1846. Don Gerónimo, a well-to-do Mexican rancher and official who professes great faith in the ideals of American democracy, slowly comes to realize that Anglo military forces intend to occupy his beloved California. His disappointment in the actions of the American government turns to resistance when it becomes clear to him that the Mexican forces cannot adequately defend their northern territory. His son Rafael, an official in the Mexican army who has repeatedly tried to warn his father of the dangers of Manifest Destiny, is a model of the Mexican patriotic spirit. Trained in Mexico City, he returns to his native California with a small military force to defend his compatriots against the advancing American army. Avendaño has taken special care to make his play historically accurate. He deftly contrasts the racism of certain American officers such as Captain Gillespie with the high sense of moral purpose of Commodore Robert F. Stockton, the commandant of the American forces. A Mr. Jenkins represents the crudeness and greed of the trappers who were eager to have the American government occupy the California territory in order to enhance their own commercial interests. The dominant American spirit of the period is most dramatically represented by the allegorical figure of America, whose appearance early in the third act augurs the defeat of the Mexicans and the triumph of expansionism. *El corrido de California* ends with the words of John C. Calhoun, who beseeched his fellow senators to reject the incorporation of the Mexican territories into the Union of the United States. Avendaño suggests that this country has and will continue to pay dearly for not heeding Calhoun's advice.

Rubén Sierra's plays *La raza pura or Racial, Racial* and *Manolo* are hard-hitting works that address two different aspects of the Chicano's social condition.[63] The first, a technically complex work made up of twenty-seven vignettes and employing films, tapes, slides, and over thirty actors, makes a powerful statement about the myth of being able to maintain racial purity in a rapidly changing society. The All-Purpose Racial Agency in the play resembles Honest Sancho's Used Mexican Lot and Curio Shop in Luis Valdez's *Los Vendidos*. The Racial Agency handles a complete Chicano line of models including Tijerina Off-White, Acapulco Gold, and Chicano Cream. Sierra's intent in this work is to provide his Chicano audience with a mirror of its foibles in a humorous way. He believes that "Seeing our own mistakes as other people see them gives us an opportunity to pause and re-examine what we are and attain a new insight into what we really are"[71]. *Manolo* deals with an internal social problem: drug addiction among Chicano Vietnam veterans. Unlike Sierra's first play, this work is written in a realistic style, presenting what is tantamount to a case history of a returning veteran whose life has been significantly altered by his war experiences and his subsequent addiction. The first scene is a retrospective view of Manolo before his return to the *barrio*. Dr. Shain, an Anglo psychiatrist, confronts the young Chicano's inability to decide whether he is going to choose to kick his habit and rehabilitate himself. The rest of the play then focuses on Manolo's struggle against tremendous odds, including the oppressive atmosphere of the *barrio*. He triumphs in the end but dies tragically, shot down by a drug pusher who has also killed his brother. The last scene in which Manolo's spirit returns to be among his friends and his sweetheart reinforces the play's positive message: that the Chicano can choose to solve the seemingly overwhelming problems that confront his daily existence.

Other Chicano playwrights who present similar social themes in their works are: Nephtalí de León, Francisco Burruel, Ysidro Macías, Octavio Romano, and Ron Arias. The five plays in León's book *Five Plays* (1972) focus exclusively on the bitter history and present-day socioeconomic situation of Chicanos. *Death of Ernesto Nerios,* like Carlos Morton's *Las Many Muertes de Richard Morales,* focuses on the murder of a young Chicano. The incident in de León's play occurred in Lubbock, Texas, in 1971. *Chicanos! The Living and the Dead!* is intended as a primer on Chicano history and as a vocal protest against injustice. De León links the struggle of Chicanos with revolutionary movements in Latin America. *Play Number 9* uses the universal figure of Prometheus but the emphasis is on the educational abuses suffered by Chicanos in the Anglo-dominated public education systems. *The Judging of Man* deals pessimistically with man's inability to survive injustice, and *The Flies* depicts the life of constant struggle against overwhelming odds. Francisco Burruel's play, *The Dialogue of Cuco Rocha,* is more hopeful. It consists of a lengthy dialogue between Cuco Rocha, an imprisoned Chicano activist, and Captain White, a prison official.[64] At first they are antagonists, with opposing viewpoints, but when they meet five years later they have developed mutual respect. In *Mártir Montezuma,* Ysidro Macías compares the mistreatment of the Aztecs by the Spaniards to the exploitation of Chicano farmworkers by Anglo growers.[65] There is an implicit criticism of union organizer César Chávez's nonviolent philosophy. His counterpart in the play, Montezuma, allowed Spaniards to subjugate the Aztecs. Macías's *The Ultimate Pendejada* focuses on a couple who have rejected their Mexican ancestry to

fanatically embrace Anglo patriotism.[66] In the end, however, they seek
authentic Chicano values in the *barrio*.

In a lighter vein, Octavio Romano's *Mugre de la canción* [The Song's
Dirt] is a hilarious satire of Anglo academics—grantsmen who study
ethnic groups with the aid of foundation grants.[67] Erica Macha—a play
on *macho*—and Handlee (Handy) Andee are deftly portrayed as a
superficially liberal couple who take advantage of Chicanos in order to
maintain their comfortable life-style. Ron Arias's short comedy *The
Interview* pokes fun at another false liberal, the Anglicized Chicano
college student whose encounter with two *barrio* derelicts leads to a
surprising conclusion.[68] Tony interviews Pete and Jess for a class
assignment on *barrio* life. Realizing how naive their interviewer is, they
feed him a distorted view of Chicano reality which he accepts as factual.
When he realizes he has been duped, Tony joins Pete and Jess for a
drink.

The works of Alfonso C. Hernández and Estela Portillo represent a
departure from the strong social current that characterizes most of
contemporary Chicano theater.

Portillo's *The Day of the Swallows* deals with human passions within a
general Hispanic context.[69] The three-act play is set in Lago de San
Lorenzo, a small village which is described in the stage directions as a
stepchild to the local *hacienda*. The village's name comes from a ritual
which is reenacted yearly when all the young women gather around the
lake to wash their hair and bathe in promise of a future husband.
Within this traditional Hispanic setting dominated for centuries by the
hacienda and the local Catholic Church, Portillo places the powerful
figure of Josefa, a middle-aged woman embittered by the humiliation
and denial females have had to endure at the hands of males. Josefa
symbolizes life, light, hope, and vitality in the play but she lives in fear
that her secret—she and another woman are lovers—will be revealed to
the townspeople. This leads to a tragic end as Josefa, driven by her fear,
cuts out the tongue of a young boy who has witnessed their lovemaking. Josefa commits suicide in the end but her spirit returns in the form
of an intense "unearthly" light. Through this device, the playwright
highlights the tragedy of her being denied her full human potential by a
repressive and rigid set of social mores. Portillo's other published play,

Sun Images, is a light musical comedy of more interest for its novelty—it is the first musical comedy to be published by a Chicano—than its content.[70]

Alfonso C. Hernández is perhaps the most artistically radical contemporary Chicano playwright in terms of his techniques. His earlier works are a harmonious combination of music, dance, film, and pantomime.[71] Stage directions and setting are elaborate. There is little dialogue as the playwright attempts to engage his audience through movement and light. Erotic scenes are common on stage. Hernández's later plays retain many of these elements but they are more fully developed. Like Portillo's *Day of the Swallows, The False Advent of Mary's Child* deals with the general state of decadence of traditional Hispanic culture, particularly its hypocritical attitude toward male-female sexuality and the hierarchical relationship between the classes.[72] These themes are presented through the members of an upper-class Mexican family. The Mother and Father maintain a socially appropriate marriage while he carries on a long sexual relationship with Lupita, a sensuous Indian woman. Only Carmen, their intelligent nineteen-year-old daughter, recognizes and vehemently protests the hypocrisy and corruption she observes in her own family and in the society at large. The mother becomes mysteriously pregnant and is saved through the intercession of a *curandero* who uses his magic to transfer her condition to Lupita's mother. The cycle of exploitation is complete; the Indian is sacrificed in order that the upper-class woman may survive.

Every Family Has One, a play in six scenes, deals in a broader way with the theme of exploitation. Man's inhumanity in social interactions is highlighted within the context of homosexual relationships. Most of the dialogue, which deals explicitly with homosexuality, is likely to alienate Chicano audiences. Nonetheless, readers will be impressed with the playwright's skill in creating a work of complex human emotions in which sexual preferences are heavily influenced by class, social, and racial differences. The tragic finale to the play—one of the men hangs himself—points to the pressures of the social predicament of people who choose to live outside of the norm.

The Imperfect Bachelor, an expressionist work, is even more explicit than the preceding play. The three female characters appear nude and there are highly erotic scenes. The author's harsh satirization of women as thoughtless and capricious beings is likely to be polemical despite his disclaimer that it is not a male-chauvinist play. In the last scene, the females become furies, pursue the play's narrator, cut out his heart, and begin eating it. The violent end suggests the male's fear of women.

Conclusion

Luis Valdez has become a major force in the establishment and development of contemporary Chicano theater. His theater group has left a heavy imprint on other *teatros* that were organized after El Teatro Campesino brought to public attention the issues of the grape strike and the general plight of the agricultural worker. But a measure of the vitality of contemporary Chicano theater is that neither El Teatro Campesino nor many other prominent theater groups have stood still; they have continued to experiment with new forms and techniques in order to more effectively dramatize social questions, cultural traditions, and themes common to all humanity. Another manifestation of the dynamic nature of contemporary Chicano theater and drama is found in the diversity of other playwrights whose works are more individual than collective creations. Whether on stage or within the covers of a book, Chicano theater and drama during the last fifteen years has grown into an artistically excellent and multi-faceted form of literary expression.

Chapter Four

Contemporary Chicano Short Story

Introduction

The period from 1930 to 1950 saw the development of different tendencies in Chicano prose. Some Chicano short-story writers of the next twenty years continue these tendencies while others experiment with different techniques and deal with themes that show a more heightened awareness of their craft. Chicano prose fiction becomes more sophisticated; yet in making this observation, we do not mean to imply that writers in general, and creators of short fiction in particular, abandon their social commitment to socio-economic change. On the other hand, it is because the art of storytelling has matured that Chicano writers are able to transmit more effectively and with greater psychological insight the multi-faceted aspects of the ethnic experience as well as of the wider human drama.

Chicano short stories from 1960 through about 1980 can be divided into the following general categories: (1) those presenting a folkloric, nostalgic view of the past. Although this view tends to be somewhat idealized, it is not always so; (2) those focusing on the negative sociological aspects of Chicano reality, both rural and urban. Many of these works, which advocate social change, are didactic. Authors place major emphasis on the creation of settings—the socioeconomic circumstances of the Chicano experience—rather than on the development of multi-dimensional characters; (3) satirical or allegorical treatments of the same reality. Through humor, several writers attempt to communicate the pathos of the plight of individuals and groups within a variety of social circumstances; (4) those mixing realism with mythological and fantastic elements resulting in a rich texture and complex narrative structure. These authors reflect a philosophical view of reality characterized by a thoughtful questioning of man's relationship to his fellow man and to a Supreme Being.

Folkloric Stories

Poet, essayist, and short-story writer Sabine Ulibarrí holds an important place in contemporary Chicano letters. All of his creative works were originally written in Spanish, although his two collections of short stories have also appeared in bilingual editions. When compared to other Chicano writers, his literary output is significant, particularly if one takes into account that he is one of a handful of contemporary Chicano writers who is completely comfortable with written literary Spanish.

Most of his short narrations are about individual personalities: relatives and acquaintances, those he knew well and those around whom local legends had developed; those he loved and those he feared as a child. All seem to have affected him strongly and together they make up a whole community of Hispanos from Tierra Amarilla in northern New Mexico. It is appropriate to compare both of his collections of short stories to Spanish-American *costumbrismo,* the literary genre which is characterized by sketches of different regional customs, language, rituals, types, and values. Local color, legends, and personalities are the stuff of his stories as he methodically sets out to re-create his world for us. His stories are not sterile reproductions, but are rendered so that his poetic sensibility shows through and enhances the sense of excitement and mystery he associates with his memories.

The first story of the volume *Tierra Amarilla* is an excellent example of how the author brings to bear his poetic sense upon his childhood memories.[1] "Mi caballo blanco" [My White Horse] reminds the reader of the Spanish poet Juan Ramón Jiménez, who immortalized a little gray donkey in his memorable prose poem *Platero y yo* [Platero and I]. Ulibarrí describes the magical qualities of a legendary horse which filled his childhood with poetry and fantasy. The young adolescent narrator tells us of the wonder with which he had heard of the marvelous

feats, some real some fictitious, of this unusual animal who roamed the
high plateaus with his harem of mares. The horse symbolizes for the
adolescent a world of masculine strength and sexuality, a world he is
about to enter himself. Ulibarrí sensitively and skillfully reconstructs a
pivotal moment in an adolescent's life—perhaps his own—where the
battle between childhood and adulthood is fiercely waged.

"Sábelo" [Know It] is a good illustration of how legends are created
in northern New Mexican communities. Once again, the story is
presented by a young narrator—nine years old in this case—who filters
reality through his child's imagination to give birth to another character endowed with fantastic powers. The story focuses on Don José Viejo
a sharp tongued old man who was "as ancient as hunger itself." After
overcoming his fear of the old man, the young narrator develops a warm
friendship with him and an almost religious respect. Don José is gifted
with an innate talent for storytelling, especially fantastic tales with
himself as the central figure. An example is how he killed a huge bear
after being badly scratched on the back. But the story that really
captures the young boy's imagination has to do with Don José's ability
to remove honey from a bee hive without receiving so much as one
sting.

"Hombre sin nombre" [Man Without a Name], the last story of
Tierra Amarilla, differs in length, form, and content from the author's
other fiction. Dealing with a number of philosophical themes such as
life as a dream, the father-son relationship, the development of the
individual personality, the story, which is divided into six short chapters, focuses on the struggle of the narrator, an author of thirty years, to
free himself from his dead father's image and domination to become an
autonomous individual.

With *Mi abuela fumaba puros y otros cuentos de Tierra Amarilla* [My
Grandma Smoked Cigars and Other Stories of Tierra Amarilla], the
author adds to his published work about his native northern New
Mexico ten more sensitively rendered tales.[2] Ulibarrí presents a tapestry of childhood memories of life among the hardy and proud Hispanos
of Tierra Amarilla. His stories are a series of carefully drawn sketches of
individuals—family, friends, acquaintances—who play an important
role in a young boy's strides toward adulthood: the matriarchal grandmother, viewed with a combination of tenderness and fear; Uncle Cirilo

under whose size and mighty voice the child lives in awe; the legendary Negro Aguilar whose feats as an indomitable *vaquero* ("cowboy") and skilled horse-tamer are reputed in the far reaches of the country; the astute Elacio Sandoval, the biology teacher who talks himself out of marrying the woman he does not love; Roberto, who one day goes to town to buy more nails and does not return for four years.

With obvious enthusiasm, Ulibarrí shares with us the wide range of the young boy's feelings and experiences: his terror upon finding himself face to face with *la llorona* herself; the profound sadness upon learning of his father's sudden death; the proud response to his heroes when they deign to talk to him. The author draws on local legends and popular superstition and combines them with vivid details from his childhood to create a rich mixture of fact and fiction. His stories are tinged with hues of longing for a past that although he cannot relive, he has brought to life with deft and broad strokes of his pen. The book thus forms a composite of the memories of a writer sensitive to the child in him who looks back nostagically to a time of closeness and warmth among people who treated him with understanding and love.

As Rudolfo Anaya points out in his introduction to this attractive volume, what emerges in all of the stories is a strong sense of daily life and tradition among the Hispanos of northern New Mexico as well as the bonds of their loving and sharing. Another important element is humor, which, while present in his earlier stories, here is more ribald.

The title story is a sensitively created and tender description of the author's grandmother, a silent matriarch who sustained the family for many decades through difficult periods and tragic events. The narrator remembers that her relationship to her husband, although somewhat tumultuous, was characterized by an underlying feeling of mutual respect and fear, "somewhere between tenderness and toughness." He affectionately recalls that after his grandfather died, the grandmother would absent herself to her bedroom after the evening chores were done to smoke a cigar, symbol to the child of his grandfather's power over his family and ranch business and also of his grandmother's longing for her husband. As so many of the characters of his stories, the grandmother seems to represent for the author a graphic and vital connection with his past: his Hispano community, his family, his language, and his cultural roots.

In his collection of short stories, *Heartland. Stories of the Southwest,*
Rubén Darío Salaz also looks back nostalgically upon the self-sufficient
way of life of the rural communities of the Southwest. Unlike Ulibarrí,
however, he also focuses on an industrialized Anglo society that destroyed much of the simple and moral pastoral existence of the
Spanish-speaking. As W. G. Shrubsall observes in his foreword, Darío
Salaz's stories present "the animosity and blanket distrust of 'civilized'
whites toward the Indian; the wastefulness of the encroaching Eas-
terner; the disappearance of a simpler and more ecological, and more
satisfying way of life; the destruction of a basic morality by a nonexis-
tent one."[3]

The opposing attitudes between the Anglos and the Indians and
Hispanos are sharply contrasted in several stories. In "The Race," the
protagonist, Corporal White of the United States Calvary, is drawn to
exemplify the deep-seated racism of American troops toward their
Indian enemies. White, a superbly trained athlete, has been selected to
join an elite corps of "Apache Fighters." He views his task as a
sportsman would approach a competition: to defeat the adversary as
soundly as possible using all the skills and tactics at his disposal. Darío
Salaz paints a sympathetic picture of the Apache nation which has
suffered great losses at the hands of the United States Army. "Liberation" is based on the Bear Flag Revolt in California on 20 February
1846. The Anglos are depicted as arrogant, uncivilized marauders
whereas the Spanish-speaking Californians are portrayed as peaceful
folk with a simple and deeply moral life-style. In "Cibolero" [Bison
Hunter] the author contrasts the Chicanos' ecologically wise attitude
toward wildlife and hunting with the Anglos' callous, shortsighted
view. The Chicano *ciboleros,* a gentle people, are dismayed when Anglo
hunters indiscriminately massacre the buffalo herd.

In several other stories, Darío Salaz casts a wistful look at the simple,
pure life of his people. "Mistress of the Plains" has to do with a young
woman's decision to allow a herd of wild mustangs to run free on the
plains. The message is quite explicit: the life of the rural Spanish-
speaking population is threatened by the advance of Anglo civilization.
"The Adobe Adobe" focuses on the dilemma of a young Chicano caught
between the traditional values of his own culture and those of the
dominant Anglo society.

Social Realism

While Sabine Ulibarrí and Rubén Darío Salaz tend to emphasize the past in their works, the writers we will discuss in this section focus on the Chicano's rural and urban experiences today. These writers include Daniel Garza, Arturo Rocha Alvarado, Nick C. Vaca, Saúl Sánchez, J. L. Navarro, Rosaura Sánchez, Carlos Morton, and Joe Olvera. Within this group there is a great variety of approaches and thematic treatments yet the element that they have in common is a decidedly critical view of the dominant culture as it affects the Chicano migrant worker, the illegal Mexican alien, and the resident of the *barrio*.

Daniel Garza's stories are illustrative of the plight of the migrant worker in Texas and the racist environment within which Chicanos in that area live. In "Saturday Belongs to the Palomía," the author describes a typical Saturday when Chicano and Mexican cotton pickers invade a central Texas town to do their weekly shopping and enjoy their weekly entertainment.[4] Their arrival changes the delicate relationship that exists between the town's Anglos and its resident Chicano population. The narrator, a young boy, is aware of his precarious position between the migrant workers and the Anglos with whom he has a comfortable relationship. He is not accepted by the former, who consider him a *pocho,* a person of Mexican descent who has left Mexico to become a permanent United States resident, yet the Anglos only accept him because he has discarded much of his Mexican identity. "Everybody Knows Tobie" also provides us with insight into the racial hierarchy that exists in Texas and throughout the Southwest.[5]

Arturo Rocha Alvarado's book *Crónica de Aztlán. A Migrant's Tale* (1977) is a series of accounts of the life of a migrant agricultural worker. Using a simple but effective style and narrative structure, the author traces the route of the thousands of Chicanos who annually leave their homes in the Rio Grande Valley in deep south Texas to join the human migrant stream that flows through much of the Midwest. One of several children in a family of migrant agricultural workers, Rocha Alvarado wryly comments that "experience is the best teacher."

In the first part of this third-person narrative, we follow the steps of a migrant family as it prepares to go north from early spring through the fall in pursuit of fields of ripening fruits and vegetables. The family is heavily in debt after a severe winter and a hot spring have devastated the crops they might have picked at home. Instead they have to compete with illegal Mexican aliens and "green-carders" (legal workers from Mexico) for the few jobs. The family confronts a number of dilemmas that are drawn as typical of those of many other families: taking the younger children out of school and leaving the older ones with friends or relatives; providing for reliable transportation for the long trek north; dealing with an insensitive Border Patrol that often treats Spanish-speaking citizens as illegal aliens. We follow the family's route through the fields of Texas, Oklahoma, South Dakota, Illinois, Michigan, Ohio, Kansas, and back to Texas from March through October, picking cotton, tomatoes, strawberries, cherries, apples—whatever the weather has dealt them for that season.

Saúl Sánchez's collection of short stories, *Hay Plesha Lichans tu di Flac* (a phonetic transcription of the attempted pronunciation of the Pledge of Allegiance), is a panoply of migrant-worker experiences ranging from a child's bewildering first day in an Anglo school to the death of a Chicano in Vietnam. Like Rocha Alvarado, his characters are uncomplicated, one-dimensional creations, yet he communicates effectively and forcefully the travails of the rural Chicano.

In this first story, "El primer día de escuela" [The First Day of School], a young boy enters the confusing world of school. A difficult step in any child's life, it is much more significant for the protagonist because he speaks poor English and is given little information on what to expect. His experience is intended to be representative of many small Chicano children from rural or *barrio* backgrounds. The young Chicano's frustration and fear begin with the Pledge of Allegiance and intensify when the Anglo teacher punishes him for not being able to pronounce the words in his reader.

Other stories in the collection reflect different migrant-laborer experiences: the miserable life in the makeshift barracks that growers rent or give to the seasonal workers; the cycle of unhappiness and instability in relationships between men and women in the migrant stream; the alienation this population feels from the political system that often acts negatively upon their lives; the uprooting of children and the repeated interruption of their education when families must travel north to harvest crops; and the futile attempts by young Chicanos to seek employment in urban areas. With the last story, "The Funeral," the author closes the circle of suffering portrayed within the pages of his collection. The body of a young Chicano soldier is returned home to be buried. His parents reflect the same bewilderment as the protagonist in the first story:

> It was hard to tell if the Mother and Father understood why or for what purpose they had given it to them. The flag, I mean. The Anglo soldier who folded it was saying something when he was handing it over to them but it didn't look like they understood at all what he was trying to tell them. I don't even think they knew how to say the "Hay plesha lichans." I bet you I know how to say it. Look, you want me to show you? "Hay plesha lichans tu di flac. . . ."[6]

Nick C. Vaca individualizes the rural experience. His characters are more subtly drawn than those of Garza, Alvarado Rocha, and Sánchez. In "The Visit," Vaca focuses on the tragedy of the forgotten and abandoned older Chicano.[7] Don Pedro, who lives alone in a dilapidated trailer on a lonely stretch of road, is visited infrequently by only one of his twelve children. Don Pedro is portrayed as a proud Mexican who is considered by his contemporaries to be an expert on the Revolution. We learn, however, that he fled Mexico to save himself. While his son Ralph believes himself to be intensely loyal to his father—he imagines sacrificing an arm as a gesture of his love—the author suggests that he, too, will soon abandon Don Pedro. The author skillfully draws a parallel between Don Pedro's "betrayal" of the Revolution and his son's betrayal of him. Having learned from bitter experience that what people say and claim to be is often very different from what they do, Don Pedro knows that Ralph's promises and declarations of love are empty ones. The story has an ironical ending as Ralph drives away thinking "if he would ever have the chance to sacrifice his right arm, his favorite arm for his father."[8]

"Martín," perhaps Vaca's most poignant story, deals with a young Chicano's discovery of human suffering.[9] The setting is the rural California community of Tracy during the late autumn when the winds portend the damp, cold, foggy days of winter. The first-person narrator recalls how, when he was a young boy, the Chicanos lived on the poor side of town in broken down frame houses which "sagged more from the weight of the sorrow from within than from the lack of adequate construction."[10] One day, he and his young *barrio* cohorts attack Martín, whose family has recently arrived from Mexico. The narrator mistakenly interprets his abnormally large belly as a sign of his prosperity, discovering in the final scene, that he suffers from malnutrition.

J. L. Navarro is the short story writer who best portrays the Chicano in an urban milieu. While his book, *Blue Day on Main Street* (1973) has several other settings, his stories about the tenuous existence of the young Chicano in the city are the most successful. "Eddie's Number," "Weekend," "Frankie's Last Wish," "Scatterbrain Johnny," "The Commission," and "Tamale Leopard," all deal with the monotony, violence, and self-destruction of hopeless and directionless young males. For example, in "Eddie's Number," the protagonist is repeatedly identified as "The Hype" to emphasize his primary characteristic: his tragic dependence on heroin. Navarro skillfully depicts the abjectness of his daily life which revolves around the vicious cycle of earning or stealing enough money to make a drug connection. The graphic detail with which the author describes his drug-induced sickness, the injecting of the heroin, and his sordid life with Carmen, a "hype-whore," contributes to the story's impact. Eddie's violent death—he is shot by an Anglo policeman—at the end of the story underscores the fragility of the young Chicano's life in the urban ghetto. "Weekend" also deals with the lowly drug culture in the urban *barrios*.

Navarro's use of flashbacks and interior monologue and his manipulation of dialogue and setting are notable. A short excerpt from his story "Blue Day on Main Street" illustrates this skill. We experience the disorientation and distress of the narrator, who has just been released from a mental institution:

Seething heat waves rise from pale walks. Cracked asphalt, soft tar oozing out of broken black veins. An erect landscape of concrete surrounds me. Windows kindle their shining visors with the reflecting blue sun. Passing people passing time, leaving their odors of sweet, cheap perfume to tussle my mind like a nickel bottle of port. Sweat stench and armpits and dirty cock and cunt. An old wino crosses the street and stops on the corner, waiting for the light to change red. His face is the color of manure and he resembles a dry fig. A Bull Durham sack sticks out of the shirt pocket. He leans against a lamp post, harks a jade oyster and blows it on the street where a lime colored cab is rounding the corner. The light turns red and he slowly skids out to a magazine stand. Up the street, a man who's the spitting image of Farmer John is coming round 5th St. herding half a dozen hogs. Vigorously, he swings a black bull whip on their backs as he drinks vodka and curses his mother.[11]

In his short stories, José Olvera uses an unorthodox style that bears some resemblance to Jack Kerouac's hip, turned-on mode. Several of his autobiographical works, set in the Chicano *barrios* of El Paso and in other cities, are montages of sights, sounds, sensations, and smells mixed with third-person narration, interior monologue, and dialogue. This blend of sensorial elements and interior/exterior narrative perspectives makes for an effective rendering of his characters' view of the city around them; sometimes it is a pleasing refuge while other times it threatens their sense of well-being. In "Homme du l'monde," a fond retrospective view of his childhood, Olvera effectively juxtaposes school, street, church, and home scenes to create a kind of invocation in praise of his *barrio*.[12] In contrast to the pleasant memories of his El Paso childhood, Olvera evokes in "My Voice" the frantic aspects of a Chicano's life in the fast-paced environment of New York City.[13]

Rosaura Sánchez's stories deal with the deep pattern of exploitation that has characterized the Anglo's treatment of the Chicano, the Chicano-male's relationship to the female, and the middle-class Chicano's attitude toward his people. In general, her stories are tersely written and carefully constructed to highlight these patterns.

In "Una mañana: 1952" [One Morning: 1952], the author establishes a parallel between United States foreign policy—its participation in the Korean War—and the Anglo racist practices at home.[14] We follow a Chicano worker's early morning preparations for a long, hard day of physical labor. Employing third-person narration, the author presents fragments of her character's thoughts as he heats the morning coffee, makes his lunch, dresses, and listens to the early news. His tenderness toward his sleeping wife and children is contrasted to his raging anger as he reflects on the North Koreans' accusation that the United States is using biological warfare.

Sánchez extends her call for the liberation of Chicanos to the release of women from oppressive relationships with males. "Una noche . . ." [One Night . . .] focuses on one woman's realization that she no longer needs to tolerate her husband's abuses.[15] Although Florencia, the mother of three, understands why Samaniego often stays out late drinking with his friends and spending his hard-earned wages, she grows less sympathetic. The author skillfully presents Florencia's dilemma: to make a stand or to continue to follow cultural tradition which dictates that she accept her man and her own lot. Her decision to end the cycle of oppression and submissiveness within the marriage comes slowly, and is therefore more credible. In "Chepa," the author also develops the theme of the liberation of the Chicana from age-old sexist practices.[16] Given an ultimatum by her husband to abort an unwanted pregnancy, Chepa asserts the right to decide what is best for her.

Social Themes Treated Humorously

Writers such as Octavio Romano and Max Martínez have published stories which portray, in a serious vein, the wide range of socioeconomic problems confronted by today's Chicano. Both writers are skillful creators of multi-dimensional characters, convincing plots, and detail-rich settings, yet it is their humorous stories which stand out as their best creative efforts. Through the judicious use of satire and allegory, Romano and Martínez have chosen a different approach to underscore the dominant social aspects of the multi-faceted Chicano experience. While we will briefly refer to some of the writers' other stories, in this section we will focus our attention on Romano and Martínez's short humorous pieces.

Stories such as "A Rosary for Doña Marina," "The Veil," and "The Forest and the Tree" reflect Octavio Romano's keen insight into the psychology of his people.[17] In the first work, he examines the stultifying religious and social attitudes of elderly women whose narrow view of the world brings them much pain and loneliness. Romano traces Doña Marina's process of self-alienation and progressive isolation. In "The Veil," he focuses on the lack of understanding between a daughter and her father, and in "The Forest and the Tree," the author examines the origin and evolution of a Chicano religious legend.

Based on his experience as a professor of anthropology at the University of California at Berkeley, Octavio Romano has been in a particularly favorable position to observe the pretentiousness and pomposity of the academic world. He takes academics, especially social scientists, to task for their dishonesty in dealing with different facets of the "Chicano Problem."

In his essay "Goodbye Revolution—Hello Slum," Romano indicts the academic community for contributing to rather than ameliorating the plight of the Chicano. He says:

> The social scientists came. They talked. The people talked with them. Then the social scientists left. They advanced in their careers because the pickers of cotton, the carriers of railroad ties, and the workers in the fish canneries took of their own time and gave it to them. More articles were written. More books were published. Then these social scientists were said to have become "experts" and "authorities." They became chairmen of their academic departments. And while their careers were advancing, the carriers of railroad ties returned to ten hours daily in the desert sun, the pickers of cotton returned to the airless cotton fields, and the cannery workers returned to the ever-stinking fish.[18]

"The Scientist" satirizes contemporary health practitioners who use ethnic groups to justify funding for their projects and who evolve theories which sometimes have little relationship to observable reality.[19] Simón Bocanegra [a name borrowed from a Verdi opera], a pompous and pontificating Chicano psychiatrist, gives up a prestigious academic position in the East to return to his native California, ostensibly to be among his people. In fact, this esteemed scientist uses the *barrio* mental-health center he creates to test out his own hypotheses which, in his moments of grandeur, he believes will bring him the international fame he desires. The story is filled with humorous exaggeration. For example, Bocanegra attempts to refine *sixteen* of his pet hypotheses! On the basis of his research in the center—absurdly named Ajúa House after a popular Mexican exclamation—he evolves a new theory: that most of the members of the community, even its most respected figures, are mentally ill. Bocanegra takes his "scientific humanism" to its illogical extreme in concluding that the rational and mentally well balanced are really those who are disturbed. His scientific methods and grand projects come crashing down around him when he commits himself to his own mental health center.

"Strings for a Holiday" is a parody of how academicians investigate what they perceive to be a social problem or a cultural phenomenon.[20]

The "strings" in the story's title refer to a high-risk game of chance that Chicano teenagers play with cars. The description of the game's rules is in itself amusing, but even more hilarious are the interpretations of the game by different classes from the university. For example, the psychology class theorizes that the cameras used to film the event symbolize a tendency for suicide, that the strings symbolize the cables on Golden Gate Bridge, and that Chicano "catcars" symbolize commuter traffic. Romano also satirizes the media—in this case, the film industry—for a tendency to exploit an ethnic event for its own gain.

"The Chosen One" is a satire of the self-righteous Anglo missionary spirit that the author associates with the disastrous policies of nineteenth-century Manifest Destiny.[21] Elizabeth Victoria Shotwell Smith, "of good New Hampshire Yankee stock," becomes a doctor in her belief that the medical profession is a calling from God. After a period of disillusionment—she discovers that many others are also called—she moves to New Mexico, where she joins with other New Englanders to save the local natives.

Max Martínez has written short stories with several themes including self-destructive *machista* behavior, violence perpetrated upon the Chicano community, loneliness in old age, and Latin American revolution. His satirical work "The Adventures of the Chicano Kid" stands out as his best effort.[22] Written in a highly hyperbolic style, it is the story of the Chicano Kid's attempts to avenge the rape of his sister by the nefarious Anglo Alf Brisket. Although humorous, the story is laced with references to the troubled racial history of Anglos and Chicanos in the Southwest. The Chicano Kid is characterized as the savior of his people, a contemporary warrior descended from proud Aztec stock. He comes to the village of Santo Gringo, a prototypical Western frontier town, searching for Brisket and resolves to let nothing stand in his way. Martínez compares him to Odysseus's majesty, Zeus's awesomeness, a sight so inspiring that he would have been the envy of Michelangelo and Carrara. The traditional American Western heroes—the Lone Ranger, the Cisco Kid, the Durango Kid, Roy Rogers, Gene Autry, Zorro, Matt Dillon, and John Wayne—are described as "mere ruffians" by comparison. The author's description of the Chicano Kid is masterful:

The wide-brimmed Charro hat, the national chapeau of the bronze people of the sun, swept upwards at the edges with the mighty force of a raging sea, made—nay, sculptured—from the finest felt, embroidered with the richest silver from the mines of Oaxaca, especially selected by management itself for its purity and lustre. And of the remainder of his attire? Attire is hardly the word! Dare I even speak of it? The poverty of language overwhelms this, your humble servant, when he tries to describe the manner of the Chicano Kid's dress. Were I Homer, Virgil, Dante, Shakespeare, Goethe, and Rod Mc-Kuen all in one, I could not do justice. Were all the languages of the world whipped together to yield the butter of the human soul, it would not be enough. What care I for words! In the Panavision of my mind, I see so clearly. I can only say, gracing his limbs, a black outfit, of the finest wool, each strand gathered with utmost care from the most heavily guarded and virgin of English sheep. Virgin English maids before the loom, weaving as they utter silent novenas. This, too, is embroidered in silver, large brilliant buttons the size of Big Mac's. The boots of highly polished, impeccable calf-skin, the toe and tops inlaid again with metal the color of moonlight. Reader, I, with all honesty, cannot go on. I beg of you, indulgent reader, to allow me the small luxury of composing myself that I may continue with the force and vigor our tale requires. (47–48)

During the course of the story, Martínez attacks Anglo hypocrisy— Puritan by day, Libertarian by night—and racism. On the other hand, his hero is gentle and patient, resorting to violence only in self-defense or when he is provoked byond human limits. As the defender of his people, his search for his sister's violator takes on larger proportions as the author posits the forces of Anglo evil against those of Chicano good. While the characteristics of each group are purposefully overdrawn, it aids Martínez's intent to treat humorously the very serious theme of exploitation. His satire penetrates deep into our consciousness.

The Masters

Due to their thematic breadth, psychological depth, and the technical mastery of their craft, the writers who stand out as the masters of the contemporary Chicano short story are Miguel Méndez, Sergio Elizondo, Estela Portillo, and Ron Arias. While other writers discussed earlier in this chapter have created stories of high artistic merit, the four writers whose works we will treat in this section reflect a greater consistency of creative excellence.

Miguel Méndez comes from a proletarian background. Born in Bisbee, Arizona, in 1930, his family returned to Mexico soon after his father lost his job due to the Depression.[23] He grew up on a communal farm in the state of Sonora, where he received all of the six years of his formal education. During his childhood he heard many stories from the people from different places who came to the farm. These stories were about the Mexican Revolution, the bloody Yaqui Indian wars from the early part of the twentieth century, and many other themes. Before he turned twenty, Méndez had returned to the United States where he worked as a laborer in the agricultural fields and in construction. His early childhood as well as his experiences as a young adult are strongly reflected in his short stories. Although he continued to educate himself—he read widely from several national literatures—and currently teaches Spanish and creative writing, his roots and his sentiments are clearly with the people. He says: "Nevertheless, with my fellow workers I spoke the same as they did, in the language of the *pachuco*. For some twenty-four years I worked in rough jobs, almost inhuman ones. Believe me, before being a writer, teacher, or intellectual, I am still a farmworker or a laborer, or both, perhaps."[24]

Méndez has felt an obligation to put forth his formative experiences in his short stories. Interestingly, he does so in a style that is highly literate, even baroque. In addition, he frequently employs interior monologues, montage, and flashbacks that add to the complexity of his expression. While the themes are predominantly proletarian, the form is not.

His collection of short stories *Tata Casehua y otros cuentos* [Tata Casehua and Other Stories (1980)], is a mixture of proletarian and poetic elements. For example, "Ahí en el desierto enterré a mi cuate" [Right There in the Desert I Buried My Buddy] is a first-person narration reminiscent of the deceptively simple stories of Juan Rulfo, the contemporary Mexican author. Like Rulfo, Méndez uses an informal conversational style to reveal deep feelings and to heighten the story's sense of inevitability. Two Mexican nationals carry on a conversation as they walk through the merciless heat of the Sonoran Desert on their way north to California. One man tries to encourage his companion, who is suffering from blisters and acute heat exhaustion, to continue walking. During the trek they have become buddies, sharing their dream of a better life in the United States. Méndez skillfully communicates the combined feelings of rage, frustration, and tenderness the narrator experiences as he watches his friend die. The story's focus on individual tragedy is set against a backdrop of social injustices: the plight of the Mexican worker and peasant who are not able to find employment in their own country, the starvation of the rural poor, the empty promises of politicians, the mistreatment of Yaquis and other Indian groups, the exploitative practices of the Mexican labor contractor, and the vicious competitive cycle among Mexicans to get jobs in the United States. The story's last paragraph, which is an excellent example of Méndez's use of interior monologue, constitutes the narrator's cathartic expression of rage over having to leave his land for a future of virtual enslavement in the United States.

In some stories, Méndez combines religious symbolism with his social messages. For example, "Jesús de Belén, Yaqui" [Jesus of Bethlehem, Yaqui"] is the allegorical tale of a contemporary Christ and his followers set along the United States—Mexican border. Christ is a Yaqui Indian whose suggestive powers to cure sinners of their guilt and physical ills are interpreted as divine. Paralleling the biblical tale, he is betrayed, arrested, and beaten by a cruel official. The narrator, a latter-day Saint Peter, denies he knows the Yaqui. In "Espaladas mojadas" [Wetbacks], Christ appears as an old man begging for water in the desert.

Related to these stories in which the author combines religious motifs and socioeconomic elements is "Tata Casehua," Méndez's best short work. Juan Manuel Casehua, the story's central figure, is a spiritual leader and a political rebel who has proclaimed himself emperor of the Sonoran Desert. Méndez suggests that after the Yaqui Indians were defeated by the Mexican army early in the twentieth century the desert became their only refuge. While many were sent to work on the plantations of southern tropical Mexico, where they died from disease and overexposure, those who remained were dispersed throughout northern Sonora. Tata Casehua is seen as a leader with a fierce pride in his Indian lineage who keeps alive the will to throw off the yoke of the oppressor to regain the Yaqui birthright: the fertile agricultural valley. Knowing that he will soon die, Juan instructs his son Jesús in the ways of Yaqui religion and shares with him the secrets of the desert. Jesús will thus become the new emperor of the desert—this is a title that Juan has proclaimed for himself—to pass on the Yaqui traditions and their spirit of independence. Méndez illustrates this spirit through his description of the mass suicide in 1900 of Chief Opodepe and his followers. Rather than submit to the Mexican troops of General Torres, the Yaquis threw themselves off a high cliff. The author suggests that this same spirit of resistance will persist until the Yaqui nation has liberated itself.

As in other stories, Méndez sees the Sonoran Desert as both treacherous and beautiful, certain death for those who do not understand it but yielding to others who, like Juan Manuel Casehua, are willing to listen and learn its secrets. The author's descriptions of the desert are highly lyrical, conveying its utter starkness and aridity on one hand and its power and majesty on the other.

Most of the stories in Méndez's other collection of short stories, *Cuentos para niños traviesos* (1979) [Stories for Mischievous Children], are directed to a young audience. Using a simpler and more direct language than in *Tata Casehua y otros cuentos,* Méndez creates fables, legends, and simple tales, some of which are designed to instruct and instill pride in the Chicano heritage while others are written to entertain his young readers. "Por qué el color chicano es el más bonito" [Why the Color of the Chicanos Is the Most Beautiful] is an example of the first type of story. Méndez narrates the legends that primitive gods left imprinted on strange inscriptions which explain why "our color is the most beautiful of all the colors of the races that fill this planet." "Lluvia" [Rain] is a delightful story in which the author describes the blend of Indian and Christian legends that characterizes the Mexican Indian's belief system. While the rain is considered to be the spittle of the indigenous Clowning God, the Indians pray to the Christian Saint Isidro, their patron, for help. The last six stories are contemporary versions of fables which have their roots in the thirteenth-century Spanish translation of the classical Indian work *Calila y Dimna.*

Although he is best known as a poet, Sergio Elizondo has made an important contribution to contemporary Chicano short fiction with the recent publication of his collection *Rosa, la flauta* [Rosa, the Flute,

1980]. With this book Elizondo explores two realms—realism and fantasy—with a sensitivity and narrative skill unusual considering it is this writer's first prose work. While he does not ignore the socioeconomic aspects of Chicano existence, his aim seems to be to bring to the surface a whole other reality: the dreams, fantasies, and intimate moments in his characters' lives. Elizondo has referred to his stories as "forms of interior and exterior life that I think are aspects of human nature."[25] In his book, he moves back and forth comfortably between these two worlds, focusing alternately on social, philosophical, supernatural, and fantastic elements. He is obviously a person with broad intellectual and artistic interest who has not been content to address only social questions. *Rosa, la flauta* can be seen as a personal search for meaning, an exploratory work of the highest calibre.

The book begins with an "Obertura," a prose overture designed to introduce the themes, motifs, and tones that follow in the individual stories. Elizondo records in a fragmentary manner pieces of dialogue, musings, perceptions, impressions, and observations which he will more fully develop later. In this introductory collage, he exposes us to the major components of his work, whetting our appetite and urging us to turn the page.

The first story, "Pos aquí estoy pa morir" [Well Here I Am to Die], is a good example of the author's effective use of dialogue with which he creates a sense of authenticity. He peels back layers of his characters' experiences and emotions to give us a more intimate view of their personalities. In this story, an older Chicana who is dying tells her nephew about the past: how it was in 1940 when her husband, a Mexican national, refused to get papers, social security, etc., for fear of being deported; how her family lost their land; her negative school experiences. While the social backdrop plays an important role, Elizondo places emphasis on the aunt's urgency to communicate the essential meaning of her life and her nephew's desire to enter into the private room of her memories. In the end, she is content knowing that she can die in peace. "Quien le manda" [Who Told Him to Do It] is also structured around a long dialogue. In the course of their conversation, two women, Chona and Agueda, reflect their bewilderment over their sons' activities in the military. Gradually revealing deeper layers of their sense of loss and confusion, the conversation takes on a more personal tone. In the final poignant scene we learn that both women have received telegrams notifying them that their sons are missing in action.

A variation on his manipulation of the long dialogue is Elizondo's use of interior monologue. The title story, "Rosa, la flauta," is a long monologue in which a fifteen-year-old woman reveals the changes she has recently undergone. The author sensitively examines his character's maturation process as she passes from the innocence and freshness of childhood into the complexities of adulthood. Rosa no longer plays the flute—a symbol of simplicity and purity—or runs, or listens to classical music, for now her body has changed and her interests are different. Elizondo captures the sadness of her passage from one age to another in the last paragraph:

Los cuatro cientos metros ahora son sólo un cuatro con dos ceros de cola, la flauta es un tubo que finge ser de plata y está llena de aire que no se mueve; de mi boca salen sólo palabras, mis dedos sirven para nada, a menos que los cuente como diez apéndices que nomás cuelgan áy; los ojos no reflejan nada, no mandan nada pa'fuera, nomás dejan entrar cosas pa' dentro. Un día reciente me puse los pantaloncillos con que antes corría, me los puse en lugar de pantaletas pero los sentía como que estaban hechos de madera con ángulos ásperos, no se moldeaban a mis caderas y muslos como que ya no querían correr conmigo, 'taban muertos: voy a tirarlos en el barril de la basura que está al lado de la pista y aunque me vean en casa voy a coger la flauta con una mano y la voy a vender para comprar más para que se complete todo eso que debe haber cuando hay terminación donde se acabó algo. Ya no hay aires, mis labios callan.[26]

(The four-hundred meters are now only a four with a tail with two zeroes, the flute is a tube that pretends to be made of silver and it is full of air that does not move; only words come out of my mouth, my fingers aren't good for anything except when I count them as ten appendages that just hang there; my eyes don't reflect a thing, they don't send anything out, they just let things come in. One day recently I put on the shorts I used to run in. I put them on instead of panties but they felt like they were made out of wood with sharp corners. They didn't fit comfortably around my hips and thighs as though they no longer wanted to run with me, as if they were dead: I'm going to throw them into the trash barrel by the field and although they see me at home, I'm going to take the flute in one hand and I'm going to sell it in order to buy more of what I needed when something has come to an end. There is no longer music, my lips are silent.)

"Ur," "Hoy no voy" [Today I'm Not Going], and "Lugar" [Place] are introspective works, more narrative essays than short stories, in which Elizondo philosophizes about the meaning of life, the structure of the universe, childhood, and a number of other related themes. In "Ur," he warns us from the outset about the dreamlike quality of his story, relating Ur to a kind of interior castle. Although it is difficult to say what, precisely, Ur represents, he gives enough direct hints to allow us to speculate. It symbolizes what we lose as we grow out of childhood. The story seems to be the author's attempt to return to, to recapture, this longed-for quality in his life. "Hoy no voy" is thematically related to "Ur." Elizondo protests that he will not continue to submit himself to the frantic, helter-skelter pace he has always followed, but resolves to slow down, to take stock, to listen to his interior voice: *Ya pagué la deuda, es hora de gozar* ("I already payed the debt, it's time to enjoy life"). In "Lugar" he addresses the cosmic meaning of life: where did we come from, what are we doing here, who or what is our creator, and similar thoughts. Elizondo speculates a great deal, gives no answers, and ends by throwing up his hands: *Inconstancia imperecedera, sinfín con orden* ("Undying inconstancy, an orderly infinity").[27]

"Pa que bailaba esa noche . . ." [In Order to Dance That Night . . .] is the author's journey into a fantastic, supernatural world. Set in a small town in the Southwest, the story concerns a young man's mysterious encounter with death. "Coyote, esta noche" [Coyote, Tonight] also falls within the realm of fantasy. Reflecting his predilection for this scruffy desert maverick, Elizondo creates a delightful tale about a wily coyote who outsmarts a rancher to get one of his mouth-watering chickens.

Estela Portillo stands out as a short-story writer due to her sensitive treatment of a variety of themes and the consistently high quality of her creative efforts. Her stories have been compared to morality plays in which conflicting forces clash, sometimes producing disharmony and destruction and other times resulting in a peaceful resolution.[28] She often infuses highly lyrical elements, striking imagery, and philosophical asides, all of which combine to highlight the disparate forces that form the basis of her stories.

One criticism of her prose is that she tends to overdraw the characters giving them an allegorical quality more proper to the theater—she is a published playwright whose work is discussed in Chapter 3—than to prose fiction. In addition, many of her stories are structured as plays in which the narrative rhythm rises and falls in the regular pattern of dramatic presentation.

Portillo has taken great care to separate politics from her literary works. Although she has been active in several social causes and outspoken on public issues in her native El Paso, she firmly believes that "all good literature is based on the human experience which is nonpolitical."[29] Her insistence that the use of literature as a political tool will ultimately bind the creative work is clearly reflected in her stories which are generally free of strictly social messages.

Liberation is an important theme in Portillo's collection *Rain of Scorpions and Other Stories* (1975). In two stories, "The Paris Gown" and "If It Weren't for the Honeysuckle," her treatment of the theme has a feminist thrust. "The Paris Gown" deals with the personal courage of a woman who is out of step with the expectations and restrictions of the Mexican society in which she is raised. Clo escapes the heavy tradition of her age by refusing to submit to the dictates of her parents who insist that she marry an elderly widower. Filled with justified resentment after years of being treated differently because of her sex, she decides to liberate herself in a most unusual but effective way—she makes a dramatic entrance at her formal engagement party completely nude! Convinced of her insanity, her father quickly accedes to her demand that she be allowed to live in Paris with his full financial support. Years later she relates the story of her unorthodox liberation to her amazed granddaughter Theresa, a young woman who is on the brink of asserting her own womanhood. "If It Weren't for the Honeysuckle," which is set in a rural Mexican hamlet, also reflects Portillo's feminist perspective. Beatriz, the story's central character, is described as an angry yet resolute middle-aged woman sensitive to the earth and the natural patterns that surround her. The honeysuckle she tends in her carefully ordered garden symbolizes, at the same time, her source and her Dionysian personality. Married young to Robles, a violent and brutal man, she finally is no longer able to tolerate his attacks on two other women he keeps in their home. The liberating act in this story is more extreme than in the preceding one: Beatriz and one of the women poison Robles. Significantly, the honeysuckle has provided the poison in the form of three white, fruiting Amanitas. With the elimination of Robles, the disharmonious force, order is restored in the lives of the three women. The Dionysian principle has triumphed over the Apollonian. A similar conflict forms the basis of "The Secret Room." Julio, a young man of German-Mexican descent, rejects the severity and rigidity of his Aryan ancestry to accept the softness and gentleness of his Latin side. Julio's liberation comes in the form of his decisions not to continue to run the family business he has inherited and not to marry Helga, a German girl who exemplifies the worst Aryan traits. Instead, he elects to be with Elsa, a curious, sensuous, and open woman of Mexican ancestry.

Related to the Dionysian-Apollonian dichotomy is the theme of the conflict between good and evil forces, which is common to several of Portillo's stories. For example, in "The Tales" she traces the break-up of a traditional Mexican family and the destructive impact on the surrounding community. After the death of the patriarchal figure Don Teófilo Anaya, his apple orchards are divided equally among his four sons. The spirit of disharmony is introduced into this peaceful environment in the figure of Nina, the wife of Ismael, the youngest son. Although she is described as an assertive woman who disdains the pattern of submissiveness of silent women within the patriarchal order, Nina is not drawn to represent a feminist viewpoint. Rather, she is seen as an Eve in the garden, her sin being one of violence growing out of her own fear of inadequacy. She turns brother against brother, creates havoc and death, and commits suicide, leaving total devastation in her wake. "Recast" has a similar evil figure in Manolo, who is appropriately compared to a brightly colored beetle whose armoring protects it from exterior danger. Like Nina and the Apollonian figures in the other stories, Manolo rejects softness, vulnerability, and openness, acquiring a hard exterior instead. He becomes a skilled manipulator of others, but in the end he dies violently, his shell penetrated.

The title story, "Rain of Scorpions," is a departure from those discussed above. While Portillo seems to deal with an aspect of social protest—a Chicano militant, a handicapped Vietnam War veteran, tries to rally his community to confront Anglo exploitation—she focuses on the quest theme and on the myth of Aztlán. The story is set in Smelter Town, close to El Paso. The Chicano community suffers from heavy doses of sulphur dioxide which the local smelter spews forth. When Fito the militant urges the residents to abandon their town, a group of young boys sets out to find a sacred green valley where their people can survive. They never find the valley, the mythical, spiritual homeland of the Chicanos, but instead discover a few artifacts in a large, cathedral-like cave. As one critic has pointed out, "the artifacts they recover reveal that the fertile valley resides within each person; one cannot flee from reality to find peace."[30] The logical extension of this message to the social situation is that Chicanos must deal with their reality not flee from it. Fito, too, discovers peace in the end, realizing that what he is searching for is internal and is not to be found in his angry militancy. He decides to stay in Smelter Town.

Best-known for his highly acclaimed novel *The Road to Tamazunchale,* Ron Arias is also a skilled short-story writer. A journalist by training, a teacher of literature by profession, and a freelance writer whose scripts have been produced by commercial television and whose other pieces have appeared in a wide variety of publications, Arias has brought to his literary craft a rich and valuable apprenticeship.[31] He began writing when he was nine, recording his impressions of a hospital after a tonsilectomy. Later, he continued writing for high-school and college newspapers, city dailies, and wire services in foreign countries. He did interviews, human-interest stories, research articles, business profiles, and travelogues. This accumulated experience is reflected in both his novel and his short stories, which have made Arias one of the most highly respected Chicano prose fiction writers.

Like the other authors discussed in this section, Arias has mastered different tones, moods, and techniques in the treatment of his subject matter. He has a keen sense of irony and humor and experiments at will with magical realism.

"El mago" [The Magician], which has the same fantastic quality as his novel *The Road of Tamazunchale,* is about a *curandero,* a wise man who lives by himself in a dark and cluttered shack.[32] Hypnotist, soothsayer, and doctor of sorts, the Chicano community comes to Don Noriega for advice and consultation. Arias gently describes the tender relationship that two young girls, Sally and Luisa, establish with the old man. One day there is a fire in his shack; Luisa enters, talks to El mago, and exits with a music box he has played for her. She discovers, however, that the musical instrument is a charred piece of wood. This ambiguous ending places the entire story within the realm of fantasy as Don Noriega suddenly takes on magical proportions. The old man of

"The Story Machine" is similarly drawn.[33] He and his nondescript green dog are discovered along a river by a group of children. Like the music box in "El mago," this old man has a wonderous machine: a tape recorder that can predict the future. The story's magical quality is played out when a group of parents, angered by the prediction of a young woman's death, pursue the old man. He escapes, seeming to fly, his feet barely touching the ground. Fausto—he is the main character in Arias's novel—in the short story "Lupe" is also endowed with mysterious powers.[34]

In each of the above stories, Arias characterizes the mysterious wise old men as perceptive and gentle observers of human nature. For the most part, their gentleness invites others, especially children, to respond positively to them, thus suggesting a relationship between their special qualities and the credulity and innocence of childhood. It is the children who most readily accept and understand the old men, who reciprocate with special attention given to their young friends. Mutual acceptance and friendship are developed as well in "The Castle."[35]

Other stories by Ron Arias that are of interest are "Chinches" [Bed Bugs], a tale of a woman's search for meaning in human relationships; "A House on the Island," in which Arias carries off a technical tour-de-force with his creation of a collective daydream; "The Interview," in which the writer pokes fun at Chicano "liberals" who have lost touch with their people; and "Stoop Labor," a satirical treatment of a Chicano's relationship to Anglo coeds.[36]

Conclusion

The Chicano short story has shown definite technical and thematic trends during the last ten years, attesting to its vitality and growth. It appears that this genre is rapidly increasing in popularity among young writers. In addition, more experienced authors such as Tomás Rivera and Rudolfo Anaya have experimented with this literary form. Another sign that points to the health of the short story is the fact that we have had to exclude several worthy authors from our discussion due to space limitations. Like all genres of contemporary Chicano literature, the study of the short story will require frequent updating and revaluation to keep pace with writers' productivity and growth.

Chapter Five
Contemporary Chicano Novel

Introduction

Unlike short-story writers, contemporary Chicano novelists have few models upon which to draw. A quick review of the development of prose fiction—discussed in Chapter 2—shows that there are few works written between the sixteenth century and the 1950s that have the characteristics of the novel. Yet, despite the paucity of models, the contemporary Chicano novel has made rapid progress in the last twenty years to become a rich and vital form of literary expression.

Beginning in 1959 with the publication of José Antonio Villarreal's *Pocho,* the novel has undergone rapid changes, developing from primarily a social document to become a compendium of modern novelistic techniques and universal themes. While Chicano novelists continue to reflect their sociohistorical circumstances, they now do so with greater emphasis on fictional characters with individual destinies, not just flat sociological creations. Against a backdrop of Chicano traditions and institutions in conflict with an oppressive Anglo society, novelists depict with increasing artistic sensitivity and psychological dimensionality their characters' dilemmas and choices. In terms of themes and techniques, the contemporary Chicano novel shows great affinity to both the American and Latin American novel. This is not surprising since most novelists have received advanced academic training in graduate programs in either English or Hispanic literature. Like the short story, as many novelists prefer to write in English as in Spanish.

While it is a difficult to discern trends in so recent a body of literature as the contemporary Chicano novel, this author has chosen to group this genre into a rough chronological schema which appears to facilitate an understanding of its evolution during the last twenty years. With a few exceptions, the writers discussed in this section continue to be productive and to develop; this makes difficult any conclusive remarks regarding a novelist's work or place within the contemporary Chicano novel. These limitations notwithstanding, a general outline of works and writers is useful. Among the early or "pioneer" novelists are José Antonio Villarreal, Richard Vásquez, Raymond Barrio, John Rechy, and Oscar "Zeta" Acosta—their early works appeared roughly between 1959 and 1972. Within a second group are those who are generally considered to be the most important novelists and whose most notable novels were published between 1972 and 1975: Tomás Rivera, Rudolfo Anaya, Rolando Hinojosa, Miguel Méndez, Ron Arias, and Alejandro Morales. Constituting a third group are the following writers, whose works, published between 1976 and 1980, shows great promise: Aristeo Brito, Orlando Romero, and Nash Candelara. In a fourth and final group are novelists writing throughout this period whom we consider to have had less impact than the above writers on the evolution of the contemporary Chicano novel: Ernesto Galarza, Floyd Salas, Edmundo Villaseñor, Isabella Ríos, Joseph V. Torres-Metzgar, and Celso A. de Casas.

Early Novelists

Although, ironically, José Antonio Villarreal does not consider himself to be a Chicano writer, his work *Pocho,* published in 1959, is, in the opinion of most critics, the first Chicano novel.[1] It is structured around the lives of Juan Manuel Rubio, a Mexican immigrant, and Richard Rubio, his son, the *pocho* identified in the book's title. In the first chapter, we see the elder Rubio, a once-proud colonel who fought valiantly with Villa during the 1910 Mexican Revolution, arriving in Ciudad Juárez from Mexico City. Discouraged with the turn the fighting has taken, he comes north to join a new offensive. Instead he is arrested in a barroom brawl and finds his way across the border to El Paso with the help of an old family friend. Juan migrates to California, where he is joined by his wife, Consuelo. For awhile they keep alive the dream of someday returning to Mexico, but gradually it becomes clear that they are destined to live out a life of disillusionment characteristic of thousands of other Mexican immigrant families. The Rubios' values are influenced by the new culture: Consuelo becomes restless as a subservient wife and demands greater sexual expression in the relation-

ship. Threatened by this challenge to his traditional patriarchal author-
ity, Juan abandons her for a young woman recently arrived from
Mexico, a woman who has not yet been acculturated.

While *Pocho* can be seen as a fictionalized account of the sociological
phenomenon of the Mexican immigrant experience, the novel offers
much more. From the second chapter on, the focus shifts to Richard's
personal development through which we see the changes that occur to
the entire family. His development through his first eighteen years is
skillfully linked with broader historical and cultural themes such as the
immigrant family's disintegration, the unrest of American workers
during the 1930s, the arrival in California of thousands of refugees from
the Dust Bowl, the emergence of the *pachucos* in Los Angeles, and the
relocation of Japanese-Americans during World War II.[2]

Pocho can best be described as a novel of initiation, a kind of Chicano
Bildungsroman, in which we follow Richard's spiritual awakening into
an often baffling alien setting. This passage from boyhood to manhood
is heightened by his perception and sensitivity to the world around
him, an unusual introspection that has led one critic to compare his
awakening to that of Stephen Dedalus of James Joyce's *A Portrait of the
Artist as a Young Man.*[3] Like Dedalus, Richard, at the tender age of
nine, begins agonizing over such questions as the existence and immen-
sity of God, suffers the guilt of childhood sexuality, reacts like a victim
to his teacher's laughter, fears the dark, and strives to answer the
unanswerable questions of the cosmos. He turns from these unfathom-
able and horrible thoughts to take refuge in the natural world of bugs
and plants available to his inquisitive mind.

As his family disintegrates and he is thrust between two cultures—
the Chicano and the Anglo—neither of which he completely accepts,
Richard's suffering becomes more intense. While he cannot accept his
mother's Catholic fatalism or his father's newly acquired materialism,
he finds some solace in Mary, his young Anglo-Protestant friend, with
whom he shares his innermost doubts. Having rejected the strictures of
his own Mexican cultural traditions, Richard seeks his answers in new
models including an agnostic Portuguese expatriate, Joe Pete, who
fuels the boy's curiosity and quest for meaningful answers. As Richard
matures and undergoes several waves of questioning and doubt, the
world around him changes rapidly: his family buys a house, thus

cutting off further links with Mexico; Juan takes up with the young Mexican woman and abandons the family; and Richard, as the eldest son, suddenly becomes the head of the household. Meanwhile his social awareness becomes more acute when he is mistaken for a *pachuco* hoodlum and beaten by the police. Richard also is a witness to the social turmoil in northern California during the years prior to World War II. Unable to respond to his new familial responsibilities and eager to strike out on his own, he leaves the family for good and joins the navy, an ambiguous act that has been variously interpreted as his final break with his heritage and his capitulation to Anglo values or his declaration of freedom.[4]

As a novel, *Pocho* has both glaring weaknesses and favorable traits. On the negative side, one critic has observed that it fails to penetrate very deeply into the full complexity of the experience which it purports to treat: the cultural identity of the Chicano people. Other technical failures are its overexplicitness, sentimentality, a flaccid journalistic style, and a tendency to assert rather than to render.[5] Richard is not an altogether convincing character, especially in his boyhood philosophical musings—he has an intellectual maturity that is well beyond his years. On a more positive note, the novel has been judged successful in dealing effectively with several universal themes, including individuality, the struggle for personal fulfillment in a world of mediocrity and compromise, and the development of a new writer.[6] Given that Villarreal did not have the advantage of a Chicano novelistic tradition and that it is his first novel, in the balance, *Pocho* is a significant literary achievement.

Villarreal's second novel, *The Fifth Horseman* (1974) is important as the only Chicano novel to treat the period prior to the Mexican Revolution. While of historical interest, it suffers for its Manichean division of pre- and postrevolutionary Mexican society into good and evil men—men because the novelist has relegated women to an inferior status as fictional characters. Villarreal also tends to overdraw his characters; for example, Heraclio Inés, the novel's protagonist, is depicted as a "super-macho," the incarnation of the Mexican male's virile traits. He is also unconvincingly honest, just, and kind besides being a legendary ferocious fighter. More successful than his characterization of Inés and others are Villarreal's realistic descriptions of revolutionary battles, his brief portraits of its principal actors, and especially his meticulous reconstruction of the social order that existed in Mexico prior to 1910.

Like Villarreal, Richard Vásquez uses the Mexican immigrant experience and the acculturation process as the basis for his novel *Chicano* (1970). It begins with the events surrounding the Mexican Revolution and struggles forward through several generations of Chicanos to the decade of the 1960s. Héctor and Lita Sandoval are forced to resettle in the United States after their son Neftalí deserts from the Mexican army. After arriving in California, where they join the growing number of Mexican crop harvesters, the family undergoes a series of degrading experiences. The two daughters turn to prostitution, Héctor dies suddenly, and Lita's childhood sweetheart takes her back to Mexico. Vásquez then focuses on Neftalí; he marries a girl named Alicia; they settle in Rabitt Town and have many children. The narrative continues through the lives of two of their children, Pedro and Angie. Pedro, who marries Minerva, climbs the social ladder as a highly paid cement finisher. The couple and their two children, Sammy and Mariana, move out of the *barrio* to the suburbs but soon return after experiencing the brunt of Anglo racism. Meanwhile, Angie has rebelled against her traditional Mexican parents. She marries Julio and starts her own restaurant, thereby declaring her independence from the family. The second part of the book focuses on Sammy and Mariana. Sammy becomes involved in drugs and Mariana falls in love with an Anglo college student, David Stiver. Their love affair is central to the second half of the novel. Sammy is arrested on narcotics charges, Julio is destroyed because of his involvement with drug pushers, and Mariana dies after an abortion that David has insisted she have.

It was apparently Vásquez's purpose to show the disastrous effects that Anglo society has had on the Mexican immigrant, especially the family. He insinuates that some members of the family, in surrendering their traditional values, have contributed to its rapid degeneration. Specifically, Pedro has given in to the neuroses of materialism by aspiring to better his social position, Pedro and Minerva have challenged the privileged position of the eldest son by clearly favoring their daughter Mariana, and Mariana has transgressed a sacred practice by establishing a relationship with a person who is not a member of the Chicano community.[7] The message is made repeatedly in the novel: the Chicano who chooses to assimilate Anglo values and who fails to express pride and live by the traditions of his own culture is condemned.

Like *Pocho*, *Chicano* suffers from a number of internal technical weaknesses. In attempting to write an epic of the immigrant experience, Vásquez diffuses the focus of his narrative and is unable to probe any of the specific psychological attitudes of his characters. Even the second part of the novel, which concentrates on Mariana and David's relationship, degenerates into a traditional love story rather than focusing in depth on their particular motivations. Several critics have taken Vásquez to task on a number of other defects as well. For example, Ralph F. Grajeda believes that *Chicano*, like *Pocho*, fails to penetrate very deeply into the cultural complexity of the Chicano people, and that the Chicano—that is, a new person who grows out of the immigrant experience—announced in the book's title never appears.[8] Another critic observes that the novel is, to a large extent, "the literary reflection of past and present Anglo-American sociological and anthropological cultural-mystical misinterpretation of the Mexican-American, coupled with an overabundance of Mexican-American stereotypic characters."[9] Regarding stereotyped characters, the one trait that figures prominently in Vásquez's descriptions of many Mexican males is the moustache. In addition to the above criticisms, the novel suffers from sketchy plot development, little progression between sections, many contrived scenes, and a style that lacks complexity and technique. It can be said that the author simply did not have the literary skill of create successfully such an ambitious novel.

Although it has a more limited focus, Vásquez's second novel, *The Giant Killer* (1978), suffers from some of the same problems as *Chicano*. The author adopts a tough, Mickey Spillane tone to relate some incidents in the life of Ramón García, a Chicano big-city reporter. The plot revolves around García's heroic actions to save Los Angeles from a bloody racial war among blacks, Anglos, and Chicanos. Although Vásquez's condemnation of racism and his plea for a peaceful solution to racial strife are laudable, he fails to construct a convincing story or to create believable characters. For example, Ramón García's salient characteristics are his physical prowess—he is an ex-boxer—and his penchant for beautiful women. *The Giant Killer* has merit only as a mediocre detective story.

The Plum Plum Pickers by Raymond Barrio has been called "the most significant novel of the '70s in American literature."[10] While this evaluation of the novel is clearly exaggerated, it does express the enthusiasm with which it was received. The statement also reflects the advances the contemporary Chicano novel had made since the publication of *Pocho* in 1959. *The Plum Plum Pickers* poignantly portrays the suffering and despair of the Chicano agricultural worker while maintaining a high artistic standard.

Focusing on a proletarian way of life, Barrio presents a panorama of an aspect of Chicano existence in this country. He does so through the lives of a migrant couple, Manuel and Lupe Gutiérrez, who are caught in the crush of agribusiness exploitation. Set in the imaginary migrant community of Drawbridge in California's Santa Clara Valley, the novel contains many of the elements of the farmworker's struggle to free himself from the wall of indebtedness, hunger, and sickness that surrounds him. Manuel, Lupe, and their two small children come to the United States from Mexico as thousands before them to seek the good life. Instead, they find themselves living in a miserable shack of the Western Grande Compound owned by the wealthy and powerful Mr. Frederick Y. Turner and operated by the pathetically insecure Morton J. Quill, a bigot whose livelihood depends on his ruthless treatment of the Mexican fruit pickers. Barrio characterizes life in the compound as a treadmill; the workers toil from dawn to dusk, chasing the ripening crops from field to field, never saving enough to escape the year-in-year-out labyrinth of monotony and disappointment.

The novelist skillfully integrates relevant sociohistorical information into his narrative. For example, he describes how Turner has acquired his lands through the cynical manipulation of Anglo law, a legal system unfamiliar to the Mexican inhabitants of California, the original owners of much of the land on which Turner has built his lucrative agribusiness. By taking advantage of tax defaults and sly but legal business deals he has slowly put together huge tracts of prime land on which his human chattel, mainly Mexicans, work themselves further into the debt of the company-owned store. Turner is helped in his enterprise by local Anglo

officials as well as by Mexican *contratistas* ("labor conractors") who sell out
their own people.

The novel is a web of appearances, facades, dreams, hopes, fantasies,
and aspirations that are played off against and contrast with the
nightmares, disappointments, and death.[11] Manuel and Lupe exist in
their own dream world of fantasies and hopes, and yet they are not
inextricably trapped. Both manage to assert their humanity and to
continue their struggle to free themselves. Lupe's dream of a better life
is one of the novel's merits and an example of Barrio's skill in highlighting the individual's plight without losing sight of the collective
Chicano struggle.

Ramiro Sánchez, a young migrant, can be seen as Barrio's spokesman. He is the character who most clearly revolts against the false world
of the Compound—Manuel and Lupe do also, but their declaration of
freedom is less dramatic—by recognizing and acting upon his conviction that change must come for his people. Through Ramiro, Barrio
suggests that a kind of humanistic revolution is a probable solution to
American society's ills and the oppression of the Chicano farmworker.

Unlike Villarreal and Vásquez, Barrio creates a sparse plot with
major emphasis on characterization, one of the novel's strongest
points.[12] He achieves this with a minimum of dialogue, depending
upon interior monologue to reveal his characters' feelings and thoughts.
Multiple point of view is another interesting technique that the novelist
uses to develop his characters. The best example is seen in the different
reactions to an obscene note that is thrown through Quill's window at
the beginning of the novel.

Barrio introduces himself directly in the narrative by overtly
editorializing on several topics. This unwarranted interruption of the
narrative flow contrasts with a much more subtle and effective editorial
technique: the use of simulated newspaper clippings and radio broad-
casts. Barrio's experimentation with this and other techniques, together with his emphasis on characterization rather than plot, makes
The Plum Plum Pickers an important work in the evolution of the
contemporary Chicano novel.

John Rechy is a writer who does not figure prominently in general
studies on contemporary Chicano literature, mainly because he does not
draw heavily on his ethnic experience in the Southwest and, related to

this, because he is a gay writer whose works deal predominantly with homosexuality in the United States.[13] To an extent, Rechy holds the same position in contemporary Chicano literature that James Baldwin does in black literature. Although Baldwin has been outspoken and visible in addressing himself to the problems of oppressed peoples in this country, not all of his works draw directly on the black experience in a narrower social sense, nor are all of his works *engagé* literature. For example, *Giovanni's Room,* set in Paris, focuses on the nature of love in America. It would be unthinkable to exclude Baldwin from a study of contemporary black literature; likewise, we include Rechy in our discussion of the contemporary Chicano novel.

John Rechy has published six novels—*City of Night* (1963), *Numbers* (1967), *This Day's Death* (1969), *Vampires* (1971), *The Fourth Angel* (1972), and *The Sexual Outlaw* (1977)—which make him the most prolific Chicano novelist. *Vampires,* which deals with the vampire myth, represents Rechy's attempt to break new literary ground for himself, to explore an aspect of reality not seen in the rest of his fiction. The other five works focus, in varying degrees, on homosexuality, the world of male prostitution, and the resultant superficial relationships and extreme aloneness of his characters. Although he vividly depicts the anguish and confusion of the homosexual in this country, viewed as a whole, in his fiction he explores the struggle of the individual to free himself from all constraints, a struggle which ultimately nets him little.

Rechy's first novel, *City of Night,* is perhaps his finest, both in terms of the breadth and the depth of its focus. Although the other novels have value as independent works, they take on greater meaning when seen as parts of Rechy's fictional world set forth in *City of Night.* This novel constitutes the anguished search for self of an anonymous young male protagonist who, setting out from his native El Paso, travels to five American cities: New York, Los Angeles, San Francisco, Chicago, and New Orleans. Each of the four parts of the novel corresponds to his stay in one of the cities with the exception of the third section, which includes both San Francisco and Chicago.

A casual examination of the novel thus reveals that its internal structure parallels the major geographical areas and that the work gives us a panoramic view of urban America. As we trace the protagonist's journey from one city to another and his encounters with the world of male hustling, dereliction, and poverty, the underside of American life begins to take shape. But related to this more obvious focus on the negative aspects of urbanized society is the exploration of the narrator's personality as it develops within the context of his experience in the Cities of Night.

The interplay of the individual and the society emerges on one level as a metaphor of the impossibility of love in America: "The particulars of the hustler's world, with its many parts, repetitions, and variations, are intended to be related to an image of America in the novel which reveals that the hustler's world and the larger American context are analogous to each other, and the male prostitute's world is the metaphor for the larger context."[14] This explanation of the metaphor is incomplete, however, because Rechy's protagonist, like Dostoevsky's Underground Man, learns through his experience that love is not possible in any context because love brings dependence on others and, finally, the destruction of the personality itself. In the final pages of the novel, the character comes to the brink of forming a relationship with another man but then rejects it, horrified by the terrible risk it will involve.

The protagonist leaves El Paso as a young man to embark on his search for a milieu in which he can live comfortably without the fear of too intense self-examination. Although he refers to his native city in the later sections of the novel with a combination of fond nostalgia and regret for having left, we come to realize that it contains the seeds of his unhappinesss: "not the great-stretching, wide plained land of the movies, but the crushing city where I had been raised in stifling love and hatred." While his mother smothered him in tender but carnivorous care and indulgence, his father, an unsuccessful composer, projected his accumulated frustration onto his son, who soon developed an intense and lasting hatred for him. The constant instability and sudden violent eruptions in his home life eventually drive him into a self-imposed isolation from which he will not return. The figure of his dead dog, Winnie, his only source of affection as a child, recurs throughout the novel as a symbol to him of hopelessness and utter misery. While craving tenderness and attention he is incapable of responding to it. A worsening home life and his inability to form adolescent friendships drive Rechy's protagonist further into himself while deepening his need for affection. Having rebelled against his family and rejected his peers, he plunges headlong into the chaotic and indifferent world of the large American cities. Male prostitution becomes a means of asserting his self-worth in an environment which will eventually deny him all expression of individuality.

The main characters of Rechy's other novels, *This Day's Death, Numbers,* and *The Sexual Outlaw,* follow essentially the same pattern. In the former the young male protagonist, Jim Girard, tries to escape the suffocating love of an overly close and overly intimate mother and the resentment of a frustrated father. He flees his family home in El Paso to explore the sexual underworld of Los Angeles. Falsely accused of homosexual solicitation, he moves back and forth between the California courts and his invalid mother in Texas. While struggling to deal with the strong societal pressures against homosexuality, he tries, in vain, to free himself from his mother's domination. In *Numbers,* a young Texan also travels to Los Angeles to reenact the scene of his earlier sexual involvement. As indicated in the title, this work describes the obsessive need for physical conquests in order to fill the lonely and despair-filled lives of individuals whose activities society has chosen to outlaw. *The Sexual Outlaw* is structured around a weekend in the life of a male hustler. In at least part of the novel we follow the protagonist's steps through the world we have come to know in his other novels.[15]

Rechy summarizes for us through his protagonists' thoughts and actions, his view of a world in which the myths of maternal, homosexual, and divine love have fallen one by one. The young male hustlers' experiences in the cities of night show it is too great a risk to explore a love which could manipulate and consume them. On the other hand, the life of superficial physical contact and nonreciprocation is not a viable solution either. This life produces in his protagonists a slow decay of their souls, a death more final than the physical death of waning youth. Rechy thus deals with more than the impossibility of love within a specific social context.

Another kind of search is that of Oscar "Zeta" Acosta, a Chicano activist lawyer turned writer, who sets forth in his two works, *The Autobiography of a Brown Buffalo* (1972) and *The Revolt of the Cockroach People* (1973), his personal odyssey to discover himself and his relationship to his cultural past. Both works are highly autobiographical but contain sufficient fictional elements to classify them as novels. In the first, Acosta becomes progressively more disenchanted with his life as an urban lawyer and aware that he is culturally rootless. His experiences with drugs and sex provide him with little relief from his anguish, and it is only through the quest and attainment of his true identity as a Chicano that Acosta reckons with his internal struggle. In the second work, after providing himself worthy of La Raza as a fierce defender of his people, his life takes on direction and meaning.

Acosta begins his six-month quest in *The Autobiography of a Brown Buffalo* by fleeing the comfortable but monotonous life of an Oakland welfare-lawyer. Although at the outset he is not aware of what ails him, he suffers from a general ennui that takes him far away from the Bay Area west to Idaho, Colorado, and Texas. He immerses himself in the psychedelic drug scene of the 1960s, experimenting with the unrestrained use of drugs and sex only to emerge as discouraged and confused as before. It is finally in Juárez, México, that he discovers his true mestizo roots and begins to take pride in himself as a "beautiful brown buffalo." He sets out for Los Angeles, "the home of the biggest herd of brown buffalos in the entire world," determined to put his newfound identity to some vague but good use.

In *The Revolt of the Cockroach People,* the former pusillanimous welfare-lawyer from Oakland becomes a militant and a fearless attorney who participates in demonstrations, marches, and dramatic courtroom defenses of activists falsely accused of crimes by the authorities. Acosta adopts his middle name, "Zeta," which comes from General Zeta, the revolutionary hero of a Mexican movie classic. The name also encompasses the traits of the nonfictional revolutionary heroes Emiliano Zapata and Francisco Villa. Another tie to the Mexican Revolution is suggested in the work's title: the cockroaches are the tenacious participants in Mexico's 1910 Revolution who marched to the tune of "La cucaracha" [The Cockroach], an inspirational song that grew out of this bloody conflict.

Revolt of the Cockroach People contains many direct or thinly veiled references to both Anglo and Chicano figures who were participants in the militant activities in Los Angeles and elsewhere in 1968 or who were government officials during this period: Rubén Salazar—Roland Zanzibar in the book—the Chicano journalist who was killed during the 29

August 1970 National Chicano Moratorium Against the Vietnam War;
Sam Yorty, the mayor of Los Angeles; "Corky" Gonzales, the Denver
Chicano activist; César Chávez; Governor Ronald Reagan; etc.

Neither of Acosta's works are fully developed novels with even
characterization and plot development, yet they effectively present a
firsthand account of an individual's search for himself within one of the
most tumultous periods of our history. Acosta enhances the interplay
between the central figure and his social context through his manipulation of cinematic techniques.[16] Of note is the manner in which he
establishes the tone and mood of an episode by striving for a cinematic
quality. He relegates settings to a secondary position, focusing on
character action. Montage is another device that he employs to establish
rapport with the movie-wise reader.

Acosta's style is energetic but often undisciplined. He shoots from
the hip, with seemingly little care for developing a refined, polished
expression. This, of course, is in concert with, in his first work, his
confused view of the world and, in his second, his rambunctious and
often irreverent attack of a hypocritical and valueless society.

1971–1975: The Maturing of the Contemporary Novel

While the novelists discussed in the previous section constitute the
pioneering efforts to establish a Chicano novelistic tradition, those
included in this section can be said to represent the maturing of this
important form of literary expression. Two related factors provide much
of the impetus for this process: the establishment of the first Chicano
publishing company, Quinto Sol, in 1969 by Octavio Romano, Herminio Ríos, and others, and the awarding of the annual literary prize
the Premio Quinto Sol. Three of the six novelists included in this
section were winners of this prestigious award: Tomás Rivera in 1970
for ". . . y no se lo tragó la tierra" [. . . and the earth did not part],
Rudolfo A. Anaya in 1971 for *Bless Me, Ultima,* and Rolando Hinojosa
in 1972 for *Estampas del valle y otras obras* [Sketches of the Valley and
Other Works]. Other important events that reflect the advances the
novel made during the 1970s are the publication of two Chicano
novelists by major Latin-American publishing houses and the awarding
of an international literary prize to one of them. Rolando Hinojosa's

Klail City y sus alrededores [Klail City and Its Environs] won the Cuban Casa de las Américas novel prize for 1976 and was published in Cuba and distributed throughout much of the Spanish-speaking world. Alejandro Morales's two novels, *Caras viejas y vino nuevo* [Old Faces and New Wine] and *La verdad sin voz* [The Voiceless Truth], were published by Mexico's important publisher Joaquín Mortiz in 1975 and 1979, respectively. The contemporary Chicano novel thus makes important advances during the 1970s.

Tomás Rivera's ". . . *y no se lo tragó la tierra*" is classified by some as a collection of short stories and vignettes, anecdotes, or sketches, but most critics who have examined the work in depth agree that its inherent unity qualifies it as a novel. For example, Ralph F. Grajeda, while conceding that the work is difficult to describe structurally, nonetheless identifies it as a novel but not in the conventional sense.[17] The book contains a set of twelve thematically unified stories—symbolic of the twelve months of the year—framed by an introductory selection, "El año perdido" [The Lost Year], and a summarizing selection, "Debajo de la casa" [Under the House]. Preceding all but one of the stories is a short anecdote, which, as Grajeda observes, is:

> directed backward (echoing or commenting on the thematic concerns of the preceding story) or sometimes pointed forward (prefacing the story that follows). In some instances the anecdote does not relate directly either to what immediately precedes or follows, but instead echoes or re-echoes values, motifs, themes, or judgments, found elsewhere in the book. The effect is incremental. Through the reinforcement, variation, and amplification provided by the twelve stories and the thirteen anecdotes, the picture of the community is gradually filled. At the end, the entire experience is synthesized and brought to a thematic conclusion through the consciousness of the central character. (71)

The book focuses on the Texas-based migrant farmworkers; however, Rivera's primary intent is not to preach social change by glorifying the Chicano and vilifying the Anglo but to create (in his own words) "an artistic world . . . in which the literary characters must move, speak, and feel as true and complex creations."[18] Rivera draws heavily on the daily lives of the people he knows best, while at the same time elevating their fears, struggles, and beliefs beyond the level of social-protest literature. Rivera does not ignore the cause of his people; rather, he gives it greater force and credibility by creating characters who have more dimensionality than those of the novelists discussed in the preceding section. Like the Mexican writer Juan Rulfo—Rulfo, along with Sherwood Anderson and William Faulkner, is one of Rivera's acknowledged masters—Rivera has rejected the stock sociological or historical model of pamphleteering literature. He avoids the Manichean trap of dividing his world into good and evil people. In some stories, he describes Chicanos cheating, robbing, and even killing their own people.[19]

The central character referred to earlier is the unnamed hero of the two frame pieces and presumably the same one who reappears in many of the stories. He is not explicitly identified with any of the other characters but the experiences and landscapes of their lives all constitute part of his past and his memories of the past. Through him, we hear the voice of the people. He remains nameless throughout the book, an indication that Rivera did not wish for him to play an important thematic role; however, he does give structural unity to the work. The experience the author wishes to create is thus a general, collective one; the central character's voice "does not ring of the individually introspective, existentially or psychologically isolated and alone, but rather of the communally active and enduring."[20]

The movement in the book is cyclical, and although there is no strict correspondence among specific months and particular stories, "the twelve stories in a general sense are symbolic representations of the year that the protagonist attempts to recapture. . . . The cyclical movement functions to delineate the cyclical and repetitive nature of the migrant farmworkers' lives as they yearly retrace the same roads to the same fields."[21]

Rivera's use of narrative techniques is notable.[22] For example, in "Cuando lleguemos" [When We Arrive], a story about the breakdown of a truck that is transporting some forty migrant workers from Texas to Minnesota, instead of a traditional narrative, he uses a series of interior monologues containing the private feelings, thoughts, memories, etc., of several of the riders. He lets each consciousness speak for itself rather than interjecting his authorial presence. The effectiveness of this technique is based on the fact that Rivera allows each worker to reveal himself without an intermediary and without the need for prior physical or external description. He gives to the farmworkers the dignity of a rich and complex internal life which sharply contrasts with the brutalizing experience of their work.

The technique used in "Cuando lleguemos" is an example of an objective experience presented subjectively through multiple points of view. In other stories, such as "Un rezo" [A Prayer], Rivera presents a subjective experience objectively by using a single perspective. In this case, we see the insider's point of view and the lack of extraneous or external statement that would detract from the authentic experience. Still in other stories he mixes a traditional third-person narrative with dialogue and interior monologue or, as in "Es que duele" [It is Painful], he combines objective reporting and subjective self-analysis interspersed with set pieces of dialogue and monologue.

In contrast to the fictional world of the migrant farmworker of ". . . *y no se lo tragó la tierra,*" Rudolfo A. Anaya has created a mythical ambience in his novel *Bless Me, Ultima* (1972). Anaya has published two other novels, *Heart of Aztlán* (1976) and *Tortuga* (1979), but his reputation as the most widely known and most popular Chicano novelist is based on his first work. In it, he describes a Chicano experience different from that delineated by Rivera, of a young boy growing up in rural New Mexico after World War II in a family whose roots go back centuries to the original Spanish settlers.

Antonio Márez, the protagonist, is almost seven when the story of his religious crisis begins. The first-person narration ends a year later after an intense period of spiritual growth for the young boy, who has been profoundly influenced by Ultima, a *curandera* ("folk healer") of indeterminate age whom Antonio's family has brought to live in their home. His father, Gabriel Márez, is an intensely independent *llanero* ("plainsman") who laments that he no longer lives on the *llano* and has not fulfilled his dream of moving to California. In contrast, Antonio's mother, María Luna, comes from a long line of farmers who are firmly rooted in the land. Critical of the wandering ways of her husband's family, she hopes that Antonio will someday become a priest in order to allow her vicariously to live out a life of cultivation and learning her marriage to Gabriel has denied her. Antonio's older brothers, all World War II veterans, are depicted as shiftless, unambitious young men who

add to their mother's disappointment. His sisters do not figure prominently in the novel.

Ultima's arrival saves Antonio from the probable psychological
torment that would have ensued as a result of his mother and father vying
to influence him. The former has already given him his faith and the latter
has imbued him with a sense of freedom, but Ultima has a more profound
impact on Antonio by inviting him to see the possibilities of a magical
world that is also a part of him. She has been described as a "pantheistic
priestess, good witch of the South, earth mother, life force and universal
spirit, all compactly molded into one small, ageless woman with glossy
braids and a magical owl."[23]

Death plays an essential role in Antonio's loss of faith in the traditional Catholic beliefs of his people and in his rebirth into the new
spirituality to which Ultima introduces him. There are four major
death scenes in the novel: Lupito, a local lunatic who kills the sheriff,
is hunted and shot by Antonio's father and a band of other men;
Narciso, the town drunk, is shot by Tenorio for protecting Ultima;
Florence, Antonio's young friend, drowns; Ultima dies. In the first
three cases, all senseless deaths, Antonio's faith is profoundly shaken,
but Ultima soothes his pain and provides a spiritual alternative to the
empty explanations his Catholicism offers.

She awakens in him the memory of the timeless, mythological
figures that inhabit his past, teaching him a profound respect for the
mystical legends and folk wisdom that have survived through the
centuries. He is finally introduced to the Golden Carp, a legendary
good god who became a fish to be near his people, who were likewise
turned into carp as punishment for their sins.

Anaya effectively uses a series of dreams to extend the novel's
narrative limits toward the realm of the magical and the fantastic.[24]
There are three kinds: those that deal with the lives of the Márez-Luna
families; those that present a conflict in which Ultima plays a reconcil-
ing role; and those that serve as prophecies and revelations. In terms of
Antonio's spiritual development, the dreams function as rites of passage, helping him through his transition and preparing him for an
answer to his doubts and for his rebirth.[25]

Another important aspect of *Bless Me, Ultima* is the importance of
the landscape. As Ultima introduces Antonio to magic, myth, and

fantasy, she also invites him to open his eyes so that he may see for the first time what Anaya calls the latent energy in landscape. Lanscape is a taking-off point for the author's exploration of magic in realism. He says: "It is the place where imagination and the image-laden memory begin their work, and the three forces—place, imagination, and memory—are inextricably wound together in my work."[26] Anaya explores his and his reader's response to land-space, labeling it an epiphany, that is, "A natural response to the raw, majestic, and awe-inspiring landscape in the Southwest, a coming together of man and that lancscape."

Anaya's concept of landscape in general and land in particular plays a pivotal role in his second novel *Heart of Aztlán.* Clemente and Adelita Chávez are forced for financial reasons to sell their land in Guadalupe, a rural New Mexican community, and move to the Albuquerque *barrio* of Barelas. As the family departs, Clemente voices his despair:

> His soul and his life were in the earth, and he knew that when he signed [the contract] he would be cutting the strings of that attachment. It was like setting adrift on an unknown, uncharted ocean. He tried to understand the necessity of selling the land, to understand that the move would provide his children a new future in a new place, but that did not lessen the pain he felt as the roots of his soul pulled away and severed themselves from the earth which had nurtured his life.[27]

Once they have settled in the city, far away from the land's benevo-lence, the family, once solid, begins to disintegrate. One daughter drops out of school, another becomes Americanized, a son gets heavily involved with drugs, and Clemente begins to drink and abuse his wife and children. All the while, another son, Jason, holds the family together. Just as Clemente is about to despair, Crispín, a mystical poet with a magical blue guitar—he is a kind of urban Ultima—shows him the path to his own salvation and urges him to assume a position of leadership among the unemployed Chicanos of his community. Crispín shares with him the sacred legend of Aztlán. The man from Guadalupe, from the land, returns to the *barrio* to preach the healing power of love.

While *Heart of Aztlán* can be interpreted as a novel of social protest, it contains too many magical and mythological elements to be so classified. It is close to *Bless Me, Ultima* in its message that the true essence of love resides with the people who are in touch with the ancient primal rhythms of the land.

Anaya's most recent novel, *Tortuga,* is about a boy's discovery of his own power coupled with his growing awareness of the magical nature of the land around him. Like *Bless Me, Ultima,* this work is the story of a young narrator's initiation into adulthood, the rites of passage being his recovery from a serious accident in a hospital for crippled children. The book begins with his arrival at the hospital after a long trip in an ambulance from his home in northern New Mexico. The first-person narration allows us an intimate view of his personal struggle to recuperate from his injuries. Nicknamed Tortuga because of the turtlelike body cast he is given, his journey back to health is a slow and painful one.

During the course of the novel, he wanders through the darkest recesses of the institution, where he discovers whole wards of grotesquely deformed children stricken by polio and other crippling diseases. He also discovers Salomón, a mute patient, who communicates with Tortuga through a mysterious telepathic process. Like Ultima and Crispín in Anaya's other novels, Salomón is a wise, shamanlike figure who introduces the narrator to the magic mountain—also named Tortuga—that can be seen in the distance and whose recuperative warm waters are piped into the hospital bringing hope and soothing the children's pain. As Tortuga moves through his despair and decides, at Salomón's urging, to embrace life, he also gets in touch with his own adolescent sexuality. He falls in love with a hospital employee, Ismelda, a sensuous young earth-mother type who is also linked with the mountain. Tortuga recovers, leaves the hospital, but vows to return someday for Ismelda. Although *Tortuga* is somewhat overwritten, in general it is a good story which flows easily within the magical-mythical New Mexican world which has become Anaya's trademark.

Rolando Hinojosa has established a solid reputation as a Chicano novelist with the publication of four novels, all of which form a part of the same fictional world of a Chicano community in south Texas in the 1960s and the 1970s: *Estampas del valle y otras obras* (1973), *Klail city y sus alrededores* (1976), *Claros varones de Belken* [The Illustrious Gentlemen of Belken] (1981), and *Miquerido Rafa* [My Dear Rafa, 1981]. In addition, he has published two other books: *Korean Love Songs* (1978), a narrative poem about the Korean conflict, and *Generaciones, notas, y brechas* [Generations, Notes and Impressions] (1980), a collection of some of his miscellaneous works.[28]

Hinojosa is the first Chicano writer to win an important international literary award and the first American citizen to be honored by the distinguished group of Latin American intellectuals who comprised the Casa de las Américas panel of judges. The judges' comments on *Klail City* are all applicable to the other works in his trilogy. The novel was cited for its importance as a testimonial to the collective experience of the Chicano community in this country, and in terms of artistry, it was praised for its richness of imagery, its sensitively created dialogues, its collagelike structure based on a pattern of converging individual lives, and the masterful control of narrative time.

Hinojosa's first novel, *Estampas . . .*, is a series of sketches forming a tapestry of the Chicano community in and around Klail City. Each *estampa* forms an integral part of the complex of lives, joys, tragedies, and struggles of the community and to consider each separately would destroy the overall effect of the author's literary creation. Hinojosa warns us at the outset of his work that his *estampas* are like individual strands of hair matted together with the sweat and dirt of generations of human toil. To separate them would be to interrupt the flow of vitality and spontaneity which surges through the work.

Estampas . . . contains a wide range in tone, from a terse, direct presentation to a rich and subtle folk humor. The work alternates between the omniscient author and the first-person narrator. It begins at an indefinite point in time and place with the marriage of Roque Malcara and Terre Tapia and then expands rapidly, growing progressively more intricate as the writer, in every sketch, adds a new character or reveals a different facet of one already presented. Over twenty-five characters appear in the work's relatively few pages.

Hinojosa intentionally obscures relationships between characters, does not identify his narrator, and blurs characterization in order to create a total impression of the community of Klail City. Only a few characters reappear throughout the pages of the novel and they serve to provide threads of unity among the many sketches.

The reader does not discover for several pages even the general location of the community described (Texas) or the time period in which the work is set. It seems to be the author's intent to create, in the place of specific time and place, the traditions and values that his Spanish-speaking community has shared for many generations and at least for as long as any of the characters in the novel can remember.

This summary of the major narrative characteristics of *Estampas* . . . provides a helpful perspective for a consideration of *Klail City* . . ., which represents the author's mastery of the techniques utilized in the first novel. He has become more adept in manipulating temporal and spatial fragmentation and the constant refocusing of the narrative on a few central figures who serve as anchors to give the work its cohesiveness. More importantly, Hinojosa is more successful in the second novel in creating a total ambience in which he allows the reader to participate through techniques such as the multiplication of point of view, convergence of individual destinies, and the use of memory as a narrative device. Structurally, *Klail City* . . . is more complex than *Estampas*. . . . We marvel that the author has packed into his relatively short novel over one hundred fictional beings and has succeeded in weaving them in and out of his narrative in a way that enhances reader participation and leaves the impression of complete naturalness and spontaneity.

Only a few characters stand out in relief: Esteban Echevarría, the old-timer with a prodigious memory who is Klail City's closest thing to a wise man and *raconteur*; Jehú Malacara, who recalls for us his youthful adventures with the fundamentalist preacher Tomás Imás; Rafa Buenrostro, a silent but ever-present narrator through whom we learn of the struggles of a young Chicano in school and, later, in the military; the good Chicano cop Don Manuel Guzmán, respected by the Chicano community for his role as counselor and friend of drunks and other unfortunate "down-and-outers"; Choche Markham, the Anglo politician who becomes a benevolent Chicano-lover during elections; the evil Leguizamón family, who were responsible for the death of Rafa Buenrostro's father, Jesús, many years ago; and a few others such as Pedro Zamudio and Celso Villalón. These few central characters give the work its continuity but they do not emerge as separate or even more important than the others. We know them better because they appear more often, but they possess little of the stuff of literary heroes or even antiheroes.

Hinojosa tells us that he wrote *Klail City* . . . in order to keep alive the memory of his youth, a memory which has taken on added importance as a new and changing world removes him further and further from his past. He does this through the use of different literary techniques. We have already discussed his effective creation of an ambience in which the reader immerses himself. By suppressing the role the individual characters play in the novel and by highlighting the function of the collective protagonist of Klail City, we are able to relate more easily and more personally to a multitude of names, relationships, happenings, etc. Further, Hinojosa's multiplication of points of view breaks down some of the barriers between reader and character reducing the narrative distance between them. This technique also allows him to give vitality to the fictional present as well as to give palpability to the fictional past. The work—the community of Klail City—is thereby transformed into a living rather than primarily a literary experience for the reader.

Through constant temporal and spatial fragmentation, the past continues to invade the present. The present is contaminated not only by memories of the past recalled in the fictional present but by the rapid alternating back and forth between the two temporal poles. The structure of the novel is neither circular nor concentric but intermingled. Characters, spaces, and times touch each other—we touch them—either casually or directly. Memories float in and out of the present, often becoming confused with it for their vividness. The novel is filled with echoes, partial glimpses of characters, snatches of dialogue, whole scenes and parts of scenes, interesting characters and some not so interesting, important events and most not so important.

In the end, the composite of the above emerges as the hermetically sealed world of Klail City and its surroundings in which we have been asked to enter and to participate not as readers by as witnesses, listeners, and friends. We, too, overhear conversations, witness scenes, listen attentively to others as they tell us about their lives or those of others we have never met. As Rafa Buenrostro, we sit and listen patiently, respectfully, in the bar as Echevarría goes on interminably about Jesús, about Choche Markham the crafty politician, about the scheming Van Meers, and about others we have never heard of or will never hear of again.

Hinojosa's recently published *Claros varones de Belken* forms the third part—the fourth part of his long narrative poem *Korean Love Songs* is included—of the series about Klail City. In this work the author

continues telling us about Rafa Buenrostro, Estaban Echevarría, Jehú
Malacara, and several minor characters. Rafa leaves the valley to go to
the university in Austin, graduates, is called up in the reserves for duty
in Korea, and returns safely to Belken County. Jehú becomes an
itinerant Baptist missionary, but his religious activities are
momentarily interrupted for service in Korea. Esteban Echevarría
grows older and weaker; however, his memory is as clear as ever as he
continues to tell Rafa about the valley's past. *Claros varones de Belken*
ends sadly with Echevarría's long lament on time and change, which
have ravished the collective life of the Chicano community. There is no
resolution at the end of the latest segment of Hinojosa's continuing
saga; rather, we close the book knowing that the novelist will continue
to unravel the lives of the characters in works that will certainly follow
this one.

Like his short story "Tata Casehua," Miguel Méndez's novel *Peregrinos de Aztlán* [Pilgrims of Aztlán, 1971] is a difficult and challenging
work due to its language and structure. The author invites us into his
complex world of oppressed Yaqui Indians and Chicano *barrio*-dwellers
on both sides of the United States—Mexican border. Although it is not
easy to struggle through the novel's pages of baroque Spanish, multiple
points of view, and stream of consciousness narration, we are rewarded
at the end by a penetrating view of various aspects of the Chicano
experience in the Southwest. *Peregrinos* has been labeled, rightfully,
"the Chicano novel of the downtrodden."[29]

The different forms of social oppression of the Yaqui Indian and the
Chicano are, in Méndez's view, war, prostitution, unemployment, and
hunger. *Peregrinos* relates the suffering of approximately a dozen victims
who live this oppression.[30] Most of the novel is narrated through the
memories of Loreto Maldonado, an old Yaqui Indian who brings into
our focus the more than half a century of his misery and that of his
people. Other important characters are El Cometa, a Chicano comic
who is sympathetic to the plight of the poor; Pedro, a Mexican who
avenges the rape of his sister; El Vate, a poet; Lorenzo, another poet who
left Mexico for the United States to save his family from starvation;
Frankie, a Chicano who is sent to Vietnam to fight his Oriental
brothers; and El Buen Chuco, an elderly alcoholic and vagrant, broken
and discouraged by a life of hard labor. The voices of these and other

characters float in and out of the entire novel, forming a complex of echoes, reminiscenses, cries of pain, and fragmented dialogues and interior monologues.

Loreto Maldonado functions as the novel's central figure. It is his consciousness which gives the work its unity and it is through his subjective thoughts, dreams, and impressions that we view various levels of border society.[31]

Peregrinos begins in an unidentified Arizona border town as Loreto begins another day of washing cars. Various valuable pieces of information are revealed during the first long sequence. We learn that Loreto is of Yaqui rather than Aztec origin—geographically, this includes the concept of the Chicano homeland of Aztlán; Loreto reflects on his enslaved condition and relates it to the Mexican wetback and to the Chicano, thus drawing together the three groups into a common bond; the city, one of the novel's leit motifs, is introduced—it often functions as an oppressive force in the work; the image of war plays a dominant role in his thoughts. Loreto remembers the betrayal of the Yaqui nation after their brave participation in the Mexican Revolution, and this is linked to Frankie's death in Vietnam, a more contemporary example of betrayal.[32]

The major theme of *Peregrinos,* that the voices of the poor and the oppressed must not be forgotten, is reflected in the novel's strong oral character which is communicated through Méndez's language, a fascinating blend of standard Spanish, *pachuquismos,* Mexicanisms, lyric prose, and empty rhetoric. The novelist allows the people from the lower strata of society to speak for themselves using the language that is closely identified with each group. This device is also used to identify the oppressors, both Mexican and Anglo, whose words ring falsely in juxtaposition with those of Yaquis, wetbacks, and Chicanos. One critic has observed that Méndez, believing that the history of the poor is found in the oral tradition, has established a human center in the character of Loreto to contain it and to be its focus.[33]

The voices of the poor are also salvaged through the novel's fragmented narrative structure. Rather than present the characters' dialogues and monologues in an orderly, linear fashion—this would falsify and contribute to our dismissing them—Méndez recovers and preserves the voices through the fragmented narrative which reflects the confusion and disorientation in the lives of Loreto and others.[34] Although the novel's sometimes disjointed structure may be the source of frustration, we should bear in mind that it is not his intention to entertain but to invite us to hear and to remember what we have heard.

While Méndez's view of the Chicano experience in the Southwest is broad, that of Alejandro Morales provices a more intimate view of life in the *barrio*. In *Caras viejas y vino nuevo* (Mexico City, 1975) he presents different scenes of the *barrio* through the double perspective of two Chicano adolescents, Julián and Mateo. Through their eyes we view celebrations—a wedding, a dance, Christmas festivities, tragedies, political confrontations, and the passage of Chicano youth into adulthood complete with their first sexual encounters and experiences with drugs. In short, the novel is a compendium of *barrio* life in the decades of the 1950s and the 1960s. The emphasis, however, is not on the collective experience but on the individual choices each young narrator is asked to make in order to decide his future. Julián is characterized as an athletically inclined young man who has the greater potential of leaving the *barrio* to join the dominant society. Despite this, he becomes involved in drugs and alcohol and ends up in jail. Mateo, on the other hand, excels as a student and leaves the *barrio,* presumably to enroll in school in the East. His end is also tragic; he dies of leukemia. Morales thus focuses on the sordid aspects of the *barrio* experience.

Like Méndez, Morales effectively uses a number of contemporary novelistic techniques—stream of consciousness, fragmentation, time and space montage, and the juxtaposition of subjective elements—in his narrative, but of greatest significance is his structural orientation, which lends originality to the novel.[35] Our vision of the *barrio* is received through Mateo, whose perception of exterior reality is affected by his personal evolution. Through the fragmentation of temporal continuity, Morales creates a complex work which is structured in reverse order.

A restructuring of the novel in chronological order reveals the basic plot line, that is, Julián's progressive involvement in drugs, the escalating conflict between him and his father, the death of his mother, and finally his own death. Interspersed between these episodes are fragments depicting the *barrio* and Mateo's personal life.[36] It is Mateo who functions as the central consciousness giving the novel unity just as Loreto does in *Peregrinos*.

A structural characteristic revealed early in the novel, in the first fragment, "is the tendency of the narrator to move without warning from the exterior perspective of direct style to an interior position attained through an indirect narrative technique."[37] Morales's borrowing of the cinematographic technique of using a zoom lens to shift the point of view rapidly from distant objective reality to a close-up of the action or the center of consciousness is often a source of confusion and a minor defect in the novel.

Language plays an important part in *Caras viejas y vino nuevo*. As one reviewer has pointed out, it is through language that the novelist "is able to capture the puppet-like existence of the inhabitants of the *barrio*."[38] Rather than being in charge of their own lives, the *barrio*-dwellers are manipulated by outside forces beyond their control. This is communicated linguistically by, for example, objects acting upon the characters rather than their controlling the objects. By dehumanizing his characters—often a part of the body or an article is the focal point of the action—and personifying objects, Morales is also able to achieve the same effect.

In his second novel, *La verdad sin voz,* also published in Mexico City (1979), Morales uses the same novelistic techniques and linguistic devices described above, but beyond these formal similarities the novels have little in common. *La verdad sin voz* is structurally more complex than the first work as the novelist broadens his fictional space beyond the *barrio* to include Mexican political corruption and repression, a materialistic and self-serving American medical establishment, and a hypocritical academic institution. As in *Caras viejas y vino nuevo,* the story line moves forward through the consciousnesses of several key characters: Michael Logan, an idealistic young Anglo doctor; Cody, his wife; El Señor Presidente, an anonymous Mexican president; Casimiro, a Mexican revolutionary; Eutemio, a Chicano literature professor; and Pistola Gorda (Fat Pistol), a corrupt Chicano sheriff. Third-person narrative sequences link these characters, whose thoughts, feelings, and impressions fill the pages of the book. The plot action alternates rapidly back and forth in a contrapuntal fashion among several focal points: a medical clinic in the Chicano *barrio* of the small Texas town of Mathis, the Mexican president's palace in Mexico City, and a guerrilla band's hideout in northern Mexico.

The novel begins as Leroy Hale, an Anglo doctor, decides to leave the Mathis medical center where he has been for only a few short months. The local authorities, both Anglo and Chicano, have carried out an intense harassment campaign to force him out. He and his family return to a comfortable job in a well-established clinic in the north. At this point Michael Logan rejects a promising lucrative career to replace Hale as director of the Mathis clinic. He and his family move to Texas. His wife, Cody, and their children remain in Corpus Christi while Michael begins the challenging task of restoring the clinic. Most of the novel deals with his relationship with the Chicano clients, his sexual involvement with Margarita, his helper, and the disintegration of his marriage. Interwoven with this main story line are several others. In Mexico, the president faces the thorny problems of increasing urban unrest and guerrilla activity in the north under the leadership of the tenacious guerrilla fighter Casimiro. Simultaneously, Eutemio faces a crisis in his academic department, where he is caught between skeptical militant students who expect him to join their demonstrations and colleagues who are critical of his efforts to write creative literature. Michael is eventually killed by Pistola Grande and Casimiro's band is decimated by Mexican troops as the forces of evil triumph over the forces of good. Those who have tried to combat the institutions that dictate much of our lives ultimately fail: a repressive Mexican government continues unabated, an inhuman medical establishment stands strong, the oppression of Chicanos by Anglos and other Chicanos persists in the *barrio*.

Morales's pessimistic view of life is moderated somewhat by Eutemio's apparent survival within his own hostile environment. At the end of the book, he resolves to write a novel about Michael Logan—appropriately, the novel's title will be *La verdad sin voz*. Against the nefarious designs of governments and institutions, Morales posits the example of the authentic person who believes and acts according to his ideals.

Besides being one of the most talented contemporary Chicano short-story writers, Ron Arias is an exceptional novelist whose *The*

Road to Tamazunchale (1975) has been singled out for its many outstanding qualities. A sample of reviewers' and critics' laudatory comments will serve to illustrate the importance of the novel as a work of art and its place within the evolution of contemporary Chicano prose fiction. Willard Gingerich calls it a masterful narrative, "a fable which extends itself out of the roots of suffering and death, a fable of real human emotions, not limited to the exhausted formulas of 'realism' or deformed by misapprehended techniques of new masters."[39] Judy Salinas characterizes the novel as "a Chicano masterpiece because Arias handles style and characterization as magically and masterfully as his Hispanic contemporaries' classics."[40] Eliud Martínez ventures that it is "a pacesetter and marks a new direction for Chicano literature."[41]

The novel's central character is Fausto Tejada, a retired bookseller and collector, who is dying. He has lived with his niece Carmela for six years in a small house in a Los Angeles Chicano community. Other characters, most of them *barrio*-dwellers, are Mrs. Rentería, a spinster; Smaldino, a fisherman; Cuca, a *curandera*; Mario, a delinquent with a good heart; Jesse, Carmela's boyfriend; Mauricio Hunca, a Peruvian shepherd who plays a flute and herds alpacas; and Evangelina, Fausto's dead wife.

Much of the action takes place in Fausto's dreams and imagination. We travel back and forth with him from a world grounded in the realism of a large, ugly metropolis and his realm of magic and fantasy. In fact, early in the novel we learn that since his retirement six years before he has been living a slow death in life, not a painful, ugly death but rather one over which Fausto has decided to take control. In Chapter 1, he literally sheds his old skin—before his niece's eyes he peels off old, wrinkled, diseased skin—to embrace the new meaning he has injected into his last days. Throughout the novel the sound of a distant flute, symbolic of death, reminds Fausto that he must hurry to enjoy life. Among his projects is a journey to Cuzco, Peru (home of the ancient Incan civilization), which he accomplishes through dreams and fantasy without ever leaving his room. Other incidents in Fausto's life interspersed throughout the novel are his encounter with Mauricio's alpacas on a busy Los Angeles freeway; a crazy ride with Mario in the car the young Chicano has stolen from Jesse—together they disrupt a funeral procession, are chased by the police, and escape; the discovery of a dead *mojado* ("wetback") who has drowned; the mysterious appearance of a cloud that selectively dumps snow on different parts of the *barrio*. Fausto dies as the end of the novel, but his death is a joyous occasion as he joins his wife, Evangelina.

Although the novel's major theme is death, it can also be seen as social commentary on the problem of the *mojados,* the illegal Mexican workers who cross the United States—Mexican border in waves each year to find better employment. The theme is poignantly introduced with the discovery of David's corpse—it is suggested that he drowned while crossing the river. Arias also intimates that Fausto himself in his younger days sheltered *mojados* from the law; however, because of the magical nature of the novel, we can never be sure if this only happens in his fantasy state. This confusion is reinforced by Fausto's unrealized plan to bring *mojados* across in ships, up the coast, and into Los Angeles. In his fantasy, Tamazunchale, the novel's central image, will become a kind of Eden, a paradise where neither he nor the *mojados* will suffer from want. Although Arias is much too subtle a novelist blatantly to shout social messages, they are implicit in the novel, veiled as they are in its magical realism.

Perhaps more than any Chicano novel, *The Road to Tamazunchale* reflects some of the most important currents in contemporary international literature and the arts.[42] We have already pointed out that much of the action takes place in Fausto's dreams and imagination. This represents Arias's preference, like that of many modern novelists, to depict interior reality and states of consciousness rather than exterior reality. This "new reality," which is the conceptual basis for many contemporary novels, is also characterized by an emphasis on play and make-believe. In Arias's novel, Fausto journeys back and forth at will in time and space. Another convention used to emphasize make-believe is a story within a story. This is seen in *The Road to Tamazunchale* in the performance of the play by the same title. The play, in an expressionistic way, unifies performers and the audience—in this case the novel's characters and the readers—by projection beyond the physical limitations of stage. This device serves to blur the borders between illusion and reality. This is also accomplished through Arias's creation of characters who are themselves illusory, contradictory, and ambiguous. Evangelina, who is officially dead but who plays a very "alive" role, is a good example of this type of character.

The Road to Tamanzunchale is a splendid combination of social commentary and artistic contemporaneity. As such, we believe that it has set a new standard for the Chicano novel and will serve as a model for young novelists.

Later Novelists: The Search for Roots

Aristeo Brito, Orlando Romero, and Nash Candelaria are three novelists who show great promise. While their works lack the artistic breadth and depth of those of the major Chicano novelists discussed above, they are nonetheless important to the development of contemporary Chicano prose fiction. While diverse technically, the novels of those writers share a common theme: the search for ancestral and cultural roots.

Aristeo Brito's *El diablo en Texas* [The Devil in Texas, 1976] is a short novel with three sections and an epilogue. Each section is structured around an important moment—1883, 1942, and 1970—in the history of the West Texas town of Presidio. The author chronicles the systematically violent and illegal acquisition of Mexican-owned lands by Anglo settlers who flooded into Texas shortly after it became part of the United States in the mid-nineteenth century. Their pastoral life destroyed by these outsiders, Brito's characters at first actively resist the invasion and abuse of their land; however, each generation becomes progressively more alienated by the futile struggle for justice and the attacks upon their traditional way of life. The young Chicanos, who become discouraged fighting Anglo domination, eventually abandon the town and the surrounding rural area.

The novel's first and longest section revolves around the conflict between an Anglo landowner and a Chicano lawyer who wages a lifelong legal and journalistic campaign to expose the atrocities committed against his people. The second section focuses on the anguish of a young Chicana who dies shortly after the birth of her child. The third part of the novel is a short confessional by a narrator who returns to Presidio after a long absence to attend his father's funeral.

In tracing the history of Presidio, the author returns metaphorically to trace his own origin.[43] The link between the two is accomplished through a narrative point of view which is alternately first-person and third-person omniscient author, individual and collective. The narrator's search for meaning in the history of his town and his people is further carried forward by the simple device of familial relationships; the town's original inhabitants are the narrator's distant relatives.

El diablo en Texas is not a static, nostalgic view of the past but a projection into the future. After the father's funeral, the narrator, who had abandoned Presidio years before, decides to stay to rekindle the flame of resistance to Anglo oppression. His mission is to reform the people of their past, to give them a historical perspective so that they might be moved to act in their own behalf.

Brito employs several techniques which raise his novel to a metaphorical level. Like Arias, he has used folk-based fantasy to transform history into myth.[44] Like Juan Rulfo's town of *Comala* in his novel *Pedro Páramo,* Presidio is suspended in time and space and, as such, requires fantastic and even surrealistic elements to describe it adequately.[45] The novel is thus a mythified dynamic search for roots firmly grounded in social reality.

Filled with reminiscences, echoes, and images of the narrator's childhood in the New Mexican pueblo of Nambé, *Nambé—Year One* (1976) is a semiautobiographical novel in which Orlando Romero, the author, attempts to come to grips with the forces of his past and to reconcile these forces with his present situation as an educated and partially assimilated Chicano-Indian. We share narrator Mateo Romero's memories of mystery, ritual, and respect for the life-giving beneficence of the land. Fertility, earth-mother imagery, religious symbolism, and magic all play important roles in the narrator's quest for meaning and stability in a modern world devoid of these elements. He ultimately comes to terms with his cultural heritage, accepting an elder's counsel to love his land, his fields, his wife, his children, and other aspects of a reality which can connect him with the past. At the end of the narrator's search we find him in touch with the collective wisdom of his people. The novel is divided into twenty-seven units of varying length, each focusing on an incident or figure from the narrator or the pueblo's life. Gradually the two become intermingled, which serves to dramatize that the narrator feels part of the cyclical renewal of hope rooted in his cultural past.

Time is an essential aspect of the novel.[46] Structurally, the work is constructed around the life-death cycle which is made up of many medium cycles—it begins in early spring and ends in early spring within a three-year cycle—and even smaller cycles falling within a year's span. Abstract time and retrospective time are also important to the author's creation of a sense of mystery and respect for things of the past.

In general, *Nambé—Year One* is an effective and sensitively written first novel; however, Romero occasionally falters, especially in the repetition of imagery, the stereotyping of the feminine personality, and the heavy reliance on the gypsy figure, the symbol of sensuousness in the work. These defects aside, Romero's novel is an important literary work for its exploration of the mythomagical aspect of Chicano culture.

Like *El diablo en Texas* and *Nambé—Year One* Nash Candelaria's *Memories of the Alhambra* (1977) is a novel about a Chicano's search for his cultural roots. Candelaria places this search within the context of the complex sociohistorical circumstances which explain why many Hispanics in the Southwest have been reluctant to identify with their Mexican Indian ancestry, preferring to consider themselves white European Spaniards. As the novel points out, this is a problem, especially for the Spanish-speaking of New Mexico.

Memories of the Alhambra begins with the funeral of José Rafa's father. Many years before José had left his native New Mexico to establish himself and his family in Los Angeles, where he had become a successful businessman. Now he returns with his wife, Theresa, and his son Joe to bury his father. Nearing his own retirement, the death and funeral serve as a catalyst for José to embark upon his search for his past. Most of the novel deals with José's frustrations and disappointments as he follows up several false leads. He pays a man in the United States to put him in contact with a Mexican genealogist who turns out to be a taxi driver. From Mexico, José goes to Spain, where he finally traces down a Señor Gómez, who is supposed to have information about his ancestry—he doesn't. Finally José goes to the province of Extremadura, home of many of the Spanish *conquistadores* who came to the New World. Finding no answers here, José dies knowing that he has failed.

Interspersed throughout the main story line are sections focusing on José and Theresa's earlier life in New Mexico and California and Joe's process of coming to grips with his identity. José and Theresa leave New Mexico to break away from the dominance of the Rafa clan, but once in California José isolates himself from the Mexican Chicanos. Denying his Mexicanness and staunchly maintaining the illusion that he is descended from pure Spanish stock, José lives a tortured existence in California. Joe his son, on the other hand, solves the problem of his cultural identitiy—he is clear and even proud of his mestizo (Mexican Indian–European Spanish) blood. He is aware—and this is the novel's essential message—that for his father, as for many other Hispanics, "Mexican," rather than being a source of pride as it is today for Chicanos, was a dirty word synonymous with the inferior status of thousands of Mexican immigrants who earlier in this century came north in search of a better life. By denying this part of his cultural background, José has effectively remained isolated from himself.

Candelaria effectively handles the third-person omniscient author narrative and deftly portrays the novel's major characters. He has succeeded in putting in a highly readable form the complex problem of cultural identity faced by many United States Hispanics.

Minor Novelists

In this section we include writers whose works have not had as much impact on the development of the contemporary Chicano novel as those discussed in the preceding sections. While the evaluative judgment of these works is open to discussion and debate, it has been our intention to establish a guide for the reader in his journey through the maze of recent Chicano novels.

Ernesto Galarza's *Barrio Boy* (1971) is an autobiographical novel which recounts the author's displacement from his boyhood Mexican home and his resettlement in the United States. The work is most important as an individual's account of the large migration of Mexicans north to this country which took place during and after the 1910 Mexican Revolution. Of note are Galarza's vivid descriptions of this human migratory wave and his moving portrayal of a young boy's bewilderment and adjustment to change. The novel advances chronologically from life in the isolated and tranquil mountain village of Jalco in central Mexico to the hectic pace of the busy port city of Mazatlán and then north to the Chicano *barrio* of an unnamed American border city. The author is at his best when he poignantly describes his gradual acceptance and assimilation into the ways of his adopted country. It is not without bitterness that he recalls his first days in an American school, the insensitivity of his teachers, and his forays into the larger Anglo society.

In *Macho* (1974), Edmundo Villaseñor describes a different aspect of the immigrant experience: a young Mexican field hand's progressive disillusionment with life as an illegal migrant worker in the United States. Roberto, his protagonist, has several negative encounters and incidents which are cast in the novel as representative of what most undocumented workers experience: he is cheated by a Mexican *coyote* (labor contractor) who breaks his promises to obtain legal status for Roberto; he is humiliated by racist immigration officers when he crosses the border; he is initiated into the brutal cycle of migrant worker life, picking from dawn to dusk in the merciless heat with only a few hours of respite at night to prepare for the following day. While these and other experiences are explicitly described, the novel is unconvincing for a number of reasons. Roberto is a one-dimensional character who blindly follows the cult of *machismo* which Villaseñor posits as the essence of the Mexican male's value system. Unfortunately, his understanding of *machismo* is limited to its negative traits. The author fails to come to grips with the question of Roberto's relationship with a group of striking Chicano farmworkers. Villaseñor's language is stiff, particularly his dialogue; when his Mexican or Chicanos speak they sound like Hollywood stereotypes.

Like Galarza, Villaseñor, and other Chicano novelists, Joseph V. Torres-Metzgar deals with a wide range of social problems encountered by the resident Chicano or the immigrant Mexican. His novel *Below the Summit* (1976), however, is unique in presenting the conflict between Anglos and the Spanish-speaking from the bigot's perspective. Roby Lee Cross, a young Anglo-Protestant Texan, is drawn to represent the worst elements of Texas racism and bigotry against Mexicans and Chicanos. The author gives him an added dimension: despite his background he marries a Mexican girl. The novel focuses on the conflict between the two antithetical elements in his personality, his hatred of Mexicans and his desire to break away from this self-destructive part of his Texas Anglo heritage. The former eventually triumphs as Roby Lee kills his wife because he suspects she has been unfaithful to him with

Dr. Serveto, a liberal Chicano college professor. Despite the author's attempt to portray the complexity of his protagonist's psychological struggle, he does not succeed. His characterization of Roby Lee is exaggerated and unconvincing. The same is true of the secondary characters. For example, Dr. Serveto, the Chicano professor who arrives in conservative Texas from liberal California, serves more as the author's spokesman than as a credible, multi-dimensional figure.[47] Roby Lee's wife is depicted as an innocent victim, a passionless creature of minimal interest.

Floyd Salas has published three novels. His earliest work, *Tattoo the Wicked Cross* (1967), is about a young Hispanic, Aaron D'Aragon, who is serving time in a penal institution. Salas portrays the inner conflict of his protagonist, who feels caught between his religious beliefs of nonviolence and the reality of having to survive in a brutalized prison environment. Another facet of his personality concerns the unresolved feelings toward his mother, whose death he has never been able to accept, and the rejection of his father, an ineffectual and irresponsible individual. Salas's two other novels, *What Now My Love* (1969) and *Lay My Body on the Line* (1978), are set in the San Francisco Bay Area during the tumultuous late 1960s. The protagonist of both novels is a turned-on but extremely paranoid college creative-writing professor—his name is Miles in the first novel and Roger Leon in the second—who has served time and has been a semiprofessional boxer. *What Now My Love* is about Miles's flight from prosecution after a Haight-Ashbury drug bust, and *Lay My Body on the Line* revolves around Roger's paranoia as an activist in antiwar and Black Panther activities. This is Salas's most interesting novel. He effectively recreates the rapidly alternating excitement and depression of one of the most volatile periods in recent American history. The novelist's eye for detail and setting is offset, however, by his weak characterization. Most of his characters are overdrawn and the presentation of their inner conflicts is repetitious.

Isabella Ríos's *Victuum* (1976) and Celso A. de Casas's *Pelón Drops Out* (1979) are a departure from the dominant trends in the contemporary Chicano novel. *Victuum* is the first Chicano novel to deal with the world of extrasensory perception and the visit of extraterrestrial beings. While the approach is interesting, Ríos fails to create a convincing plot, much of which seems disorganized and gratuitous. Casas's work, a zany satire on Carlos Castaneda's books on the Yaqui shaman Don Juan, is much more successful. The author's expressed intention is to make his readers laugh by creating a novel which he describes as "organic insanity."[48] The novel is about a young Chicano's apprenticeship under two master masons who take advantage of his apprehension and naiveté. The tone is mirthful and ribald throughout. Casas has created the novelistic version of the famous Cheech and Chong movie series.

Conclusion

The contemporary Chicano novel has made significant advances in the last twenty years, an evolution all the more exciting when we consider that writers had a poor novelistic tradition upon which to draw for models. Beginning with the first tentative efforts of Villarreal and Vásquez, the Chicano novelists very quickly moved away from the creation of flat, one-dimensional characters who functioned predictably within nondynamic sociological circumstances. While not losing sight of their role as *engagé* writers committed to social change, novelists acquire the literary tools with which to produce artistically more sophisticated works which, due to their breadth and depth, were to be more convincing social documents than earlier novels. Using novelistic techniques found in the American, European, and Latin American contemporary novel, and dealing with themes common to all cultures, Chicano novelists begin to establish themselves on the American and international literary scenes. The contemporary Chicano novel thus holds out great promise for the future as young writers can now refer proudly and with confidence to mentors such as Rivera, Anaya, Méndez, Morales, Honojosa, and Arias, who in a few short years have created a strong and vital base.

Chapter Six

Contemporary Chicano Poetry

Introduction

Like theater, contemporary Chicano poetry is both a reflection and an outgrowth of the special sociohistorical circumstances that had an impact upon the Chicano people in the mid-1960s. Chicano poets became participants, many of them militant activists, in the Chicano Movement. Their poetry is socially committed, written to uphold the positive aspects of Chicano culture and its indigenous roots and to denigrate the negative traits of Anglo-American society and its value system. While they use a variety of styles, metaphorical language, imagery, modes, and tones, most of the prominent poets are committed to a combative poetics in the service of the sociopolitical aims of the Movement. Around the mid-1970s, new poets emerge and old ones change, both groups moving away from the clearly delineated militant-activist expression toward the exploration of different themes or even the same themes within a wider humanistic context. The spirit is still revolutionary but the shift is toward an artistic competence that frees the poet to develop a more complete image of the Chicano experience. About the same time, Chicana poets come into their own offering a different perspective of the Chicano people. Much of this poetry is decidedly feminist, communicating the profound dissatisfaction with the secondary status of the Chicana and her role within the larger society. All contemporary Chicano poets reflect to varying degrees the influence of recent trends in Anglo-American—especially black—and Latin American poetry.

Social Poetry of the 1960s and Early 1970s

An important vehicle for the collective expression of social unrest of the Chicano people in the 1960s is the Spanish-language newspaper.

Continuing in the tradition of the many newspapers that were published throughout the Southwest, California, and elsewhere from the mid-nineteenth century on (see Chapter 2) the dawning of the Chicano Movement brought a renewed activity in this printed medium.[1] Community groups, unions, political and social associations, students, and other organizations began publishing newspapers of varying lengths and quality, in English and in Spanish, to report cultural and political news to their readers. It was common to see creative literature within the pages of these publications, and poetry was by far the most common form.

El malcriado [The Brat], the official publication of the United Farmworkers Union at Delano, California, provided many examples of popular expression such as *corridos, décimas,* and anonymous poems.[2] Although much of this poetry was unsophisticated by academic standards, it provided an outlet for the collective creative spirit of Chicano farmworkers and their allies. *El grito del norte* [The Cry of the North], published in Española, New Mexico, circulated many poetic compositions created to commemorate and celebrate the activities of Reies López Tijerina and his Alianza party. The work of Cleofas Vigil, a local New Mexico poet, folklorist, and rancher, was representative of the popular oral *corrido* poetry that appeared in this newspaper. What this bard sacrificed in the formal aspects of poetry, he gained in the simple, effective expression of the accumulated frustration of the Chicanos of northern New Mexico. Vigil posits as an alternative to the rampant materialism of American society the communal life of the rural working population.[3]

Other examples of Chicano Movement publications that carried poetry on their pages are *Con Safos, El Pocho Che,* and *El Grito,* all mentioned in Chapter 1. Each represented a slightly different political emphasis and intellectual orientation, but all provided an outlet for many of the young Chicano poets whom we will discuss below.

Joel Hancock has provided an excellent overview of the poetry published in Chicano journals, magazines, and newspapers during the 1960s and the early 1970s.[4] He characterizes Chicano poetic expression of this period as essentially a definition and description of the Chicano people. The predominant themes are the identification with both contemporary Mexico and its indigenous Aztec and Mayan cultures; the life of the Chicano in the United States today, particularly the *barrio* experience; the Chicano family as a source of cultural continuity, strength, and love; *carnalismo* ["brotherhood") among Chicanos; and political action achieved through unity and solidarity in order to maintain the Chicanos' identity and protect their values. In addition to these cultural and political concerns, poets have also drawn on currents in world literature for thematic inspiration. For example, Chicano poetry of this period includes cultured and refined expression.

Language is of paramount importance to the poets whose works appear in Chicano Movement publications. Poetic expression shifts away from the florid, resonant, and affected style of earlier poetry to become more simple and direct. For the first time the particular syntactic blend of English and Spanish characteristic of the speech of many Chicanos is elevated to a level of authentic poetic expression. In addition to this combined form of the two languages—variously known as the binary phenomenon or line, code-switching, and inter-lingualism—the unique argot of the *pachuco* and the *vato loco* as well as prison language become vehicles for the authentication of the *barrio* experience and sources of cultural affirmation. Indeed, some poetry is unintelligible even to the Spanish speaker who is not familiar with the expressions and nuances of *caló* and *pachuco* which linguistically are to the Chicano what black English and "jive talk" are to the black American. The language of the Chicano people, particularly the *barrio*-dweller, is thus an essential characteristic of Chicano poetry during the period under discussion.

The social consciousness reflected in the poetry published in Chicano Movement publications during the 1960s and early 1970s is an essential characteristic of the individual collections of poetry which appeared during this period. Most of the poets we will discuss in this section were frequent contributors to these publications and were actively involved in the political activities of the Movement. The themes, sources, language, etc., of their works are thus the same as those found in the newspapers, magazines, and journals discussed above.

The Major Social Poets

The most important socially committed poets are Rodolfo "Corky" Gonzales, Abelardo Delgado, Alurista (Alberto Urista), Ricardo Sánchez, and Sergio Elizondo. Rodolfo "Corky" Gonzales, the organizer of the Denver-based Crusade for Justice, is one of the principal spokesmen for the Chicano Movement. His epic poem *I am Joaquín,* published in 1967, is important both as a social document and as a literary work that synthesizes many of the themes and motifs of Chicano poetry of the 1960s and early 1970s. As Gonzales says in his introduction, the poem is a search for identity and cultural roots.[5]

Joaquín is the collective voice of the Chicano who resists assimilation into Anglo society and subjugation to its oppressive forces and who searches for strength in his cultural heritage in order to continue the struggle. In tracing the history of the Chicano from his Spanish and Indian past through Mexican history to the present era in American history, Gonzales offers a frank appraisal of the "villains and heroes," that is, both the positive and negative aspects of this historical composite. With his dual ancestry, Joaquín was both tyrant and slave, the exploiter and the exploited, the revolutionary and antirevolutionary, the victor and the vanquished. The poet exalts the heroic dimensions of men such as Cuauhtémoc, Benito Juárez, Emiliano Zapata, and Joaquín Murieta, offering them as models for inspiration for the modern Chicano.

The dominant theme running throughout the work is endurance. As Joaquín has survived the many travails, conquests, wars, etc., in his past, he will continue to endure in the future. Gonzales ends the poem with a crescendo, calling Chicanos to join in solidarity, triumphantly to seize their destiny.

Like Gonzales, Abelardo Delgado is a poet-activist whose actions and words have made him one of the most respected and influential figures in contemporary Chicano poetry. His four books of poetry, all published before 1975, have left their mark on many of his peers who often speak of him as a model and inspiration.[6]

Delgado sees himself as a kind of chronicler of Chicano history, "a recorder for Chicano events, happenings, victories, defeats, struggles from a poetic perspective absent from newspapers and prose journals," and as an "animator" to give spirit, philosophical direction, and criticism.[7] He admirably fulfills these dual roles. While much of his poetry is characterized by a militant, critical view of the dominant society and its cultural values, he attempts to bring together the alienated Chicano and the Anglo in a spirit of harmony and revindication.

Many of Delgado's poems have become standard anthology selections. He is best known for his terse, direct work "Stupid America." Expressing himself simply, almost prosaically, Delgado issues a warning to Anglo-America to recognize and encourage the potential of the Chicano people lest it explode and be wasted. While remaining hopeful that he will be heard, the poet's tone is unconciliatory.

While both Gonzales and Delgado make important contributions to the evolution of contemporary Chicano social poetry, three other figures—Alurista, Ricardo Sánchez, and Sergio Elizondo—stand out for their ongoing creative development. While there can be no doubt about their social commitment, which can be easily substantiated in their poetry as well as in their political activism, at the same time they have emerged as consummate artists devoted to the practice of their craft.

Tomás Ybarra-Frausto characterizes Alurista as "a seminal figure in the contemporary fluorescence of Chicano poetry," singling out his creative participation in the tumultuous phase of the Chicano Movement (1965–1969), his experiments with bilingualism and the incorporation of indigenous themes in his work, and his key role as philosopher and ideologist in the formulation of the conceptual basis of the nationalist phase of the Movement.[8]

Alurista has been more successful than any other contemporary Chicano poet, experimenting linguistically with a combination of English, Spanish, and *barrio* slang. His experimentations with language have served to add an oral dimension to his poetry, one of its key characteristics and in keeping with Alurista's view that the poet is a public rather than a private artist whose work should be communal in nature with an outward social thrust.[9] He has also used his interesting bilingual forms to help create a bicultural world in which he juxtaposes pre-Columbian Mexican Indian and *barrio* images. Alurista believes that the former nurtures and vitalizes the latter.

Alurista's four books span the last ten years of Chicano poetry testifying to his artistic versatility and vitality: *Floricanto en Aztlán* [Flower and Song in Aztlan, 1971], *Nationchild Plumaroja* [Nationchild Redfeather, 1972], *Timespace Huracán* [Timespace Hurricane, 1976], *A'nque* (1979), and *Spikin Glyph* (1981).

Floricanto en Aztlán is dominated by vivid imagery which depicts two worlds in conflict: the indigenous, *mestizo* world of the Mexican-

Chicano and the materialistic, traditionless world of the Anglo. Alurista's poems are replete with references to the Aztec gods, whose names he
invokes as regenerative forces in the life of the contemporary Chicano.
Quetzalcoatl, Ometeutl, Tlaloc, and Tonantzín are called forth to
inform, vitalize, and remind him of the dynamism of his cultural
heritage. Periodically throughout the book, Alurista urges his brothers
to take up spiritual arms to resist the continued subjugation to Mr.
Jones, an archetypal Anglo who is the incarnation of the worst qualities
of a valueless, plastic world. He urges the Chicano to reassert his pride
in indigenous symbols as a way of combating the dehumanization of a
mechanized society. "Mis ojos hinchados" [My Swollen Eyes] synthesizes Alurista's view of accumulated pain of generations of suffering,
its source, the demise of the Anglo world, and the triumphant cry of
Chicano freedom. The poem is a good example of his poetic
bilingualism:

> mis ojos hinchados [my swollen eyes]
>   flooded with lágrimas [tears]
> de bronze [of bronze]
> melting on the cheek bones
> of my concern
>   razgos indígenas [indigenous traits]
> the scars of history of my face
>   and the veins of my body
> that aches
>   vomita sangre [vomits blood]
> y lloro libertad [and I cry liberty]
>   i do not ask for freedom
> i am freedom
>   no one
> not even yahweh
>   and his thunder
> can pronounce
>   and on a stone
> la ley del hombre esculpir [man's law
>   no puede   cannot sculpture
> mi libertad   my freedom]
> and the round tables
>   of ice cream
>   hot dog

                        meat ball lovers meet
                to rap
                        and rap
                and i hunger
                        y mi boca está seca [and my mouth is dry]
                el agua cristalina [clear water]
                        y la verdad [and truth]
                        transparent
                in a jarro [pitcher]
                        is never poured
                dust gathers on the shoulders
                        of dignitaries
                y de dignidad [and of dignity]
                        no saben nada [they know nothing]
                muertos en el polvo [dead in the dust]
                        they bit the earth
                and return
                        to dust[10]

Alurista's second book, *Nationchild Plumaroja,* has been described as
"a work of synthesis and ongoing dialectic in which he continued to
experiment with bilinguality and with the linking of indigenous
themes of Chicano actuality."[11] While his poetry becomes somewhat
more introspective, the poet continues to call for collective resistance to
Anglo exploitation. Nature and the ancient indigenous cultures are
seen as a refuge from the sterility of the modern capitalist world.
Alurista develops his concept of Amerindia, that is, the source of
spiritual inspiration for the Chicano people, a metaphor for the sense of
cultural pride and *carnalismo* that resides within each of us. His tone is
more urgent than in his first book as he exhorts *la raza* to find itself
before it disappears. "Because la raza is tired" communicates this
urgency:

                        because la raza is tired
                        i find time in molasses thick
                        we cannot wait
                            because la raza is tired
                        we cannot wait
                        the moving red sun is out

    to shine a crystal dream
to walk an autumn leaf to earthly drought
to bring water in cubetas [pails]
    put out fire of red uniform
arriving to feed on ashes
en las ruinas calaveras rocas [in the skeleton ruins rocks]
    tristes recuerdos vacíos of a dead people [sad empty memories]
genocide, genocide
we cannot wait, because
wait because la raza
tired, torn we cannot wait
while la raza's being born[12]

Timespace huracán offers both a synthesis of Alurista's previous thematic concerns and experimentation with the visual aspects of form including shaped poetry, serial poems, prose poems, and haiku.[13] While most of the poetry has the same oral quality that dominates in his first two books, the poet now includes more selections meant for a more private, quieter experiencing. Visual transfigurations and typographical innovations correspond to and enhance our understanding. In this book, Alurista continues to articulate his view that the isolated individual in the modern world will be saved from his alienation through his adherence to indigenous spiritual values. As such, Amerindia plays a dominant role in *Timespace huracán* as an alternative to the cold plasticity and hopelessness created by Anglo culture.

Alurista's recent book, *A'nque,* is a restatement of the key concepts elaborated in his earlier works. He continues to indict Anglo cultural values and the Yankee oppression of Chicanos and other Third World peoples, calls for solidarity and unity, and urges the Chicano to reaffirm himself in his indigenous past. What is new is Alurista's view of the transformation of the world: the decline of Yankee dominance and the dawning of a new age represented by Amerindia. In the poem " 'Taba,' " Alurista's vision is symbolized in the metamorphosis of the caterpillar into a free and beautiful butterfly.[14] While he is not blind to the difficulties that lie ahead, it is as though the poet has finally let himself translate his hope into concrete imagery.

Like Alurista, Ricardo Sánchez attacks the injustices perpetrated by the Anglo on the Chicano and urges his brothers to band together in unity, within the spirit of *carnalismo*, to resist continued subjugation. The similarity between the two poets ends, however, with the common view they share of the dialectic between the two cultures. Whereas Alurista draws on indigenous imagery, plays with sound and visual poetry, and creates a mythological ambience, Sánchez is a trumpeter blasting loud, strident notes as he noisily calls our attention to the mostly grim side of social reality. His language and form are often jarring and jagged, his tone almost always irreverent, and his images shocking. Sánchez is unfettered in his opinions, extreme in his views, and sometimes undisciplined in his form.

His three books—*Canto y grito mi liberación* [I Sing and Shout my Liberation, 1971], *HechizoSpells,* (1976) [*hechizo* is Spanish for spells], and *Milhuas Blues and Gritos Norteños* [Milhuas Blues and Cries from the North, 1978]—all present the poet's personal travails imposed upon him by an insensitive society more interested in profit than compassion, but his life is drawn in his poetry to represent the collective Chicano experience. Many of the poems in *Canto y grito mi liberación* deal with the brutality and dehumanization of prison life—Sánchez spent several years in jails and penitentiaries—and the poet's odyssey to find himself in a fragmented world where violence and inhumanity reign. Sánchez finds some solace in the nurturing love of the *barrio* and his family.

HechizoSpells, a combination of prose and poetry, can best be described as a literary happening. It is a panoply of images, shocking statements, feints, attacks, and glimpses of personal anguish that is sometimes self-indulgent but never dull. Sánchez comes across as an admittedly biased iconoclast who sets out to attack an absurd world of anomie, plasticity, insensitivity, and rampant materialism. Social scientists, politicians, educators, and prison wardens all come under his scrutiny, but in addition to his many antiestablishment diatribes against Anglos, Sánchez also takes on a number of sacred cows within his own culture. For example, he debunks the myth that drugs are a positive part of the Chicano tradition or that the superiority of the male is a desirable aspect of Chicanismo.

Sánchez can be direct, incisive, and perfectly coherent, but most of his poetry in the three books is impressionistic and visceral, filled with phantasmagoric imagery and personal symbolism. The poem "Mish/Mesh" is an example:

bumbling along,
rumble started   late
        (pero muy tarde, compa) [(but very late, comrade)]
in awry east el paso   turbulent pachuquismo venting
desafío [challenge] y desmadre [and disgrace], hurting
aquí dentro [very deeply] en mis entrañas [in my guts]
it was youth
enflamed
como quemaduría [burning]
tintinnabulating social change;
                it was año de juventud [a year of youth]
                dressed in frenchtoed shoes
                con filero en vivorocha vaisa, carnal,
                [with knife in lively hand, brother]
and caló anger exploded
                volcanically
spurting social vengeance
like spermatozoic madness
                into the gringo's social ven-tri-cle;
incertidumbre [uncertainty]
dancing, prompting
response,
conundrum contigent
on social structure continuity,
linkage of hollow-eyed children
festering in social cranny cloisters
fomenting revolución y venganza [revolution and revenge]
                ventilated minds circumventing,
                    circumlocution negating,
                    willy-nilly idiocy obviating,
y la justicia existe [and justice exists]
                nomás en sueños [only in dreams]
                y aspiraciones sonámbulas.
                [and somnambulistic aspirations]
tal fue la vida loca [that's how the crazy life was];
tal es la vida ahora [that's how life is now].[15]

Sergio Elizondo is reluctant to call himself a writer, preferring to be
identified as a teacher.[16] This is evident in his two books of poetry,
Perros y antiperros [Dogs and Antidogs, 1972] and *Libro para batos y*

chavalas chicanas [A Book for Chicano Guys and Girls, 1977], which are directed at the Chicano people as an educational instrument. He is unpretentious in this purpose and he carries this personal trait over into his poetry as he goes about the task, at least in *Perros y antiperros,* of providing a global view of Chicano history. His second book is more personal.

Like the poets already discussed, Elizondo has actively participated in the Chicano Movement since its inception. In 1969 he was instrumental in formulating the Plan de Santa Barbara, an intellectual manifesto which focuses on the education of the Chicano. Since then, Elizondo has had high visibility as a spokesman on a variety of other issues affecting La Raza.

In *Perrros y antiperros,* which has the same epic quality as *I am Joaquín,* the poet identifies himself as the voice through which the people speak, the bard whose task, an act of love toward the Chicano people, is to transmit what he hears. He is the carrier of news, some good but mostly bad, of how the Anglo came to the Southwest and California in the nineteenth century and robbed the land from the Chicano. Most of the book is then a chronicle of this legacy of inustice, including the bitter tale of the Alamo, the return of Chicano veterans after the Great Wars to an unyielding racist land, and the endless cycle of work in the agricultural fields. This bitter history is punctuated with poems announcing the hope: the son who rejects his father's submissiveness toward the Anglo, the raising of the black union eagle flag at Delano, and other signs that times are changing. As in Alurista and Delgado's poetry, *carnalismo* and other nurturing aspects of Chicano culture provide a refuge from the cold, inhospitable Anglo world.

Libro para vatos y chavalas chicanas, like Elizondo's first work, contains social poetry but its thematic focus is love. In the first part of the book, the poet preaches love to Chicanos as a regenerative and unifying force that can give them the strength to life's difficulties. Then, in contrast to this didactic, moral treatment of love, the second part emphasizes its sensual aspects. Elizondo characterizes the woman as an earth mother, a life-source who provides care and tenderness to the male, the warrior of the species, who must deal with a hostile social environment.

Other Social Poets

Other poets who produced influential Chicano social poetry during the 1960s and early 1970s are Luis Omar Salinas, José Montoya, Tino Villanueva, Raymundo "Tigre" Pérez, and Heriberto Terán. Like most of the poets discussed earlier in this chapter, each of these writers is thematically diverse, having written poetry which, even in the broadest sense, cannot be classified as social. They are included here, however, because of their general stance toward the dominant Anglo culture and because they have chosen to identify themselves, through their creative efforts, as part of a dissident (and sometimes militant) Chicano opposition.

Luis Omar Salinas takes on the persona of a "crazy gypsy" who, in his book of the same title, writes poems about the existential suffering of the Chicano in a bewildering and compassionless world. Related themes are death, loneliness, and despair.[17] The most striking aspect about his poetry is its somnambulant quality—the poet wanders through a devastated landscape in a half-awake stupor searching for evidence of life's value. A surrealistic, phantasmagoric imagery and intensely personal symbolism heighten the anguish of this lonely quest. Salinas, however, grounds himself, ties himself back into concrete reality with frequent references to historical figures such as Cortés, Pedro Infante (a famous Mexican singer), Che Guevara, the Chilean poet Pablo Neruda, and specific places such as contemporary Mexico, Vietnam, and the *barrio*.

José Montoya's sole book of poems, *El sol y los de abajo* [The Sun and the Underdogs, 1972], falls squarely within the current of Chicano Movement social protest poetry. The poet takes a humorously irreverent swipe at different aspects of what he considers to be a society that alienates the individual, particularly in the form of the Catholic Church. Montoya's heroes, the true representatives of a combative, resilient Chicano spirit, are the *vatos locos* who are rejected by many of their own people and harassed by Anglos who do not understand their rebelliousness. In addition to satire, Montoya's book has another, grimmer side which focuses on the Chicano as an underdog, the descendant of the oppressed Mexican peasant. The poet looks for something that will sustain him in his struggle. He finds it in an understanding of his cultural roots, symbolized by the Aztec sun in the book's title.

The high respect for Montoya as a poet is based principally on a single poem, "El Louie," which has been anthologized and cited many times. It is an elegy to Louie Rodríguez, a *pachuco* leader from Fowler, California, in the 1940s and 1950s. Like the *vatos* of his book poems, Louie is depicted as a Chicano hero who has refused to assimilate into mainstream American life. Montoya praises his positive qualities and laments his tragic end—he dies alone from drug addiction. The poem is an excellent example of the integration of *pachuco* argot, English, and Spanish. We quote only a portion:

Hoy enterraron al Louie [They buried El Louie today]
And San Pedro o sanpinche
are in for it. And those
times of the forties
and the early fifties
lost un vato de atolle [a real neat guy].
Kind of slim and drawn,
there toward the end,
aging fast from too much
booze y la vida dura [and the hard life].
But class to the end.
En Sanjo [In San Jose] you'd see him
sporting a dark topcoat
playing in his fantasy
the role of Bogart, Cagney or Raft.
Era de Fowler el vato [the dude was from Fowler],
carnal del Candi y el [Candi and Ponchi's buddy]
Ponchi—Los Rodriguez—
The Westside knew 'em
and Selma, even Gilroy
48 Fleetline, two-tone—
buenas garras [nice threads] and always
rucas—como la Mary y [chicks—like Mary and
la Helen . . . siempre con [Helen . . . always with]
liras bien afinadas [well-tuned song]
cantando La Palma, la [singing La Palma, the

que andaba en el florero   [one who was in the pot].
Louie hit on the idea in
those days for tailor-made
drapes, unique idea—porque [—because
Fowler no era nada como   Fowler wasn't anything
Los, o'l E.P.T. Fresno's   like Los Angeles, El Paso]
westside was as close as
we ever got to the big time,
But we had Louie and the
Palomar, el boogie, los
mambos y cuatro suspiros [the mambos and four breaths
del alma—y nunca faltaba   [of the soul—and there was always]
the gut-shrinking love-
splitting, ass-hole-up
tight-bad news—
    Trucha, esos! Va 'ber [Watch out, you guys! Theres going
    pedo!   to be trouble!
    Abusau, ese!   Be alert, guy!]
    Get Louie[18]

Over the years, Tino Villanueva has established a solid reputation for himself as a fine poet and perceptive scholar. His only book of poetry, *Hay otra voz Poems* [There Is Another Voice Poems, 1972], is a combination of two aesthetic approaches: poems that deal with historical realism—aspects of the Chicano experience—and those that are philosophical about time, death, love, beauty, and other personal themes. The book's thirty poems are divided into three sections: the first section deals with different levels of human existence, from intrapersonal to extrapersonal; the second, which is structured as a diary, is at once a reaffirmation of the priorities of the first section and a movement toward social poetry; the third section consists of poems on Chicanos.[19] Time plays a key role in the first sections, which are replete with images such as the hourglass and the wristwatch. The poet struggles to escape its grip, which he finally achieves through his commitment to denounce injustice and racism. The poems in the third section focus on Chicano farmworkers as victims of their work, schools, and poverty. Like Montoya and others, Villanueva sees the *pachuco* as a symbol of resistance, an eloquent spokesman who through his dress, language, and mannerisms rejects assimilation. The book's last poem, "Chicano Is an Act of Defiance," dedicated to Rubén Salazar, a Chicano journalist killed in 1971 in Los Angeles during the Chicano Moratorium against the Vietnam War, is an affirmation of the importance of the spoken word for the Chicano. Buce-Novoa sees the significance of both the journalist and the poet's willingness to speak out: "yet, because he [Salazar] had enunciated his views publicly, his words remain, and Villanueva transforms them into poetry. The Chicano has found a voice, and though he can still be killed, he leaves a memorable historical presence."[20]

Other poets whose works have a decidedly social orientation are Raymundo "Tigre" Pérez, Heriberto Terán, Nephtalí de León, Carlos Morton, Raúl Salinas, Juan Gómez-Quiñones, Juan Felipe Herrera, Reyes Cárdenas, and José Antonio Burciaga. Pérez was one of the earliest poets to speak out against the Vietnam War and other oppressive forms of racism.[21] He advocates revolution as the only probable solution and portrays the Chicano Movement as a focal point for this process. Terán's protest poetry is less strident and more thoughtful than Pérez's, yet he is no less committed to change.[22] He characterizes himself as a metaphysical rebel within a social context. De León energetically attacks what he believes to be the worst aspects of "Amerika" and offers images of "Chicano beauty."[23] Morton's poetry focuses on the Chicano urban scene. He sees urban America as the source and breeder of violence and dehumanization and in *White Heroin Winter* (1971) creates images that reflect the city's horrifying character. Salinas's sole book, *Viaje Trip* (1973), written during his imprisonment, traces the development of his social conscience and calls for solidarity. Like Villanueva, Gómez-Quiñones traces his evolution as a Chicano poet and his political awakening. His poetry, which alternates between personal and social themes, is characterized by a fine lyricism expressed in intimate glimpses of the poet's feelings and experiences.[24] Juan Felipe Herrera's *Rebozos of Love* (1974) reminds us of Alurista's invocation dedicated to Amerindia. The poet seeks reintegration of the Chicano with his Indian cultural traditions. Herrera freely experiments with neologisms, original combinations of English and Spanish, and calligrams. Reyes Cárdenas writes upsetting, jagged, fragmented poetry that expresses his overriding bitterness growing out of his prison and *barrio* experiences.[25] Like Ricardo Sánchez, José Antonio Burciaga's poetry is outrageous, scandalous in tone and content. His *Restless Serpents* (1976) is an energetic collage of cool jive, hip *pachuco* language, fractured images, and litanies in which he attacks the bankruptcy of Anglo values.

The Mid-1970s: A New Direction

After the withdrawal of troops from Vietnam in the mid-1970s, political activism in this country declined or at least took on a less militant, less activist form. Due, in part, to this general change in political climate and responding to its own internal forces, the Chicano Movement also entered a new phase in its development. Mass rallies, demonstrations, and marches yielded to grass-roots political organizing as social and political manifestos of a few years before were translated into concrete forms. This is not to say that the social ills affecting the Chicano population were solved—they were not. In fact, a worsening economic situation and the rise of more virulent strains of racism in the mid-1970s actually intensified this minority group's secondary status in American society.

As the approach to socioeconomic problems and the formulation of solutions changed, so did Chicano poetry. In general, poets became less strident in their tone, less focused on specific societal ills, and more open in the expression of a broad range of more general preoccupations. They were no less committed than before, but they ceased to be primarily spokesmen and activists to become artists conscious of both the social and more broadly humanistic potential of their dedication to a literary craft. Older poets such as Alurista and Elizondo evolved while younger poets emerged to give Chicano poetry a new creative impetus. The thematic emphasis shifted from an outer to an inner reality, and the poetic image took on greater importance than before. The major poets who signaled this new orientation were Richard García, Rafael Jesús González, Miguel Méndez, and Gary Soto.

Richard García eschews social reality to create an internal dream world filled with a rich collage of astral bodies—the moon and the sun, the sea, stones, hands, and other personal and fanciful images. Some of his poems are based on his world travels while others are evocations of inner feelings generated by love, death, suicide, and fear. García's talent for creating poetry around the commonplace is notable. A common technique is his effective use of synechdoche, especially hands, with which he communicates the floating, unsure part of his personality. His dreams provide not so much an escape as an access to the warmth and closeness he seems unable to achieve in human relationships. They also allow him to present and to deal with the horrifying, cataclysmic images of destruction, war, and death. "It Is Always Morning" illustrates this process:

> It is always morning
> Or perhaps sunset
> Always the end of the world
>
> But I am not the first man
> Although I have forgotten everything
> Even your name
>
> Awake I see myself dreaming
> Climbing the stairway of my throat
> Entering my head
>
> Always the half-light stains me
> Always I hear blue doors
> Opening and closing in my body
>
> I have walked too long
> Beneath the wax face of a sleeper
> Have slept too long without dreams.[26]

Rafael Jesús González's one book of poetry is called *El hacedor de juegos/The Maker of Games*. It might more aptly have had the title "The Maker of Images," for this poet is a master of the creation of the image whose importance and function he proclaims in his poem "Coin," subtitled "Ars Poética":

> A moon of silver
>   to buy
>   a drop of baptism

a 1st son from priesthood
one's way to death
(remembrance)

The value depends
not on the explanation
(25 weights
720 fine)
a limited mint

but the image:

the sky-eagle
devouring the earth-serpent
as a sign.

The Aztec ball player
losing the game lost his heart
to keep alive the gods.

The wells claim it:

Li Po
would die
needing it
for the moon.[27]

In addition to indicating the economical and synthetic quality of the image, González also refers to other essential aspects of his poetry: the pre-Columbian Mexican Indian world and non-Western philosophy. In general, his poetry is made complex by the many references to abstract philosophical concepts and figures with which most readers will not be familiar. But the effort of trying to understand these aspects as well as his surrealistic images is rewarding. González, who is as expressive in English as he is in Spanish, deals with a wide variety of themes, including the Nahuatl view of death, truth, exhilaration and disappointment in human relationships, anger, social injustice, and the aging process. Some of his poems are simply playful and highly inventive. "Departure" is a good example of his poetry. González manipulates surrealistic images on the page with the same ease that Chirico (to whom he refers in the poem) does on canvas:

> The leaving was unspoken
>   yet contained the words
> like the leather of drums,
> faces muscles taut drawn
>   against a bursting skull.
>
> The great bird
> left white excrement
>
> like the hungers of jazz
>   & the white tatters
> of the pennants of speech
>   flapping in the bone cage
>   of the brain.
>
> (I speak thru my headless hat)
>
> & words like crimson beasts
>   faded by fate
>   crawl rattling thru lead
>
> the anguish of Chirico.[28]

Miguel Méndez is also a masterful creator of images. While the title of his one book of poetry, *Los criaderos humanos (Epica de los desamparados) y Sahuaros* [The Human Nurseries (Epic of the Helpless) and Sahuaros], would seem to indicate that it has a social focus, it is actually the quest of a man who wanders through the world in search of his being, his roots, and his fate. Méndez is sharply critical of a stratified Anglo society—represented in his long poem by the Glass Men, Rapine Men, and their servants the Goads—but the poem's overall tone is contemplative as the poet ponders the nature of man.[29] The narrator never identifies with the collective struggle of the Chicano but instead sees social injustice and oppression as a kind of purgatory through which Man, who is innately evil, must pass. Man's ultimate salvation is his reintegration with the natural world.

As in his prose works, Méndez's richly textured language is replete with images, in this case mainly images of toil and despair, apocalyptic in their force. A section from early in the poem illustrates this:

> Letanías de cigarras secas
> chillan estridencias que se apagan.
> Vana crucifixión
> sin sangre sin agua
> Riveras y milpas
> ansían el torrente
> cual hembras olvidadas.
> Tejen la atmósfera
> sollozos secreteados
> ruido de arroyos
> ramajes rezando
> desde parejes perdidos
> en las entrañas de antaño.
> Siluetas de ataúdes
> andan el filo del alba.
> Cubren los sombreros
> los rebozos guardan
> dolor pertrificado
> llanto de estatuas.
> Allá va la procesión.
> Pisa campos cadavéricos.³⁰

> (Litanies of dried locusts
> scream stridencies that die out.
> Vain crucifixion
> without blood without water
> Brooks and fields
> long for the downpour
> like forgotten females.
> Secretive sobs
> the sound of gullies
> branches praying
> from lost places
> in the core of yester-year
> braid the atmosphere
> Silhouettes of coffins

walk along dawn's edge.
Hats protect
shawls shelter
petrified pain
the weeping of statues
There goes the procession
stepping on cadaverous fields.)

Gary Soto is the most promising of the group of Chicano poets of the 1970s. He has won several literary prizes including the United States Award, the Academy of American Poets Prize, Discovery—THE NATION Award, *Poetry*'s Bess Hokin Prize for 1977, and *Nuestro*'s poetry selection of 1977. His books, *The Elements of San Joaquín* (1976), *The Tale of Sunlight* (1978), *Father Is a Pillow Tied to a Broom* (1980), and *Where Sparrows Work Hard* (1981) are written in a clear, chiseled English without any of the linguistic characteristics found in the work of the preceding group of Chicano poets. His intent seems to be to address the pain around individual memories rather than to speak collectively. He generalizes rather than particularizes the Chicano cultural experience, rejecting both blatant political content and rhetorical excesses. One reviewer observes that he "carries his ethnicity with an almost studied inconspicuousness." Another comments that his poetry lacks the strong resonance of the Chicano oral tradition.[31]

Soto, however, does not turn his back on his Chicano heritage. Raised in Fresno, California, in the midst of a rich agricultural area, he reflects in his poetry much of the degradation and misery of the life of the Chicano farmworker as well as the squalor of urban existence. In *The Elements of San Joaquín,* he brings to the fore the dominant aspects of the natural world—fog, sun, dust—that lend to the oppressiveness and monotony of the life of the individual who must survive within it. Reminiscences of his childhood in a Fresno neighborhood reinforce the poet's sad-eyed view of his world. These pleasant memories of a child's past, which contrast starkly with the bleakness of the present, seem to be the poet's only refuge.

The Tale of Sunlight is divided into three sections. In the first and the third sections, two characters, Molina and Manuel Zaragoza, represent different parts of the poet's desires and fantasies. In the first section, Molina, Soto's childhood alter ego, leads us through a world of adventure and innocence. In the third section, Manuel relies on magic to transform the depressing conditions of poverty and human tragedy into a form he can live with. The second section consists of journeys, both literal and symbolic, over distant lands and closer, more familiar landscapes.

Other poets who have had an impact on Chicano poetry during the last five years are Juan Bruce-Novoa, Leroy Quintana, Rolando Hinojosa, Ricardo Aguilar, Armando Vallejo, and Leonard Adame. The twenty-one selections in Bruce-Novoa's *Inocencia perversa*. *Perverse Innocence* (1977) are sensitively rendered, reflecting the poet's control of his craft and his intellectual breadth. Many of the poems are erotic. The imagery is exquisite, the tone delicate, the themes varied and provocative. Leroy Quintana's poetry speaks of the simplicity of cultural values buried beneath layers of misinformation and deliberate deceit.[32] Quintana has the ability to go directly to the core of this simplicity, holding it up for the reader to behold. He offers lightly humorous, gentle commentary on traditions, customs, and the old people of his youth as he plumbs the wealth of local New Mexico history. Rolando Hinojosa's *Korean Love Songs* (1978), a slim volume based on the writer's personal experiences, brings into sharp focus the cruel myth of the glory of war. The memories of buddies lost in battle are set against a backdrop of endless days of pounding artillery batteries, eerie nights on patrol, and worse, the burial details. Hinojosa skillfully integrates battlefield scenes and historical facts to make a poignant antiwar, prohumanity statement. Ricardo Aguilar's *Caravana enlutada* [Mourning Caravan, 1975] is a pleasing combination of playful verse, linguistic and graphic experimentation, intimate poetry, and social statement. The dominance of surrealistic imagery reminds us of Latin American vanguard poetry of the 1930s. Although Armando Vallejo, in *Luna llena* [Full Moon, 1979], deals with social issues such as the miserable lot of the farmworkers, he stands out for his use of images drawn to communicate the simplicity and warmth of those whose daily toil fills the pages of his book. Leonard Adame's work has appeared in magazines, journals, anthologies, and a chapbook. His *Cantos pa' la memoria* [Songs for Memory, 1979] are among the most moving Chicano poetry of the contemporary period. Of note are his tender poems devoted to his daughter, his father, and his sister.

The poetry of Sabine Ulibarrí deserves special consideration. While chronologically his two books fall within the early period of contemporary Chicano poetry—*Al cielo se sube a pie* [You Get to Heaven on Foot]

and *Amor y Ecuador* [Love and Ecudor] were published in 1966—
poetically he has a greater affinity with the later poets discussed in this
section. *Al cielo se sube a pie* includes selections that deal with love,
woman, Ulibarrí's native Tierra Amarilla, uprootedness, solitude, the
tragic consequences of progress, life as a transitory state, and other
themes. His poetry is filled with color and finely rendered images, and
his language, a precise, deliberate Spanish, is always appropriate to the
content. As the title indicates, *Amor y Ecuador* has two major themes:
love and the poet's impressions of Ecuador. Ulibarrí touches lightly on
social reality in this book—he draws a parallel between the Andean
Indian's centuries-long suffering and the exploitation that the New
Mexican Chicano has endured.

Chicana Poets

Women writers have been most visible as poets in contemporary
Chicano literature. While only a handful of Chicanas have made their
mark in drama and prose fiction, there is a significant, identifiable
group whose works offer a different view of the Chicano experience.
This is most evident in their exploration of the role of the Chicana
within contemporary society in general and within Chicano culture in
particular. Attitudes in this general area run the gamut from strong
declarations of independence and calls for adherence to a women's
liberationist stance to more gentle expressions of criticism and dissatisfaction with their status of inferiority. In addition to women's issues,
these poets also offer socially committed poetry as decidedly critical of
the dominant culture as that of their male counterparts of the 1960s and
early 1970s. Contemplative, introspective poetry is also common to
this group's writings.

The author of three books of poetry, Angela de Hoyos is the most
prolific Chicana poet.[33] Her first two works deal with social themes
related to the Anglo oppression. The second poem of *Chicano Poems for
the Barrio* (1975) is representative of the tone and subject matter of both
works. "Hermano" [Brother] presents a panoramic historical view of
Anglo-Chicano relations; the poet laments the rape of the land and the
culture. Other poems contrast Anglo and Chicano values and warn
Chicanos not to forget their culture and to resist the false promises of

assimilation. De Hoyos exhorts her brothers and sisters to be more aggressive in the assertion of their rights. Her third book, *Selected Poems* (1979), is more philosophical, the poetic expression more purified, and the vocabulary and images more stark than in the first two books; however, the poet confronts other adversaries—death, disappointment in love—with the same defiant, rebellious stance.

Nina Serrano's book of poems, *Heart Songs* (1980), presents a broader view of social struggle. Her poetry is devoted to men and women who suffer from political oppression and who have valiantly opposed it. Included in the latter group are Roque Dalton, the Salvadorean revolutionary poet who was killed in battle; Lolita Lebrón, a Puerto Rican freedom fighter; Lucio Cabañas, a Mexican guerrilla leader; and Pablo Neruda, the Chilean poet. Many of her poems reflect the social unrest and political ferment of the last decade in Latin America as well as in Chicano *barrios* in this country.

Lin Romero is another Chicana poet who deals with social themes. *Happy Songs Bleeding Hearts* (1974) is an unusual book in which she deftly combines narrative prose, poetic imagery, and photography to create a composite picture of centuries of Mexican and Chicano history. The book's title aptly catches the duality of this collective experience: beneath the happy sounds of song and dance reside both the memory and daily encounters with poverty and other forms of human suffering.

Establishing a separate identity as a woman and as a Chicana and transforming oppressive roles into productive individual efforts are constants in Chicana poetry. Bernice Zamora couches her feminist issues within a broader philosophical context; she creates a world of limitations and definitions imposed from the outside by strangers as well as by those we love. She believes our power lies in the ability of love, the metaphor for all the life impulses, to free us from the rigid limits which restrict life.[34] In a general way, Anglo society represents these oppressive forces, but within the Chicano context, it is the male who denies the Chicana the realization of her full potential. Traditional cultural values dictate a double sexual standard and very early in her girlhood channel the young Chicana into acceptable behaviors and roles.

Dorinda Moreno, Inés Hernández Tovar, Margarita Cota Cárdenas, and Miriam Bornstein-Somoza are more militant than Zamora in their insistence that the Chicana must liberate herself from the dual constraints of Anglo society and the Chicano's sexism. A constant theme in Moreno's poetry is woman as the giver of life, the sustaining force in the Chicano family and in the Movement.[35] She advocates that the Chicana become politically active, rejecting the passive female roles her culture offers her and assuming a position of leadership. Sor Juana Inés de la Cruz, the assertive seventeenth-century Mexican poet, is held up as a model.

Hernández Tovar focuses on the interrelational dynamics between the Chicano and the Chicana, attacking the male's deep-seated need to cast woman in a nurturing role. The poet recognizes that this helps maintain her inferior status in the relationship, an awareness that she transfers into an angry protest. "Untitled" expresses her accumulated frustration and decisiveness:

So you say to yourself,
"She needs to know that
    I'm really angry."

So you sulk
    and smoke
    and stalk around

But you're hurt inside
    I mean *bién* sentido [*really* hurt]
And you want my arms
    around you
And later on you'll
    even say "I love you"

And the same damned
    confianza [confidence]
that says you're right
is the same that tells
    you I'll come back

Pués, sabes qué, bato? [Well, you know what, dude?]
Not this time
this time the ice froze over
y aunque el miedo me resfría [and although fear may freeze me]
This time, I won't go.[36]

Margarita Cota Cárdenas asserts her independence and establishes her identity as a Chicana through eroticism. Reversing the traditional male-female sexual roles, she takes the initiative in lovemaking and urges her sisters to enjoy their bodies and to reject the shame traditionally associated with sexual pleasure. Her poetry is bawdy and mischievous in its tone and strong in the poet's declaration of her newfound freedom to be herself. Cota Cárdenas chides males for their sexual expectations of women. She creates highly satirical poems out of their fantasies. Specifically, she addresses the cultural myths that the woman should remain virginal until married and that she should then become a long-suffering mother of many children who result from only the male's sexual pleasure. Her militancy is clearly expressed in "Manifestación tardia" [A Late Declaration].[37]

Bornstein-Somoza rejects the male world as being too rigidly defined and emotionally restrictive. She hungers for the lover who is able to drop his facade of masculinity to reach across the barrier that exists between them, spontaneously to reveal his inner self. Fear of being trapped in this kind of relationship without her own identity intact is a dominant theme in her poetry. This identity is also threatened by the self-imposed role of the long-suffering wife-mother who has thoughtlessly sacrificed her own fulfullment for her husband and children. Bornstein-Somoza's poetry is tinged with a sadness not found in the other Chicana poets already discussed. The recognition that, for much of her life, she has turned away from herself to seek meaning in roles and in other's expectations heightens the longing for communion and self-actualization. "Recogiendo recuerdos" [Gathering Memories] poignantly expresses this sentiment:

han callado mis poemas
a llegar a tu cintura
cuerpo deshojado
que fue llenando mis caminos de tristeza
han marcado mis noches taciturnas
y poblado el silencio con sus ecos
los he visto recostarse
en la ausencia de tus ojos
abrazando el oleaje de tu alma

la vida como el olvido
llega acompañada de palabras

ay
   tanto amor
      perdido en las huellas del destino[38]

(my poems have become silenced
upon reaching your waist
stripped body
that filled my paths with sadness
and have marked my taciturn nights
and populated the silence with its echoes
I have seen them recline
in the absence of your eyes
embracing the surge of your soul

Life like oblivion
   arrives accompanied with words

Oh
   so much love
      lost in destiny's tracks)

Marina Rivera, Lucha Corpi, and Alma Villanueva represent an introspective current in contemporary Chicana poetry. While they do not ignore social themes, their poetry is dominated by a search for meaning in self. In general, their language is measured and precise without rhetorical devices.

Marina Rivera deals with the loss of essences, that is, the tragic surrendering of family and cultural rootedness in the process of changing one's priorities.[39] Specifically, she laments the split that occurs in herself as she has become more educated and less able to maintain a healthy perspective on the Chicano values she seems to surrender in the transition. Forgiveness, acceptance, self-responsibility, and warmth are replaced by lack of communication, jagged interrelationships, and, ultimately, alienation from self.

Lucha Corpi's poetry is diverse. In the prologue to her book *Palabras de mediodía, Noon Words,* the Mexican author Juan José Arreola says: "The poetry of Lucha Corpi moves from daily and domestic experience to the experience—also daily—of consciousness and feeling; from the hazards of friendship and love to involvement in the collective longing for renewal and liberation, the search for a better world."[40] Her poetry is replete with both delightfully optimistic and starkly horrifying

images that communicate her alternating states of hope and despair of
finding "a place filled with sunlight and love." Corpi rejects easy
answers, slogans, false prophets, demagoguery, and a generation "that
rushes out in search of absolutes." She knows that her search for
tranquillity will be a long and solitary one:

> Caminando a solas
> en el paréntesis
> entre placer y padecer
> no hay mayor gloria
> que la ausencia del dolor,
> ni mayor pena
> que la ausencia del amor.[41]

> (Walking alone
> in the parenthesis
> between pleasure and suffering
> there is no glory greater
> than the absence of pain,
> no pain greater
> than the absence of love.)

Alma Villanueva's poetry stands out for its universal quality and its
tone of undaunted exploration of a wide variety of themes. As James
Cody remarks in the preface to her first book of poetry, *Bloodroot*, "she
takes the same insouciant joy in the crude, the ordinary, while elevating
it, or accepting it equally with the rest of life. There are no subjects that
she does not embrace unhesitatingly."[42] While her poems make basic
statements about her family, her womanhood, her Chicanismo, she is
never prosaic but instead is able to elevate her self-perceptions and
observations of others to eloquent poetic statements. Unlike most of
the Chicana poets discussed in this section, Villanueva expresses deep
joy and excitement even as she remembers difficult times of her
girlhood. While her poetry contains feminist sentiments, she is always
gentle (yet firm) in expressing her convictions.

Conclusion

Contemporary Chicano poetry is diverse thematically, technically,
and linguistically. Poets during the last fifteen years adhere to no single

artistic doctrine, and this has been the major factor contributing to the vitality and growth of this important genre. While remaining committed to social change—the release from the oppressive bonds of a racist society or from the constraints of sexism—poets have demanded and acted upon their right to be artistically independent. They have been as revolutionary in the practice of their craft as in their expressions of protest in the sociopolitical sphere. This spirit to remain, above all else, true to themselves as both artists and Chicanos has given their poetry an invigorating forward motion and a sense of constant renewal. Chicano poetry in the decade of the 1980s remains healthy and dynamic, a source of cultural and artistic inspiration for future generations.

Chapter Seven
Overview—Past Achievements and Future Promise

The origins of contemporary Chicano literature are found in the sixteenth century, when the Spaniards brought to the Southwest both their oral and written literary traditions. Folk poetry, folk drama, and folk tales in their varied forms quickly took root in the fertile ground of Spain's newly acquired northern territories, and thrived for the next four hundred years. Today, many of these original oral forms survive in relatively isolated geographic areas such as northern New Mexico and southern Colorado while others have become transformed in response to changing literary conventions and socioeconomic circumstances. The *corrido,* for example, reflects social reality to a much greater extent than did its predecessor, the *romance.* Concurrent with the flowering of oral forms was the development of the written tradition. The prose writings of the chroniclers, explorers, soldiers, and missionaries who ranged far and wide across the Southwest and California until the nineteenth century provide the richest source of written expression. Professional theater activity dates from as early as the late-eighteenth century and seems to be well established by the 1840s.

Mexico's loss of much of the Southwest and California to the United States in the mid-1850s had a profound and lasting effect on the area's Spanish-speaking population. The establishment of hundreds of Spanish-language newspapers is a dramatic manifestation of their will to survive culturally. The literature published in these newspapers sometimes reflects the sociopolitical conditions of the time but mostly avoids dealing with controversial themes. Exceptions are the prose series on Joaquín Murieta and the social poetry of the late-nineteenth and early-twentieth century. Artistically, prose and poetry become more sophisticated in the twentieth century, reflecting a developing consciousness among writers of the practice of their craft. At the same time, professional theater troupes and acting companies are found in many large cities of the Southwest, California, and even the Midwest. By the 1950s there exists a substantial body of literary expression in the three important genres of prose fiction (especially the short story), poetry, and theater.

Due to a combination of sociopolitical circumstances, the 1960s and early-1970s are a time of intense intellectual ferment for Chicanos in general and for writers in particular. Social protest, the search for identity, and other concerns are channeled into an unprecedented burst of literary activity with the formation of publishing houses, the establishment of magazines and journals, and the holding of annual festivals to celebrate a renewed sense of cultural and artistic pride.

Organized to support the farmworkers in the agricultural fields of California, Luis Valdez's El Teatro Campesino establishes a new direction in Chicano theater. The group has a major impact on other *teatros* whose creators follow El Teatro Campesino's example of taking social messages to the people through the simple but dynamic vehicle of the *acto*. Chicano theater undergoes changes in the next few years as groups begin to experiment with the *mito* and to broaden their repertoires thematically and technically.

While some contemporary short-story writers continue the trends set by their predecessors in the preceding decades, others deal with different themes with a more heightened awareness of themselves as creative artists. The folkloric, nostalgic view of the past is still preferred by some, but most boldly explore the negative aspects of Chicano life in this country. Social realism and humor and allegory are common approaches to these problems. Other writers expand the borders of the short story by introducing mythological and fantastic elements to develop more broadly philosophical short works.

Since the publication of Villarreal's *Pocho* in 1959, the Chicano novel has made rapid progress to become a rich and vital form of Chicano literary expression. While the earlier novels tended to be historical and sociological in their focus, those of more recent publication reflect a greater awareness by novelists of the possibilities of modern novelistic techniques. Flat, one-dimensional characters have been replaced by multi-dimensional and more credible fictional beings as writers have begun to particularize the Chicano experience. Temporal and spatial fragmentation, stream-of-consciousness, and montage are now commonly used to enhance a more fully developed view of social reality and the individual psyche.

Like theater, contemporary Chicano poetry grows out of the special sociohistorical context of the 1960s and early 1970s. Poets, many of them active participants in the demonstrations, rallies, and other political activities of this era, write socially committed, combative poetry that attacks Anglo society and plumbs the cultural richness of their own. Around the mid-1970s a subtle shift occurs as poets move away from a clearly delineated militant expression toward an emphasis on thematic variety and greater creative flexibility. Chicana poets emerge as an important identifiable group with a different perspective of their culture as well as human relationships.

Like the literature, Chicano literary criticism, as the bibliography which follows suggests, is in a healthy state. A polemic among critics with diverse approaches goes on, fueling the critical process and giving rise to vital creative tensions. Those who study, analyze, and define the multiple forms of Chicano literary expression no longer feel bound to defend or protect works that do not measure up to high artistic standards, nor are they reluctant to offer critical views which may not be currently popular or acceptable. Like Chicano writers, the critics have, for the most part, remained true to their own sense of integrity and intellectual honesty. The future promises a systematic revaluation of today's strongly felt and fiercely defended critical approaches and the emergence of new theories to deal with a body of literature that is itself in constant transition.

Contemporary Chicano literature flows out of a long tradition, becomes renewed in the 1960s, and enjoys an exciting period of richness and productivity during the 1970s. Its future promises growth and change as writers remain committed to social change and artistic renovation.

Notes and References

Chapter One

1. Carey McWilliams, *North from Mexico* (1948; rpt. New York, 1968), p. 19.
2. See Arthur L. Campa, "Mexican Interlude," in *Hispanic Culture in the Southwest* (Norman: University of Oklahoma Press, 1979), for an excellent summary of this period.
3. Rodolfo Acuña, *Occupied America. The Chicano's Struggle Toward Liberation* (San Francisco: Canfield Press, 1972), p. 9.
4. Ibid., p. 82.
5. "The Treaty of Guadalupe Hidalgo," in *A Documentary History of the Mexican Americans,* ed. Wayne Moquin (New York: Bantam Books, 1972), p. 247.
6. Acuña, *Occupied America,* p. 29.
7. Julián Samora et al., *Gunpowder Justice. A Reassessment of the Texas Rangers* (Notre Dame, Ind.: University of Notre Dame Press, 1979), p. 2.
8. Acuña, *Occupied America,* p. 61.
9. See McWilliams, *North from Mexico,* pp. 227–43, for a summary of the Sleepy Lagoon incident and its aftermath. As an organizer of the Sleepy Lagoon Defense Committee, McWilliams provides probably the most authoritative accounts of this troubled period in the history of California race relations.
10. See Pedro Castillo and Albert Camarillo, *Furia y muerte: los bandidos chicanos* [Fury and Death: The Chicano Bandits] (Los Angeles: Chicano Studies Center of UCLA, 1973), for an excellent revaluation of these "bandits," which the authors view as social rebels.
11. Acuña, *Occupied America,* p. 52.
12. Ibid., p. 59.
13. Leonard Pitt, *The Decline of the Californios* (Berkeley and Los Angeles: University of California Press, 1966). See chapter 11 for a biography of Ramírez.
14. Acuña, *Occupied America,* Chapter 7.
15. Ibid., chapter 8.
16. Tomás Ybarra-Frausto, "The Chicano Movement and the Emergence of a Chicano Poetic Consciousness," *New Scholar* 6 (1977):82.

17. Acuña, *Occupied America*, p. 176.
18. Ibid., p. 236.
19. Ybarra-Frausto, "Chicano Movement," pp. 93–94.
20. Francisco J. Lewels, *The Use of Media by the Chicano Movement: A Study in Minority Access* (New York: Praeger Publishers, 1974), 65ff.
21. Ybarra-Frausto, "Chicano Movement," p. 97.
22. Ibid., pp. 99–100.

Chapter Two

1. Nicolás Kanellos, "El teatro profesional hispánico: orígenes en el Suroeste," *La palabra* 2, no. 1 (Spring 1980):16–24. Kanellos gives an excellent overview of early Spanish-speaking professional theater.
2. Gaspar Pérez de Villagrá, *Historia de la Nueva México* (México: Imprenta del Museo Nacional, 1900), 1:canto 13.
3. Ibid., canto 16.
4. Mary Austin, "Folkplays of the Southwest," *Theater Arts Monthly*, August 1933, p. 606.
5. Most of the information in this section on Spanish folk drama is based on two long articles by Arthur L. Campa: "Spanish Religious Folktheatre in the Spanish Southwest (First Cycle)," *University of New Mexico Bulletin* 5, no. 1 (15 February 1934):1–71, and "Spanish Religious Folktheatre in the Southwest (Second Cycle)," *University of New Mexico Bulletin* 5, no. 2 (15 June 1934):5–157. We have also used the following sources: John E. Englekirk, "Notes on the Repertoire of the New Mexican Spanish Folktheatre," *Southwestern Folklore Quarterly* 4 (1940):227–47; Edwin B. Place, "A Group of Mystery Plays Found in a Spanish-Speaking Region of Southern Colorado," *University of Colorado Studies* 18 (1930):1–8; and Mary Austin's article cited in note 4.
6. Don Pedro Pino, Don Carlos Fernández, and Juan de Padilla, *Los comanches*, ed. Aurelio M. Espinosa, *University of New Mexico Bulletin* 1, no. 1 (1907):5–46.
7. Ibid., p. 17.
8. Aurelio M. Espinosa, "*Los tejanos,*" *Hispania* 27 (1977):219–314.
9. Kanellos, "El teatro profesional," p. 16.
10. Ibid., p. 18.
11. John W. Brokaw, "Teatro Chicano: Some Reflections," *Educational Theatre Journal* 29 (December 1977):535–44. Two of Brokaw's other articles are sources for more specific information: "A Mexican-American Acting Company, 1849–1924," *Educational Theatre Journal* 27 (1975):23–29, and

"The Repertory of a Mexican-American Theatrical Troupe, 1849–1924," *Latin American Theatre Review* 8, no. 1 (Fall 1974):25–35.

12. Nicolás Kanellos, "Mexican Community Theatre in a Midwestern City," *Latin American Theatre Review* 7, no. 1 (Fall 1973):43–48.

13. Ibid., p. 46.

14. Nicolás Kanellos, "Fifty Years of Theatre in the Latin Communities of Northwest Indiana," *Aztlán* 7 (1976):255–65.

15. Aurelio E. Espinosa, *Cuentos populares españoles* [Popular Spanish Folk Tales], *Stanford University Publications* 1–2 (1923):3–4 (1926); Juan B. Rael, *Cuentos populares de Colorado y Nuevo México* [Spanish Folk Tales of Colorado and New Mexico], 2d ed., 2 vols (Santa Fe: Museum of New Mexico Press, 1977); Aurora Lucero-White Lea, *Literary Folklore of the Hispanic Southwest* (San Antonio, Texas: The Naylor Company, 1953); Elaine K. Miller, *Mexican Folk Narrative From the Los Angeles Area* (Austin: University of Texas Press, 1973).

16. Rael, *Cuentos populares*, p. 4.

17. See Percy M. Baldwin's translation, "Fray Marcos de Niza and His Discovery of the Seven Cities of Cibola," *New Mexico Historical Review* 1 (1926):193–223.

18. See the multiple-volume set of the Coronado Cuatro Centennial Publications, 1540–1940, published by the University of New Mexico Press.

19. See George P. Hammond and Agapito Rey, *The Rediscovery of New Mexico, 1580–1594* (Albuquerque: University of New Mexico Press, 1966).

20. Fray Junípero Serra, *Writings of Junípero Serra*, ed. Antonine Tibesar, O.F.M. (Washington, D.C.: Academy of American Franciscan History, 1955).

21. Francisco Palou, *La vida de Junípero Serra* [The Life of Junípero Serra] (Mexico: La Imprenta de don Felipe de Zúñiga y Ontiveros, 1787).

22. *Diary of Gaspar de Portolá During the California Expedition of 1969–1770*, ed. Donald E. Smith and Frederick J. Teggart, *Publications of the Academy of Pacific Coast History* 1, no. 3 (1909):31–89.

23. Miguel Costansó, *The Costansó Narrative of the Portolá Expedition. First Chronicle of the Spanish Conquest of Alta California*, tr. Ray Brandes (Newhall, Calif.: Hogarth Press, 1970), p. 9.

24. Excellent translations of these diaries are found in Herbert Eugene Bolton, tr., *Anza's California Expeditions*, Vol. 2 and Vol. 3 (Berkeley: University of California Press, 1930).

25. Bolton, *Anza's*, 245–306.

26. Ibid., p. 339.

27. Gerónimo Boscana, *Chinigchinich. A Historical Account of the Origin, Customs, and Traditions of the Indians at the Missionary Establishment of San Juan Capistrano, Alta California.* The work was translated by Alfred Robinson and is included in his *Life in California during a Residence of Several Years in That Territory* (New York: Wiley and Putnam, 1846).

28. Luis Leal, "Cuatro siglos de prosa aztlanense," *La palabra* 2, no. 1 (Spring 1980):7.

29. Hermino Ríos and Guadalupe Castillo, "Toward a True Chicano Bibliography: Mexican-American Newspapers, 1848–1942," *El Grito* 3, no. 4 (Summer 1970):17–24; Herminio Ríos, "Toward a True Chicano Bibliography—Part II," *El Grito* 5, no. 4 (Summer 1973):38–47.

30. Most of the information and prose examples from newspapers were taken from the retrospective newspaper collection housed in the Chicano Studies Library at the University of California, Berkeley. Microfilms were generously made available to us by Francisco García, the Head Librarian.

31. "Las aventuras de Joaquín Murieta," *La Gaceta* [Santa Barbara, Calif.] 4 June–23 July 1881.

32. *La crónica* [San Francisco], 10 December 1910, p. 3.

33. *El cronista del valle* [Brownsville, Texas], 19 September 1925, p. 2 (hereafter abbreviated CV).

34. *El eco de México* 26 October 1924, p. 6, and *La estrella,* 7 September 1929, p. 1.

35. *El eco de México,* 3 October 1924, p. 1.

36. *CV*, 6 November 1924, p. 2.

37. Ibid., 6 December 1924, p. 2.

38. Ibid., 20 December 1924, p. 2.

39. Clara Lomas, "Resistencia cultural o apropiación ideológica," *Revista Chicano-Riqueña* 6, no. 4 (Fall 1978):48. See also Juan Rodríguez, "Jorge Ulica y Carlo de Medina: escritores de la bahía de San Francisco," *La palabra* 2, no. 1 (Spring 1980):25–46.

40. *CV,* 10 December 1924, p. 2.

41. Ibid., 16 December 1924, p. 2.

42. Ibid., 19 November 1924, p. 2.

43. Ibid., 4 March 1925, p. 2.

44. Ibid., 6 February 1925, p. 2.

45. Ibid., 3 January 1924, p. 2.

46. Ibid., 16 November 1924, p. 2; *La estrella,* 7 May 1927, p. 1; *El cronista del valle,* 7 May 1927, p. 1.

47. *CV,* 4 May 1925, p. 2.

48. *La estrella,* 17 September 1927, p. 1; *La estrella,* 4 June 1927, p. 1; *La estrella,* 12 March 1927, p. 1.

49. *CV,* 25 April 1925, p. 2.

50. Ibid., 13 January 1925, p. 2.

51. Ibid., 21 September 1927, p. 3.

52. Ibid., 25 November 1925, p. 2.

53. Ibid., 19 May 1925, p. 2.

54. Ibid., 7 December 1925, p. 2.

55. Ibid., 13 April 1926, p. 2.

56. Ibid., 23 July 1927, p. 3; *El cronista del valle,* 24 July 1927, p. 3; *El cronista del valle,* 6 August 1927, p. 3.

57. *CV,* 6 January 1925, p. 3.

58. See Estevan Arellano, *"La historia de un caminante, o sea Gervacio y Aurora* (Capítulo 19)," *La palabra* 2, no. 1 (Spring 1980):57–66.

59. Eusebio Chacón, *El hijo de la tempestad* (Santa Fe, New Mexico: Tipografía "El Boletín Popular," 1892); *Tras la tormenta la calma* (Santa Fe, New Mexico: Tipografía "El Boletín Popular," 1892). See Francisco Lomelí, "Eusebio Chacón: eslabón temprano de la novela chicana," *La palabra* 2, no. 1 (Spring 1980):47–56.

60. See Doris Meyer, "Felipe Maximiliano Chacón: A Forgotten Mexican-American Author," *New Scholar* 6 (1977):111–26.

61. Miguel Antonio Otero, *My Life on the Frontier 1864–1882. Incidents and Characters of the Period When Kansas, Colorado, and New Mexico Were Passing through the Last of Their Wild and Romantic Years,* 2 vols. (New York: The Press of the Pioneers, 1935), p. 11.

62. Miguel Antonio Otero, *The Real Billy the Kid. With New Light on the Lincoln County War* (New York: Rufus Rockwell Wilson, Inc., 1935).

63. Miguel Antonio Otero, *My Nine Years as Governor of the Territory of New Mexico 1897–1906* (Albuquerque: University of New Mexico Press, 1940).

64. I am indebted to Professor Raymond Paredes of UCLA, who has collected many of the stories referred to in the following pages. See his article "The Evolution of Chicano Literature," *MELUS* 5 (1978):71–110.

65. Ibid., p. 85.

66. Nina Otero, "Count La Cerda's Treasure," in *Old Spain in Our Southwest* (New York: Harcourt, Brace, Jovanovich, 1936), pp. 129–34.

67. Josefina Escajeda, "Tales from San Elizario," in *Puro Mexicano,* ed. J. Frank Dobie (Austin: University of Texas Press Society, 1935), pp. 115–21.

68. Jovita González, "Among My People," *Tone the Bell Easy,* ed. J. Frank Dobie (Austin: Texas Folklore Society, 1932), pp. 99–108.

69. Juan A. A. Sedillo, "Gentlemen of Rio en Medio," *New Mexico Quarterly* 9 (August 1939):181.

70. Mario Suárez, "El hoyo," *Arizona Quarterly* 3 (1947):114–15.

71. Mario Suárez, "Señor Garza," *Arizona Quarterly* 3 (1947):116.

72. Angélico Chávez, *From an Alter Screen. El Retablo: Tales From New Mexico* (Freeport, N.Y.: Books for Libraries Series, 1943); *New Mexico Triptych* (Santa Fe, N.M.: William Gannon, 1976).

73. A *retablo* is a wood panel on which religious motifs are painted.

74. Robert H. Torres, "Mutiny in Jalisco," *Esquire* 3, no. 3 (March 1935):37ff.

75. Robert H. Torres, "The Brothers Jimínez," *Esquire* 5, no. 6 (June 1936):139 (begins on p. 90).

76. Roberto F. Salazar, "Nobody Laughs in Yldes," *Esquire* 9, no. 3 (March 1938):84ff.

77. See Arthur L. Campa, *Spanish Folk-Poetry in New Mexico* (Albuquerque: University of New Mexico Press, 1946), pp. 16–27.

78. For a thorough treatment of the romance, see Aurelio M. Espinosa, *Romancero de Nuevo Méjico* [New Mexican Ballads] (Madrid: Revista de Filología Española, 1953).

79. Lucero-White Lea, *Literary Folklore of the Hispanic Southwest,* p. 115.

80. Ibid., p. 117.

81. Raymond Paredes, "The Evolution of Chicano Literature," p. 73.

82. Américo Paredes, *"With His Pistol in His Hand." A Border Ballad and Its Hero* (Austin and London: University of Texas Press, 1971).

83. Paredes, "Evolution of Chicano Literature," p. 19. This is a longer unpublished version of his article referred to in note 64.

84. Campa, *Spanish Folk-Poetry,* p. 127.

85. Ibid., p. 182.

86. Ibid., pp. 23ff.

87. Aurelio M. Espinosa, "Los trovos del Viejo Vilmas," *Journal of American Folklore* 27 (April–June 1914):217–94.

88. See note 2 in this chapter.

89. Salvador Rodríguez del Pino cites these works in his study "La poesía chicana: una nueva trayectoria," in *The Identification and Analysis of Chicano Literature,* ed. Francisco Jiménez (New York: Bilingual Press, 1979), p. 71.

90. "A mi amada" [To My Beloved], *El clamor público* [Los Angeles], 6 December 1856, p. 4.

91. "Tus ojos y tu sonrisa" [Your Eyes and Your Smile], *El clamor público,* 27 September 1856, p. 4.

92. "No con ligero labio" [Not With a Light Lip], *El clamor público,* 23 August 1856, p. 4.

93. E. Montalván, "Para ti," *El bejareño,* (San Antonio) 8 December 1855, p. 2.

94. "A ti" [To You], *El bejareño,* 10 November 1855, p. 3.

95. Julio Flores, "Mis negras flores," *La bandera americana,* 15 August 1902, p. 3.

96. Felipe M. Chacón, "Desengaños," *El eco del valle,* (Albuquerque) 16 July 1906, p. 2.

97. Felipe M. Chacón, "A mi Elvira," *La bandera americana,* 24 January 1935, p. 3.

98. Felipe M. Chacón, "Celos y amor," *La bandera americana,* 24 January 1935, p. 3.

99. Dantés, "A una desconocida," *La gaceta,* 9 April 1881, p. 1.

100. J. J. Pesado, "El dolor," *El clamor público,* 26 July 1856, p. 4.

101. Manuel Caballero, "Entrevistando a Cristo," *El cronista del valle,* 9 April 1925, p. 2.

102. Doris Meyer, "Early Mexican-American Responses to Negative Stereotyping," *New Mexico Historial Review* 53, no. 1 (January 1978):75–91.

103. "Allá en la Corte Suprema," *El clamor público,* 29 March 1856, p. 1.

104. "Oración a Dwyer," *El tiempo,* 28 October 1886, p. 2.

105. "Saludo a Dwyer," *El guía de Santa Fe,* 9 October 1886, p. 1.

106. "Que entienda . . .," *El guía de Santa Fe,* 16 October 1886, p. 2.

107. "Composición poética en relación al asesinato de Faustín Ortiz" [A Poetic Composition on the Assassination of Faustín Ortiz], *El Nuevo Mexicano,* 13 September 1890, p. 1.

108. J. Marroquín, "Paráfrasis de la convención democrática del condado" [A Paraphrase of the County Democratic Convention], *El Nuevo Mexicano,* 11 October 1890, p. 1.

109. Doris Meyer cites this example in her article, referred to in note #102, p. 79. The translation is hers.

110. López Ayllón, "Mi raza," *El cronista del valle,* 14 June 1927, p. 2.

111. "Composición poética en loor del idioma castellano," *La estrella,* 22 February 1914, p. 1.

112. M. P. Mondragón, "Salutación a la Sociedad Hispano Americana," *La estrella,* 3 January 1914, p. 1.

113. Doris Meyer cites this example in her article, referred to in note #102, p. 84. The translation is hers.

114. Eleuterio Baca, "A la unión americana," *Los pobladores nuevo mexicanos y su poesía, 1889–1950* [The New Mexican People and Their Poetry, 1889—1950], ed. Anselmo F. Arellano (Albuquerque, N.M.: Pajarito Publications, 1976), pp. 87–88.

115. Alfredo Lobato, "Patria querida," *La bandera americana,* 26 July 1918, p. 3.

116. See the following poets for examples: Felipe Maximiliano Chacón, Eleuterio Baca, José Inés García, Víctor Anaya, Margarito Roybal, Ricardo Montoya, and Daniel García in *Los pobladores nuevo mexicanos y su poesía, 1889–1950.*

117. José M. Arellano, "Juan Cristóbal," *Los pobladores nuevo mexicanos y su poesía, 1889–1950,* p. 19.

Chapter Three

1. Most of the biographical information on Luis Valdez is taken from Beth Bagby, "El Teatro Campesino. Interviews With Luis Valdez," *Tulane Drama Review* 11, no. 4 (Summer 1967):70–80.

2. Ibid., pp. 74–75.

3. Luis Valdez, *Actos. El Teatro Campesino* (San Juan Bautista, Calif.: Cucaracha Press, 1971), p. 5.

4. Ibid., p. 6.

5. Jorge A. Huerta, "Chicano Agit-Prop: The Early *Actos* of El Teatro Campesino," *Latin American Theatre Review* 10, no. 2 (Spring 1977):46.

6. Valdez, *Actos,* p. 2.

7. Luis Valdez, "El Teatro Campesino," *Ramparts,* July 1966, p. 55.

8. Francis Donahue, "Anatomy of Chicano Theater," *San Jose Studies* 3, no. 1 (February 1977):43.

9. Luis Valdez, *Program for Radical Theatre Festival* (San Francisco: San Francisco State University, September 1968), p. 12.

10. Francisco Jiménez, "Dramatic Principles of the Teatro Campesino," *The Identification and Analysis of Chicano Literature,* p. 125.

11. Huerta, "Chicano Agit-Prop," p. 46.

12. John Gregory Dunne, *Delano* (New York: Farrar, Straus and Giroux, 1971), provides an excellent overview of this and other aspects of the grape strike.

13. This and other *actos* discussed below were published in *Actos. El Teatro Campesino.*

14. Huerta, "Chicano Agit-Prop," p. 48.

15. Ibid., p. 52.

16. "Chicano Group at ICCC," *Los Angeles Times,* 27 September 1969, Part 2, p. 9.

17. Huerta, "Chicano Agit-Prop," p. 56.

18. This succinct definition is given by Yvonne Yarbro-Bejarano in her article "From *acto* to *mito:* A Critical Appraisal of the Teatro Campesino," in

Modern Chicano Writers. A Collection of Critical Essays, ed. Joseph Sommers and Tomás Ybarra-Frausto (Englewood Cliffs, N.J.: Prentice-Hall, Inc., 1979), p. 177.

19. Valdez, *Actos,* p. 5.

20. Yarbro-Bejarano, "From *acto* to *Mito,*" p. 178.

21. Theodore Shank, "A Return to Aztec and Mayan Roots," *Drama Review* 18, no. 4 (December 1967):61.

22. Yarbro-Bejarano, "From *Acto* to *Mito,*" p. 185.

23. The complete play is not available in published form. Scene 3 was published in *Aztlán. An Anthology of Mexican American Literature,* ed., Luis Valdez and Stan Steiner (New York: Vintage Books, 1972), pp. 364–76.

24. Ibid., p. 361.

25. Luis Omar Salinas and Lillian Faderman, eds., *From the Barrio. A Chicano Anthology* (San Francisco: Canfield Press, 1973), pp. 79–98.

26. Françoise Kourilsky, "Approaching Quetzalcoatl. The Evolution of El Teatro Campesino," *Performance* 2, no. 1 (Fall 1973):39, 41.

27. This play has not been published.

28. Jorge A. Huerta gives a list and a summary of critical reviews of "Zoot Suit" in *TENAZ Talks Teatro* 2, no. 2 (Spring 1979):7–9.

29. Jorge A. Huerta, "From the Temple to the Arena: Teatro Chicano Today," in *The Identification and Analysis of Chicano Literature,* pp. 90–116.

30. See David Coplin, "Chicano Theatre: El Festival de Los Teatros Chicanos," *Drama Review* 17, no. 4 (December 1973):73–89, for a critical summary of the Fourth Annual Festival.

31. Ibid., p. 80.

32. Nicolás Kanellos, "Chicano Theatre to Date," *Tejidos* 2, no. 8 (Winter 1975):40.

33. Ibid., p. 42.

34. See Theodore Shank's article "A Return to Aztec and Mayan Myths" for an overview of the Fifth Annual Festival.

35. Kanellos, "Chicano Theatre to Date," p. 43.

36. Nicolás Kanellos, "Séptimo Festival de los Teatros Chicanos," *Latin American Theatre Review* 10, no. 1 (Fall 1976):72–76.

37. Jorge A. Huerta, *TENAZ Talks Teatro* 1, no. 1 (Winter 1978):1–2.

38. Jorge A. Huerta, *TENAZ Talks Teatro* 1, nos. 3 and 4 (Summer and Fall 1978):1–4.

39. Jorge A. Huerta, *TENAZ Talks Teatro* 2, no. 3 (Summer 1978):1–2.

40. See *El Teatro de la Esperanza. An Anthology of Chicano Drama,* ed. Jorge A. Huerta (Goleta, Calif.: El Teatro de la Esperanza, 1973), pp. 1–5,

for a brief history of this theater group. Most of El Teatro de la Esperanza's plays were published in this anthology.

41. Ibid., p. 13.

42. Ibid., p. 74.

43. *Nuevos Pasos. Chicano and Puerto Rican Drama,* ed. Nicolás Kanellos and Jorge A. Huerta, *Revista Chicano-Riqueña* 7, no. 1 (Winter 1979):9–17.

44. Ibid., p. 9.

45. Huerta, "From the Temple to the Arena," p. 102.

46. Lucia Fox, "El Teatro de la Esperanza en East Lansing, Michigan," *Latin American Theatre Review* 13, no. 2 (Spring 1980):107.

47. *Chicano Theatre Two,* Summer 1973, pp. 16–17.

48. Nicolás Kanellos, "Chicano Theatre: A Popular Culture Battleground," *Journal of Popular Culture* 13 (1980):544–46.

49. *Chicano Theatre Two,* p. 50.

50. Copelin, "Chicano Theatre," p. 84.

51. Ibid., p. 85.

52. *Chicano Theatre Two,* p. 30.

53. Kanellos, "Chicano Theatre: A Popular Culture Battleground," p. 549.

54. *Chicano Theatre Two,* p. 29.

55. See "Los Pelados," *Teatro Libertad* (Tuscon: Teatro Libertad, 1978).

56. Printed in *El grito* 7, no. 4 (June–August 1974):7–37.

57. Ibid., p. 37.

58. Printed in *Grito del Sol* 1, no. 3 (July–September 1976):39–85.

59. Ibid., p. 67.

60. Printed in *Tejidos* 4, no. 1 (Spring 1977):28–50.

61. *Nuevos Pasos,* pp. 43–63.

62. *Racist Rag,* appears in *Caracol* 2, no. 1 (September 1975):6; *Buzzardville,* in *Caracol* 2, no. 5 (January 1976):16–17.

63. *La Raza Pura, or Racial, Racial, Contemporary Chicano Theatre,* ed. Roberto J. Garza (Notre Dame, Ind.: University of Notre Dame Press, 1976), pp. 60–101; *Manolo, Nuevos Pasos,* pp. 65–109.

64. Printed in *El Grito* 3, no. 4 (Summer 1970):37–45.

65. *Contemporary Chicano Theatre,* pp. 165–190.

66. Ibid., pp. 135–164.

67. Printed in *El Grito* 3, no. 2 (Winter 1970):50–55.

68. *Nuevos Pasos,* pp. 2–7.

69. *Contemporary Chicano Theatre,* pp. 205–45.

70. *Sun Images,* in *Nuevos Pasos,* pp. 19–42.

71. *The Lemon Tree, The Wedding Dress,* and *The Potion* all appeared in *El Grito* 7, no. 4 (June–August 1974):38–54.

72. All of Hernández's plays discussed are collected in *The False Advent of Mary's Child and Other Plays* (Berkeley, Calif.: Editorial Justa Publications, 1979).

Chapter Four

1. Sabine Ulibarrí, *Tierra Amarilla: Stories of New Mexico. Cuentos de Nuevo México* (Albuquerque: University of New Mexico Press, 1971).
2. Sabine Ulibarrí, *Mi abuela fumaba puros y otros cuentos de Tierra Amarilla* (Berkeley, Calif.: Quinto Sol Publications, 1977).
3. Rubén Darío Salaz, *Heartland. Stories of the Southwest* (Santa Fe, N.M.: Blue Feather Press, 1978); p.x.
4. Daniel Garza, "Saturday Belongs to the Palomia" in *The Chicanos,* ed. Ed Ludwig and James Santibáñez (Baltimore: Penguin Books, 1972), pp. 25–30.
5. Daniel Garza, "Everybody Knows Tobie," *We Are Chicanos,* ed. Philip D. Ortego (New York: Washington Square Press, 1973), pp. 301–10.
6. Saúl Sánchez, *Hay Plesha Lichans tu di Flac* (Berkeley, Calif.: Editorial Justa Publications, 1977), p. 100.
7. Nick C. Vaca, "The Visit," *El Espejo. The Mirror,* ed., Octavio Ignacio Romano V. (Berkeley, Calif.: Quinto Sol Publications, 1969), pp. 150–60.
8. Ibid., p. 160.
9. Ibid., pp. 139–44.
10. Ibid., p. 140.
11. J. L. Navarro, *Blue Day on Main Street* (Berkeley, Calif.: Quinto Sol Publications, 1973), p. 65.
12. José Olvera, "Homme du l'monde" *Grito del Sol* 2, no. 1 (January–March 1977):39–45.
13. José Olvera, "My Voice," *Grito del Sol* 1, no. 3 (July–September 1976):21–26.
14. Rosaura Sánchez, "Una mañana: 1952." *Revista Chicano-Riqueña* 6, no. 4 (Fall 1978):23–25.
15. Rosaura Sánchez, "Una noche . . ." *Bilingual Review* 3, no. 3 (September–December 1976):245–48.
16. Rosaura Sánchez, "Chepa," *Grito del Sol* 2, no. 3 (July–September 1977):46–49.
17. Octavio Romano, "A Rosary for Doña Marina," *El Espejo. The Mirror,* 1972, pp. 75–93; "The Veil," *Grito del Sol* 3, no. 4 (October–December 1978):57–58; "The Forest and the Tree," *Grito del Sol* 3, no. 4 (October–December 1978):63–68.

18. Octavio Romano, "Goodbye Revolution—Hello Slum," *El Espejo. The Mirror,* 1969, pp. 81–82.

19. Octavio Romano, "The Scientist," *Grito del Sol* 1, no. 1 (January–March 1976):85–108.

20. Octavio Romano, "Strings for a Holiday," *El Grito* 5, no. 1 (Fall 1971):45–54.

21. Octavio Romano, "The Chosen One," *El Grito* 5, no. 3 (Spring 1972):37–41.

22. Max Martínez, "The Adventures of the Chicano Kid," *Revista Chicano-Riqueña* 7, no. 2 (Spring 1979):45–57.

23. This and other biographical information on Méndez is taken from Bruce-Novoa, *Chicano Authors. Inquiry by Interview* (Austin: University of Texas Press), pp. 83–93.

24. Ibid., p. 87.

25. Ibid., p. 79.

26. Sergio Elizondo, *Rosa, la flauta* (Berkeley: Editorial Justa Publications, 1980), p. 25.

27. Ibid., pp. 46, 61.

28. Bruce-Novoa, *Chicano Authors,* p. 164.

29. Ibid., p. 174.

30. Ibid., p. 164.

31. Ibid., pp. 235–52.

32. Ron Arias, "El mago," *El Grito* 3, no. 2 (Spring 1970):51–55.

33. Ron Arias, "The Story Machine," *Revista Chicano-Riqueña* 3, no. 4 (Fall 1975):9–12.

34. Ron Arias, "Lupe," *El cuento Chicano,* ed. Rudolfo A. Anaya and Antonio Márquez (Albuquerque: New America, 1980), pp. 55–59.

35. Ron Arias, "The Castle," *Bilingual Review* 3, no. 2 (May–August 1976):176–82.

36. Ron Arias, "Chinches," *Latin American Literary Review* 5, no. 10 (Spring–Summer 1977):180–85; "A House on the Island," *Revista Chicano–Riqueña* 2, no. 1 (Winter 1974):2–6; "Stoop Labor," *Revista Chicano-Riqueña* 2, no. 1 (Winter 1974):7–14; "The Interview," *Revista Chicano-Riqueña* 2, no. 1 (Winter 1974):2–6.

Chapter Five

1. José Antonio Villarreal, (New York: Doubleday and Co., 1959). A *pocho* is a derogatory term used to describe a Mexican who has abandoned his country for life in the United States, rejecting, as least in part, his customs, traditions, and language and assimilating those of his adopted country. A

pocho is seen as a traitor of his Mexican culture and is therefore not respected in Mexico.

2. Ralph F. Grajeda, "José Antonio Villarreal and Richard Vásquez: The Novelist Against Himself," in *The Identification and Analysis of Chicano Literature*, p. 332.

3. Luther S. Luedtke, "*Pocho* and the American Dream," *Minority Voices* 1, no. 2 (Fall 1977):2.

4. In his forward to the novel, Ramón E. Ruíz interprets this as an escape. On the other hand Juan Bruce-Novoa sees it as an act of rebellion, an affirmation of life. See his article "*Pocho* as Literature," *Aztlán* 7, no. 1 (Spring 1976):74.

5. Grajeda, "J. A. Villarreal," p. 334.

6. Bruce-Novoa, *Chicano Authors*, p. 66.

7. See Sister H. Monahan, "The Chicano Novel: Toward a Definition and Literary Criticism," Diss., St. Louis University 1972, p. 58.

8. Grajeda, "J. A. Villarreal," p. 340.

9. Herminio Ríos, review of *Chicano, El Grito* 3, no. 3 (Spring 1970):68.

10. Philip D. Ortego, unpublished letter to literature professors (San Francisco: Canfield Press, November 3, 1971) praising *The Plum Plum Pickers* (Sunnyvale, Calif.: Ventura Press, 1969).

11. See Vernon E. Lattin, "Paradise and Plums: Appearance and Reality in Barrio's *The Plum Plum Pickers*," *Selected Proceedings of the Third Annual Conference in Minority Studies*, ed. George E. Carter and James R. Parker (La Crosse, Wisc.: Institute for Minority Studies, 1976), p. 165.

12. Monahan, "Chicano Novel," p. 106.

13. For a more detailed analysis of Rechy's works, see my study "The Sexual Underworld of John Rechy," *Minority Voices* 3, no. 1 (Fall 1979):47–52.

14. Stanton Hoffman, "The Cities of Night: John Rechy's *City of Night* and the American Literature of Homosexuality," *Chicago Review* 17 (1964):200.

15. For a full treatment of this novel, see Juan Bruce-Novoa, "In Search of the Honest Outlaw: John Rechy," *Minority Voices* 3, no. 1 (Fall 1979):37–45.

16. See Norman D. Smith, "Buffalos and Cockroaches: Acosta's Siege of Aztlán," *Latin American Literary Review* 5, no. 10 (Spring–Summer 1977):91.

17. See his excellent study, "Tomás Rivera's '. . . *y no se lo tragó la tierra*': Discovery and Appropriation of the Chicano Past," *Hispania* 62

(1979):71–81. Much of our discussion of the novel is based on this study.

18. Tomás Rivera, "Into the Labyrinth: The Chicano in Literature," a paper presented at the Conference on Chicano Literature held 7–8 October 1971 at Pan American University in Edinburg, Texas, p. 22.

19. See Seymour Menton, review of ". . . y no se lo tragó la tierra," Latin American Literary Review 1, no. 1 (Fall 1972):112.

20. Grajeda, "Tomás Rivera's '. . . y no se lo tragó la tierra,'" p. 72.

21. Ibid.

22. See Daniel Testa, "Narrative Technique and Human Experience in Tomás Rivera," Modern Chicano Writers, pp. 86–93.

23. Dyan Donnelly, "Finding a Home in the World," Bilingual Review 1, no. 1 (January–April 1974):115.

24. See Roberto Cantú, "Estructura y sentido de lo onírico en Bless Me, Ultima," Mester 5, no. 1 (November 1974):41.

25. Vernon E. Lattin, "The Horror of Darkness: Meaning and Structure in Anaya's Bless Me, Ultima," Revista Chicano-Riqueña 6, no. 2 (Spring 1978):53.

26. Rudolfo A. Anaya, "The Writer's Landscape: Epiphany in Landscape," Latin American Literary Review 5, no. 10 (Spring–Summer 1977):98.

27. Rudolfo A. Anaya, Heart of Aztlán (Berkeley, Calif.: Editorial Justa Publications, 1976), p. 3.

28. Rolando Hinojosa, Estampas del valle y otras obras (Berkeley, Calif.: Quinto Sol Publications, 1973); Klail City y sus alrededores (La Habana, Cuba: Casa de las Américas, 1976)—this novel was published in the United States in 1977 by Editorial Justa Publications as Generaciones y semblanzas [Generations and Sketches]—Claros varones de Belken (Berkeley, Calif.: Editorial Justa Publications, 1981); Korean Love Songs (Berkeley, Calif.: Editorial Justa Publications, 1978); Generaciones, notas, y brechas (San Francisco: Casa del Libro, 1980); Mi querido Rafa (Houston: Arte Publico Press, 1981).

29. Francisco A. Lomelí and Donaldo W. Urioste, review of Peregrinos de Aztlán, in Chicano Perspectives in Literature: A Critical and Annotated Bibliography (Albuquerque: Pajarito Publications, 1976), p. 43.

30. See Juan Bruce-Novoa, "Miguel Méndez: Voices of Silence," De Colores 3, no. 4 (1977):64.

31. Marvin A. Lewis, "Peregrinos de Aztlán and the Emergence of the Chicano Novel," Selected Proceedings of the Third Annual Conference on Minority Studies, ed. George E. Carter and James R. Parker (La Crosse, Wisc.: Institute for Minority Studies, 1976), p. 151.

32. Ibid., pp. 151–52.

33. Bruce-Novoa, "Miguel Méndez . . . ," p. 66.

34. Ibid., p. 67.

35. See Erlinda Gonzales-Berry, *"Caras viejas y vino nuevo:* Journey through a Disintegrating Barrio," *Latin American Literary Review* 7, no. 14 (Spring-Summer 1979):62–72, for an excellent treatment of this and other technical aspects of the novel.

36. Ibid., p. 64.

37. Ibid., p. 65.

38. María Herrera Sobek, review of *Caras nuevas y vino nuevo, Latin American Literary Review* 5, no. 10 (Spring–Summer 1977):149.

39. Willard Gingerich, "Chicanismo: The Rebirth of a Spirit," *Southwest Review* 62, no. 3 (Summer 1977):vii.

40. Judy Salinas, "Review of *The Road to Tamazunchale, Latin American Literary Review* 4, no. 8 (Spring–Summer 1978):111.

41. Eliud Martínez, "Ron Arias' *Road to Tamazunchale*: A Chicano Novel of the New Reality," *Latin American Literary Review* 5, no. 10 (Spring–Summer 1977):61.

42. Ibid., p. 52. Much of our discussion of this aspect of the novel is based on Martínez's fine study.

43. See Ernestina Eger, review of *El diablo en Texas, Latin American Literary Review* 5, no. 10 (Spring–Summer 1977):162.

44. Ibid., p. 165.

45. Salvador Rodríguez del Pino, "Lo mexicano y lo chicano en *El diablo en Texas,"* in *The Identification and Analysis of Chicano Literature,* pp. 368–69.

46. See Nasario García, "The Concept of Time in *Nambé–Year One,"* *Latin American Literary Review* 7, no. 13 (Fall –Winter 1978):20–28, for an enlightening treatment of this aspect of the novel.

47. Ricardo A. Valdez, review of *Below the Summit, Latin American Literary Review* 5, no. 10 (Spring–Summer 1977):160.

48. Celso A. de Casas, *Pelón Drops Out* (Berkeley, Calif.: Tonatiuh International Publications, 1979), p. 14.

Chapter Six

1. Guillermo Rojas, "Serials Listing: Chicano/Raza Newspapers and Periodicals, 1965–1972," *Hispania* 58 (1975):851–63. Rojas lists 191 titles. Francisco J. Lewels's *The Use of the Media by the Chicano Movement. A Study in Minority Access* (New York: Praeger, 1974), is an excellent overview of Chicano Movement publications during the 1960s and early 1970s.

2. See Ybarra-Frausto, "Chicano Movement," for a study of this and other newspapers.

3. Ibid., p. 91.

4. Joel Hancock, "The Emergence of Chicano Poetry: A Survey of

Sources, Themes, and Techniques," *Arizona Quarterly* 29, no. 1 (Spring 1973):57–73.

5. Rodolfo Gonzales, *I Am Joaquín* (New York: Bantam Books, 1972), p. 1. The poem was originally published in 1967 by the Crusade for Justice.

6. Bruce-Novoa, *Chicano Authors*, p. 95. The books are *Bajo el sol de Aztlán: 25 soles de Abelardo* (El Paso: Barrio Publications, 1973); *Chicano: 25 Pieces of a Chicano Mind* (Denver: Barrio Publications, 1969); *It's Cold: 52 Cold Thought-Poems of Abelardo* (Salt Lake City: Barrio Publications, 1974).

7. Bruce-Novoa, *Chicano Authors*, p. 101.

8. Tomás Ybarra-Frausto, "Alurista's Poetics: The Oral, The Bilingual, The Pre-Columbian," *Modern Chicano Writers*, p. 117.

9. Ibid., p. 118.

10. Alurista, *Floricanto en Aztlán* (Los Angeles: Chicano Studies Center of UCLA, 1971), p. 40.

11. Ybarra-Frausto, "Alurista's Poetics," p. 127.

12. Alurista, *Nationchild Plumaroja* (San Diego: Toltecas en Aztlán Publications, 1972); the book is not paginated.

13. Ybarra-Frausto, "Alurista's Poetics," p. 128.

14. Alurista, *A'nque* (San Diego: Maize Publications, 1979), p. 6.

15. Ricardo Sánchez, *HechizoSpells,* (Los Angeles: Chicano Studies Center of UCLA, 1976), p. 127.

16. Bruce-Novoa, *Chicano Authors,* p. 75.

17. Luis O. Salinas, *Crazy Gypsy* (Fresno, Calif.: Orígenes Publications, 1970); a later book is *I Go Dreaming Serenades* (San Jose, Calif.: Mango Pulbications, 1979).

18. José Montoya, "El Louie," *Literatura chicana: texto y contexto,* ed. Antonia Castañeda Shular, Tomás Ybarra-Frausto, and Joseph Sommers (Englewood Cliffs, N.J.: Prentice-Hall, 1972), pp. 173–74.

19. See Bruce-Novoa, "The Other Voice of Silence: Tino Villanueva," in *Modern Chicano Writers,* pp. 133–40, for a thoughtful study of Villanueva's poetry.

20. Ibid., p. 140.

21. Pérez has published three books of poetry: *Free, Free at Last* (Denver: Barrio Publications, 1970); *Phases* (n.p., 1971); *The Secret Meaning of Death* (Lubbock, Texas: Trucha Publications, 1972).

22. Terán has published three books of poetry: *Tlacuilos* (Salt Lake City: n.p., 1975); *Trece Aliens* (Austin: Trece Aliens, 1976); *Vida de ilusiones* (Corpus Christi: El Tercer Sol Book Store, 1971).

23. Nephtalí de León, *Chicano Poet* (La Puente: Calif.: Sunburst Enterprises, 1973).

24. Juan Gómez-Quiñones, *5th and Grande Vista* (Staten Island, N.Y.: Editorial Mensaje, 1974).

25. Juan F. Herrera, *Chicano Territory* (published by the author, 1975); *Anti-bicicleta haiku* [Anti-Bicycle Haiku] (San Antonio, Texas: Caracol, 1976).

26. Richard García, *Selected Poetry* (Berkeley, Calif.: Quinto Sol Publications, 1973), p. 2.

27. Rafael Jesús González, *El hacedor de imágenes/The Maker of Images* (San Francisco: Casa Editorial, 1977), p. 31.

28. Ibid., p. 11.

29. See Laura Flores and Mark McCaffrey, "Miguel Méndez: el subjetivismo frente a la historia," *De Colores* 3, no. 4 (1977):51.

30. Miguel Méndez, *Los criaderos humanos (épica de los desamparados) y Sahuaros* (Tucson: Editorial Peregrinos, 1975), p. 2.

31. Raymond Paredes, review of *The Elements of San Joaquín, Minority Voices* 1, no. 2 (Fall 1977):106. Juan Rodríguez, review of *The Elements of San Joaquin, New Scholar* 6 (1976):269.

32. Leroy Quintana, *Hijo del pueblo* (Las Cruces, N.M.: Puerto del Sol, 1976).

33. Angela de Hoyos, *Chicano Poems for the Barrio* (Bloomington, Ind.: Backstage Books, 1975); *Arise Chicano* (Bloomington, Ind.: Backstage Books, 1975); *Selected Poems. Selecciones* (San Antonio: Dezkalzo Press, 1979).

34. Juan Bruce-Novoa, review of *Restless Serpents, Latin American Literary Review* 5, no. 10 (Spring–Summer 1977):153.

35. Dorinda Moreno, *La mujer es la tierra. La tierra de vida* [Woman Is Earth. The Earth of Life] (Berkeley, Calif.: Casa Editorial, 1975).

36. "Untitled," *Con razón corazón* [Rightly Heart] (Notre Dame, Ind.: published by the author, n.d.), p. 17.

37. Cota Cárdenas, "Manifestación tardía," in *Noches despertando inconsciencias* [Nights Awakening Unconsciousness] (Tucson: Scorpion Press, 1975), the book is not paginated.

38. Miriam Bornstein-Somoza, *Bajo cubierta* [Under Wraps] (Tucson: Scorpion Press, 1976), p. 28.

39. Marina Rivera, *Sobra* (San Francisco: Casa Editorial, 1977).

40. Juan José Arreola, *Palabras de mediodía. Noon Words* (Berkeley, Calif.: El Fuego de Aztlán Publications, 1980), p. xx.

41. Ibid., p. 143.

42. James Cody, *Bloodroot* (Austin, Texas: Place of Herons Press, 1977), p. ii.

Selected Bibliography

PRIMARY SOURCES

1. General Bibliographies

Barrios, Ernie, et al. *Bibliografía de Aztlán: An Annotated Chicano Bibliography.* San Diego: Centro de Estudios Chicanos Publications, 1971. The result of the collective efforts of nineteen experts. Comments are thorough and incisive. An abundance of Mexican materials.

Cabello-Argandoña, Roberto, et al. *The Chicana: A Comprehensive Bibliographical Study.* Los Angeles: The Chicano Studies Center of UCLA, 1976. By far the most thorough bibliographical work on the Chicana.

Chavarría, Jesús. "A Precise and a Tentative Bibliography of Chicano History." *Aztlán* 1, no. 1 (Spring 1970):133–41. Author suggests a schematic view of Chicano history based on a basic chronology and divided into different historical periods.

Clark Moreno, Joseph. "A Bibliography of Bibliographies Relating to Studies of Mexican-Americans." *El Grito* 5, no. 2 (Winter 1971–1972):47–79. 457 entries are listed. Not annotated but useful.

Gómez-Quiñones, Juan, and Camarillo, Albert. *Selected Bibliography for Chicano Studies.* Los Angeles: Chicano Studies Center of UCLA, 1975. Not annotated but excellent, especially in history.

Heisley, Michael. *An Annotated Bibliography of Chicano Folklore From the Southwestern United States.* Los Angeles: Center for the Study of Comparative Folklore and Mythology, University of California, 1977. The most complete Chicano folklore bibliography available. Annotations are informative and succinct.

Maciel, David R. *Mexico. A Selected Bibliography of Sources for Chicano Studies.* Los Angeles: Chicano Studies Center of UCLA, 1973. Not annotated but a good reference work for the individual interested in integrating Chicano Studies and Mexican history, literature, art, etc.

Nogales, Luis G., et al. *The Mexican American: A Selected and Annotated Bibliography.* Stanford, Calif.: Stanford University, 1971. Comments are generally thorough and well balanced. Indexes add to the value of this work.

Pino, Frank. *Mexican Americans: A Research Bibliography.* 2 vols. East Lansing: Michigan State University, 1974. Contains over 8,500 entries in 35 different areas. Useful for being comprehensive but lack of annotations makes it somewhat cumbersome to the uninitiated.

Riós, Herminio, and Castillo, Guadalupe. "Toward a True Chicano Bibliography: Mexican-American Newspapers, 1848–1942." *El Grito* 3, no. 4 (Summer 1970):17–24. A valuable resource list of newspapers published in the Southwest and California.

Riós, Herminio. "Toward a True Chicano Bibliography—Part II." *El Grito* 5, no. 4 (Summer 1972):38–47. An addition to earlier bibliography. Includes newspapers published between 1881 and 1958.

Robinson, Barbara J., and Robinson, J. Cordell. *The Mexican-American: A Critical Guide to Research Aids.* Greenwich, Conn.: JAI Press, 1980. Highly recommended reference work. Divided into general works and subject bibliographies. Comments are concise and useful.

Rojas, Guillermo. "Serials Listing: Chicano/Raza Newspapers and Periodicals, 1965–1972." *Hispania* 58 (1975):851–63. Contains 191 titles.

Talbot, Jane, and Cruz, Gilbert R. *A Comprehensive Chicano Bibliography, 1960–1972.* Austin: Jenkins Publishing Company, 1973. Concentrates on works published between 1960 and 1972. Emphasis on literature and education.

Tatum, Charles M. *A Selected and Annotated Bibliography of Chicano Studies.* Lincoln, Nebr.: Society of Spanish and Spanish-American Studies, 1979. Emphasis on the humanities, especially literature; 526 entries.

Teschner, Richard V., et al. *Spanish and English of United States Hispanos: A Critical, Annotated, Linguistic Bibliography.* Arlington, Va.: Center for Applied Linguistics, 1975. Bulk of entries concerns works on Chicano Spanish and English. Thorough and frank annotations.

Trejo, Arnulfo D. *Bibliografía de Aztlán: A Guide to Information Sources.* Detroit: Gale Research Company, 1975. Excellent sections on general reference works and social sciences.

Woods, Richard D. *Reference Materials on Mexican Americans: An Annotated Bibliography.* Metuchen, N.J.: Scarecrow Press, 1976. Annotations on 387 items are informative and concise. Bibliographer does not hesitate to make critical comments.

2. Background and General Interest

Acuña, Rodolfo. *Occupied America: A History of Chicanos.* New York: Harper and Row, 1981. Revaluation of Chicano history following the theory that Chicanos are a colonized people in the United States in a way similar to how other Third World groups are dominated by technologically superior societies.

Barrera, Mario. *Race and Class in the Southwest. A Theory of Racial Inequality.* Notre Dame, Ind.: University of Notre Dame Press, 1979. Focuses on the economic foundations of race and class inequality of Chicanos in the Southwest. Develops a theory as a synthesis of class and colonial analyses.

Burma, John H., ed. *Mexican-Americans in the United States. A Reader.* Cambridge, Mass.: Schenkman Publishing Company, 1970. Forty-one articles by both Anglo and Chicano scholars in several fields ranging from family and religion to prejudice and political behavior.

Camarillo, Albert. *Chicanos in a Changing Society.* Cambridge, Mass.: Harvard University Press, 1979. Focuses on the dynamics of change from Mexican *pueblos* to American *barrios* in Santa Barbara and Southern California from 1848 to 1930. An excellent case study.

Campa, Arthur. *Treasure of the Sangre de Cristo. Tales and Traditions of the Spanish Southwest.* Norman: University of Oklahoma Press, 1963. Stories dating from the sixteenth century.

Castillo, Pedro, and Camarillo, Albert. *Furia y muerte: los bandidos chicanos.* Los Angeles: Chicano Studies Center of UCLA, 1973. A revaluation of the important Chicano "bandits," whom the authors consider social rebels, precursors of today's political militants.

Castro, Tony. *Chicano Power: The Emergence of Mexican America.* New York: Saturday Review Press, 1974. A journalistic account of the entire spectrum of the Chicano Movement. Long and generally balanced treatment of Movement leaders.

Cotera, Marta. *Diosa y Hembra. The History and Heritage of Chicanas in the U.S.* Austin: Information Systems Development, 1976. A historical perspective of the Chicana from pre-Columbian times to the present and a general socioeconomic profile of the Chicana in this country today.

Durán, Livie I., and Bernard, H. Russell, eds. *Introduction to Chicano Studies.* New York: The Macmillan Company, 1973. A fine collection of articles on many aspects of the Chicano experience and background including pre-Columbian heritage, Spanish colonization, loss of Aztlán, health, literature, language, and the migrant experience.

Forbes, Jack D., ed. *Aztecas del Norte: The Chicanos of Aztlán.* Greenwich, Conn.: Fawcett Publications, 1973. Contains sections on the Indian heritage of the Chicano, life in the Southwest, discrimination, and self-identity.

Gómez-Quiñones, Juan. *"On Culture." Revista Chicano-Riqueña* 5, no. 2 (Spring 1977):29–47. A thought-provoking essay dealing with the concept of culture among Chicanos. Emphasizes polemics, definitions, and analysis rather than specific data. Written to generate debate.

González, Rafael Jesús. *"Pachuco*: The Birth of a Creole Language." *Arizona Quarterly* 23, no. 4 (Winter 1967):343–56. Author traces the origin of *pachucos* and their language from the underworld of El Paso dope traffic to the 1943 Los Angeles race riots. Discusses current significance of *pachuco* language.

Griswold del Castillo, Richard. *The Los Angeles Barrio. 1850–1890.* Berkeley: University of California Press, 1979. Traces the emergence of the Los Angeles *barrio* during the period of Americanization of California. Focuses on the bases for modern Chicano communities.

Guzmán, Ralph C. *The Political Socialization of the Mexican–American People.* New York: Arno Press, 1976. Study is organized to examine the dominant external majority group ideologies and the ideological reaction of Chicanos.

Hernández, Carrol A., et al., eds. *Chicanos: Social and Psychological Perspectives.* Saint Louis: The C. V. Mosby Company, 1976. An excellent compendium of scientific and research works on the Chicano.

Hernández Chávez, Eduardo, et al. *El lenguaje de los chicanos* [Chicano Language]: *Regional and Social Characteristics of Language Used by Mexican-Americans.* Arlington, Va.: Center for Applied Linguistics, 1975. Includes several important theoretical and descriptive studies of Chicano Spanish.

Lea, Aurora Lucero-White. *Literary Folklore of the Hispanic Southwest.* San Antonio: The Naylor Company, 1953. Author interprets almost a hundred traditional Spanish plays, ballads, stories, customs, and popular sayings, many from the sixteenth century.

Lewels, Francisco J. *The Use of Media by the Chicano Movement: A Study of Minority Access.* New York: Praeger Publishers, 1974. Focuses on various media strategies developed by the Chicano Movement during the 1960s and early 1970s.

McWilliams, Carey. *North from Mexico: The Spanish-Speaking People of the United States.* New York: Greenwood Press, 1968. Originally published in 1948, this is a seminal work on Chicanos. Author deals with false myths and levels of misinformation about this minority group. Basic reading.

Maciel, David R., ed. *La otra cara de México: El Pueblo Chicano* [The Other Face of Mexico: The Chicano People]. México, D.F.: Ediciones "El Caballito," 1977. Essays by distinguished scholars deal with Chicanos and history, politics, psychology, women's liberation, economics, folklore, education, and literature. In Spanish.

Martínez, Joe L., ed. *Chicano Psychology*. New York: Academic Press, 1978. Mainly Chicano scholars examine several areas of psychology vis-à-vis the Chicano.

Miller, Elaine K. *Mexican Folk Narrative From the Los Angeles Area*. Austin: University of Texas Press, 1973. A compilation of sixty-two legends and twenty traditional tales with a brief preliminary study.

Mora, Magdalena, and Castillo, Adelaida R., eds. *Mexican Women in the United States. Struggles Past and Present*. Los Angeles: Chicano Studies Center of UCLA, 1980. An excellent collection of essays on different aspects of the Chicana including integration and development, sterilization, labor activity, past struggles, and profiles.

Paredes, Américo. *"With His Pistol in His Hand": A Border Ballad and Its Hero*. Austin: University of Texas Press, 1958. A study of the ballad and life of its hero, Gregorio Cortez, a Chicano social rebel of the nineteenth century.

Peñalosa, Fernando. "Toward an Operational Definition of the Mexican-American." *Aztlán* 1, no. 1 (Spring 1970):1–12. Offers a flexible definition of the Chicano and raises several important cultural and historical questions.

Quirarte, Jacinto. *Mexican-American Artists*. Austin: University of Texas Press, 1973. A comprehensive and scholarly study of important figures and trends in Chicano painting. Emphasis is contemporary, but author traces the evolution of Spanish and Mexican art in the Southwest.

Rael, Juan B., ed. *Cuentos españoles de Colorado y Nuevo México* [Spanish Tales from Colorado and New Mexico]. Santa Fe: Museum of New Mexico Press, 1977. A marvelous collection of tales collected from Spanish-speaking farmers, stock raisers, farm laborers, etc., in an area where the oral tradition still thrives.

Romano-V, Octavio I. *Voices: Readings From El Grito*. 2nd ed. Berkeley, Calif.: Quinto Sol Publishers, 1973. A collection of some of the best scholarly articles from the journal *El Grito*. An excellent reader which deals mainly with social science concepts and methodology, bibliographies, penal reform, history, education, and the arts as they relate to the Chicano.

―――. "The Historical and Intellectual Presence of Mexican-Americans." *El Grito* 2, no. 2 (Winter 1969):32–46. A discussion of the importation of important trends of revolutionary and philosophical thought with the emigration of artists and intellectuals from Mexico to the Southwest and its impact on contemporary Chicano culture.

————. "The Anthropology and Sociology of the Mexican-Americans." *El Grito* 2, no. 1 (Fall 1968):13–26. A provocative essay on several major social science studies of Mexican-Americans. Author takes issue with underlying assumptions of these studies.

Sánchez, Rosaura, and Cruz, Rosa Martínez, eds. *Essays on La Mujer.* Los Angeles: Chicanos Studies Center of UCLA, 1977. A collection of well-researched essays on the Chicana with special attention given to health, history, and labor.

Steiner, Stan. *La Raza: The Mexican-Americans.* New York: Harper and Row, 1969. A captivating journalistic account of Chicano history, traditions, and current status.

SECONDARY SOURCES

Note: along with the burgeoning of Chicano literature during the last twenty years there has been a surge in the publication of scholarly criticism of Chicano literary texts. Indicative of the keen interest among critics in this body of literature is the large number of articles and reviews that has appeared in Chicano as well as non-Chicano journals, the creation of special sections at the meetings of regional and national professional associations, and the many dissertations and theses written at major graduate schools. Journals such as *Latin American Literary Review, New Scholar,* and *De Colores* have devoted whole issues to Chicano literary criticism, and several recently published bibliographies deal entirely or partially with this essential critical process of bringing Chicano literature into public awareness.

Chicano literary criticism is in its nascent stage, with critics falling principally into two broad groups: those who are young and relatively inexperienced academics who seem to be searching for their own critical approach or critics already established in their own fields—usually Latin American or Peninsular literature—and who are now applying their generally well-defined critical approaches to a body of literature which still has not been adequately studied either historically or generically.

The following overview of this criticism provides a guide to the bibliographies, anthologies, and individual criticisms most useful in approaching this new and rapidly developing field.

1. Bibliographies

Cárdenas de Dwyer, Carlota. "Chicano Literature: An Introduction and Annotated Bibliography." Austin: Departments of English and

Mexican-American Studies, University of Texas, 1975. Offers comments on over fifty literary works divided into the following categories: autobiography, novel, short story, poetry, Chicano anthologies, and multi-ethnic anthologies.

Eger, Ernestina. *A Bibliography of Criticism of Chicano Literature.* Berkeley, Calif.: Chicano Studies Library, 1982. A monumental work with over a thousand entries. Only criticism on creative genres is included. Emphasis is post-1966. Not annotated but highly recommended as an essential research tool.

Lomelí, Francisco A., and Urioste, Donaldo W. *Chicano Perspectives in Literature. A Critical and Annotated Bibliography.* Albuquerque: Pajarito Publishers, 1976. Long and incisive comments on individual works. Selections are carefully chosen. A valuable research tool.

Rojas, Guillermo. *Toward a Chicano/Raza Bibliography: Drama, Prose, Poetry.* Berkeley, Calif.: Quinto Sol Publications, 1973. The most comprehensive bibliography of pre-1973 creative literature available. Also includes an appendix of Chicano/Raza newspapers and periodicals from 1965–1972.

Tatum, Charles M. "Toward a Bibliography of Chicano Literary Criticism." *Atisbos,* Winter 1976–77, pp. 35–59. A bibliography of the major critical works on Chicano literature published through 1975. Introductory comments to each section.

2. Anthologies

Arellano, Anselmo, ed. *Los pobladores nuevo mexicanos y su poesía, 1889–1950* [The New Mexicans and Their Poetry, 1889–1950]. Albuquerque: Pajarito Publications, 1976. A collection of New Mexican poetry from newspapers.

Cárdenas de Dwyer, Carlota, ed. *Chicano Voices.* Boston: Houghton Mifflin, 1975. Concentrates on Chicano writers productive during the 1960s and early 1970s. Instructor's Guide provides thought-provoking questions and suggestions for discussion.

Castañeda Shular, Antonia; Ybarra-Frausto, Tomás; and Sommers, Joseph. *Literatura chicana: texto y contexto* [Chicano Literature: Text and Context]. Englewood Cliffs, N.J.: Prentice-Hall, 1972. Editors broaden the perspective of Chicano literature by including Mexican and other Latin American works. Reader is organized around three major points: social protest, the essence of Chicano culture, and the migratory experience.

Harth, Dorothy E., and Baldwin, Lewis M., eds. *Voices of Aztlán: Chicano Literature of Today*. New York: New American Library, 1974. Selections are representative of some of the best Chicano poets, novelists, dramatists, and short-story writers.

Kanellos, Nicolás, and Huerta, Jorge A., eds. *Nuevos Pasos. Chicano and Puerto Rican Drama. Revista Chicano-Riqueña* 7, no. 1 (Winter 1979). Contains several important examples of contemporary Chicano drama.

Keller, Gary D., and Jiménez, Francisco, eds. *Hispanics in the United States. An Anthology of Creative Literature*. Ypsilanti, Mich.: Bilingual Review Press, 1980. Includes creative literature by both established and unpublished Chicano writers. Selections are excellent.

Ludwig, Ed, and Santibáñez, James, eds. *The Chicanos: Mexican-American Voices*. Baltimore: Penguin Books, 1971. Contains a wide variety of selections about literature, education, and sociology.

Mestizo. Anthology of Chicano Literature. Albuquerque: Pajarito Publications, 1979. Unique among the newer anthologies for the wide variety of literary forms it contains: theater, short stories, translations, children's stories, parables, folk stories, novel excerpts, essays, prison writings, poetry.

Ortego, Philip D., ed. *We are Chicanos: An Anthology of Mexican-American Literature*. New York: Washington Square Press, 1973. Includes a wide and varied selection of Chicano literature and other readings as well as editor's incisive commentaries. Traces the roots of Chicano literature and offers a valuable perspective.

Paredes, Américo, and Paredes, Raymund, eds. *Mexican-American Authors*. Boston: Houghton Mifflin, 1972. Contains a broad range of literary works, all in translation. Brief introductions to each section are valuable.

Romano-V, Octavio I., ed. *El espejo. The Mirror: Selected Mexican-American Literature*. Berkeley, Calif.: Quinto Sol Publications, 1972. Directed to Chicanos who might profit from seeing their own reflection in the panorama of cultural and social experiences portrayed in the carefully chosen selections. All literary genres are represented.

Salinas, Luis Omar, and Faderman, Lillian, eds. *From the Barrio: A Chicano Anthology*. San Francisco: Canfield Press, 1973. Twenty-seven writers included represent a broad spectrum of Chicano political militancy, literary experience, and age.

Valdez, Luis, and Steiner, Stan, eds. *Aztlán: An Anthology of Mexican-American Literature*. New York: Vantage Books, 1972. Offers a variety of readings ranging from creative literature and essay to selections dealing with the roles of the church and women in contemporary Chicano culture.

Villanueva, Tino, ed. *Chicanos. Antología Histórica y Literaria.* Mexico, D.F.: Fondo de Cultura Económica, 1980. Is unusual in two respects: it is the first work of its kind entirely in Spanish; it brings together a broad sampling of literary and nonliterary works offering a panoramic view of the Chicano people. Highly recommended.

3. Criticism

A. General and Theoretical Studies

Armas, José. "Role of Artist and Critic in the Literature of a Developing Pueblo." *De Colores* 3, no. 4 (1977):5–11. Develops the idea that Chicano literature must be measured and appreciated within its own cultural and historical concept.

Brown, Carl R. V. "Cultural Democracy and Cultural Variability in Chicano Literature." *English Education* 8, no. 2 (Winter 1977):83–89. Author expresses his concern that a culturally democratic atmosphere be created in English classrooms in which minority students may more easily achieve their desired educational goals.

Bruce-Novoa, Juan. "The Space of Chicano Literature." *De Colores* 1, no. 4 (1975):22–42. Perhaps the most persuasive and clearest exponent of the formalist approach to Chicano literature is Juan Bruce-Novoa. Originator of the concept of literary space as applied to Chicano literature, he cautions against the definition of Chicano literature within "limiting characteristics based on narrow criteria" (23). Basing his discussion of literary space upon the concept developed by such contemporary Western thinkers as Mircea Eliade, George Bataille, and the Mexican writer Juan García Ponce, Bruce-Novoa advocates that Chicano writers define and fill their own space rather than limiting themselves to either Mexican or American literary models.

————. *Chicano Authors. Inquiry by Interview.* Austin: University of Texas, 1980. In-depth interviews with fourteen important Chicano writers including Villarreal, Hinojosa, Elizondo, Rivera, Anaya, and Alurista. This valuable source of biographical information as well as writers' insights is basic reading.

Dávila, Luis. "Chicano Fantasy through a Glass Darkly." In *Otros Mundos, Otros Fuegos: Fantasía y realismo mágico en Iberoamérica* (East Lansing: Michigan State University Latin American Studies Center, 1975), pp. 245–48. Although in this general study of the use of fantasy in Chicano literature, Davila does not deal with any specific philosophical theme, he advocates the universalizing of Chicano literature through the use of literary and philosophical themes.

De La Garza, Rudolph O., and Rivera, Rowena. "The Sociopolitical World of the Chicano: A Comparative Analysis of Social Scientific and Literary Perspectives." In Dexter Fisher, ed. *Minority Language and Literature: Retrospective and Perspective.* New York: Modern Language Association, 1977, pp. 42–64. Compares and contrasts the writings of social scientists and literary critics.

Elizondo, Sergio. "Myth and Reality in Chicano Literature." *Latin American Literary Review* 5, no. 10 (Spring-Summer 1977):23–31. Traces the use of the myths of Indian and Hispanic cultures in Chicano literature, showing that while the works of writers such as Alurista, Miguel Méndez, Tomás Rivera, and Rolando Hinojosa are solidly rooted in these myths, they also reflect the social reality from which they come.

García-Girón, Edmundo. "The Chicanos: An Overview." In *Proceedings, Comparative Literature Symposium.* Lubbock: Texas Tech University, 1978. Traces the history of the Chicano people from their Mexican-Indian roots and then discusses the major genres, figures, and trends in Chicano literature since the 1950s.

Gerdes, Dick, and Ulibarrí, Sabine. "Mexican-American Literature and Mexican Literature: A Comparison." In Wolodomyr T. Zyla and Wendell M. Aycock, eds. *Ibero-American Letters in a Comparative Perspective.* Lubbock: Texas Tech University, 1977. A carefully researched and well-documented study that considers a number of theoretical questions regarding the interrelationship of Chicano, Mexican, and American literatures within the larger context of the three interrelated cultures and then examines the various ways in which Chicano and Mexican literatures are similar.

Hinojosa-S., Rolando. "Mexican-American Literature: Toward an Identification." *Books Abroad* 49 (Summer 1975):422–30. An internationally known Chicano writer addresses the questions of the origins of Chicano literature, the area of literature to which it belongs, and its major characteristics. Most informative for the general reader.

Jiménez, Francisco. "Chicano Literature: Sources and Themes." *Bilingual Review* 1, no. 1 (January-April 1974):4–15. A well-documented general introduction to Chicano literature that traces its cultural heritage and delineates its major characteristics.

———. ed. *The Identification and Analysis of Chicano Literature.* New York: Bilingual Press, 1979. An impressive collection of twenty-three critical essays by important literary critics, divided among these subjects: identification of Chicano literature; its origins, background, and development; critical trends, and critical applications. An essential research tool.

Leal, Luis. "Mexican-American Literature: A Historical Survey." *Revista Chicano-Requena* 1, no. 1 (1973):32–44. A significant article since the author does not limit himself to published literature, that is, he does not assume that literature as an artistic phenomenon is a practice of the wealthy, educated classes, but rather an outgrowth of an oral tradition, which, he shows, has its roots in pre-independence Hispanic America. Discusses such popular forms as *romances, corridos,* folk tales, and religious as well as later written forms.

Ortego, Philip D. "The Chicano Renaissance." *Social Casework,* May 1971, pp. 294–307. A well-documented pioneering study that makes a convincing case that in recent years, Chicanos who are more politically and socially aware than before have also become more conscious of their literary heritage. Ortego discusses sensitively and knowledgeably the loss of a literary birthright by Chicanos systematically denied an identity by the shapers of the American literary tradition. (Ortego also wrote a pioneering dissertation on the history of Chicano literature since the sixteenth century, "Backgrounds of Mexican-American Literature," University of New Mexico, 1971.)

Paredes, Raymund A. "The Evolution of Chicano Literature." *MELUS* 5 (1978):71–110. This long account of major historical and literary developments concludes that a sense of ethnicity and a concern for the portrayal of the ethnic experience are essential to the categorization and definition of Chicano literary works.

———. "The Promise of Chicano Literature." In Dexter Fisher, ed. *Minority Language and Literature: Retrospective and Perspective.* New York: Modern Language Association, 1977, pp. 29–41. Contrasts Chicano literature to mainstream American literature and discusses several distinctive qualities of Chicano literature including its rich cultural heritage.

Rivera, Tomás. "Chicano Literature: Fiesta of the Living." *Books Abroad* 49 (Summer 1975):439–52. A respected creative writer defines his own work as a ritual and joyous ceremony of the living. He believes that the most important function of Chicano literature is to be found in the articulation of past experiences, real and imagined.

Robinson, Cecil. *Mexico and the Hispanic Southwest in American Literature.* Tucson: University of Arizona Press, 1977. This carefully documented study contains a short chapter on Chicano literature, but it is more important for documenting the image of the Mexican and the Chicano in American literature.

Rodríguez, Juan. "El florecimiento de la literatura chicana." In David R. Maciel, ed. *La otra cara de Mexico: el pueblo chicano.* México, D. F.: Ediciones "El Caballito," 1977, pp. 349–69. A panoramic article that makes the case that Chicano literature historically and within the preceding decade is a literature of protest against the strictures of Anglo society.

Salazar Parr, Carmen. "Current Trends in Chicano Literary Criticism." *Latin American Literary Review* 5, no. 10 (Spring-Summer 1977):8–15. Categorizes the major trends of Chicano literary criticism into five discernible approaches—ethnogeneric, comparative, Marxist, archetypal, and thematic—and sees Chicano critics polarized into two groups: those who view Chicano literature as reflecting the sociohistorical and cultural circumstances of the Chicano people and those who choose to emphasize the universal values present in Chicano literature.

Salinas, Judy, "The Image of Woman in Chicano Literature." *Revista Chicano-Requeña* 4, no. 4 (Fall 1976):139–48. Discusses how Chicano literature has succeeded in breaking away from the traditional stereotypic depiction of the woman and has presented her rather as a total person.

————. "Recommended Resources for Teaching Chicano Literature and Culture." *Popular Culture Association Newsletter* 6, no. 1 (March 1977):62–75. Excellent introduction to the resources available in the field.

Sánchez, Rosaura. "La crítica marxista: propuestas para la crítica literaria chicana." *Revista Chicano-Requeña* 8, no. 3 (Summer 1980):93–96. Discusses the appropriateness of the application of Marxist criticism to Chicano texts.

Sommers, Joseph. "From the Critical Promise to the Product: Critical Modes and Their Applications to a Chicano Literary Text." *New Scholar* 6 (1977):51–80. This most thorough article first analyzes three general modes of criticism—traditional formalist, culturalist, and historically-based and dialectically formulated—in terms of the adequacy of each as applied to Chicano literature, which, in Sommers' view, can best be understood within specific historical and cultural contexts. In the second part of this thought-provoking essay, he applies each of the three critical modes to Tomás Rivera's ". . . y no se lo tragó la tierra."

————, and Ybarra-Frausto, Tomás, eds. *Modern Chicano Writers: A*

Collection of Critical Essays. Englewood Cliffs, N.J.: Prentice Hall, 1979. A wide range of essays by prominent scholars divided into those providing a conceptual framework and articles on the narrative (with a focus on Tomás Rivera), poetry, and theater (focus on El Teatro Campesino). Highly recommended.

Tatum, Charles, ed. *Latin American Literary Review* 10 (1977). A special issue devoted to Chicano literature.

B. Drama and Theater

Bagby, Beth. "El Teatro Campesino: Interviews with Luis Valdez." *Tulane Drama Review* 11, no. 4 (Summer 1967):70–80. Contains much valuable biographical information on Valdez, who reflects on the early years of El Teatro Campesino.

Bruce-Novoa, Juan, and Valentín, David. "Revolutionizing the Popular Image: Essay on Chicano Theater." *Latin American Literary Review* 10, no. 5 (Spring–Summer 1975):42–50. Dispels the popular conception that Brecht's epic theater influenced El Teatro Campesino.

Donahue, Francis. "Anatomy of Chicano Theater." *San Jose Studies* 3, no. 1 (February 1977):37–48. Author contrasts the militant nature of Chicano theater with the relatively innocuous character of established theater in this country.

Huerta, Jorge A. "Chicano Agit-Prop: The Early Actos of El Teatro Campesino." *Latin American Theater Review* 10, no. 2 (Spring 1977):45–58. Focuses on the first years of El Teatro Campesino during its period of political commitment.

————. "Chicano Theater: A Background." *Aztlán* 2, no. 2 (Fall 1971):63–78. A brief history of pre-Columbian and Hispanic roots of Chicano theater and an analysis of El Teatro Campesino, TENAZ, and the annual theater festivals.

————. *Chicano Theater. Themes and Forms*. Ypsilanti, Mich.: Bilingual Press, 1982. The most complete study available on Chicano theater. Highly recommended as both an introductory work and a research tool.

————. "From the Temple to the Arena: Teatro Chicano Today." In Francisco Jiménez, ed. *The Identification and Analysis of Chicano Literature*. New York: Bilingual Press, 1979. Traces the development of El Teatro Campesino from 1965 to the present. Also discusses TENAZ and other theater groups with emphasis on El Teatro de la Esperanza. Good introduction to Chicano theater.

Jiménez, Francisco. "Dramatic Principles of the Teatro Campesino." *Bilingual Review* 2, nos. 2 and 3 (January–August 1975):98–111. Traces the changes El Teatro Campesino has undergone in terms of objectives, content, form, language, style, technique, funding, and its influence on other *teatros.*

Kanellos, Nicolás. "Chicano Theatre: A Popular Culture Battleground." *Journal of Popular Culture* 13 (1980):541–55. A discussion of popular aspect of contemporary Chicano theater. Author sees *teatro chicano* as a vehicle for sensitizing Mexican-American communities and involving them in various political struggles and cultural concerns.

————. "Fifty Years of Theatre in the Latino Communities of Northwest Indiana." *Aztlán* 7, no. 2 (Summer 1976):255–65. An important survey of both Chicano and Puerto Rican theater groups and their activities in Gary and East Chicago since the 1920s.

————. "El teatro profesional hispánico: orígenes en el suroeste." *La Palabra* 2, no. 1 (Fall 1980):16–24. A discussion of the origins of Chicano professional theater in California in the late-eighteenth and nineteenth century. A seminal study.

Kourilsky, Françoise. "Approaching Quetzalcoatl. The Evolution of El Teatro Campesino." *Performance* 2, no. 1 (Fall 1973):37–46. Probably the best general study of El Teatro Campesino. Focuses on its transition from *acto* to *mito.* Highly recommended.

C. Poetry

Campa, Arthur L. *Spanish Folk-Poetry in New Mexico.* Albuquerque: University of New Mexico Press, 1946. Cites and discusses many examples of *romances, corridos, décimas,* and *canciones.*

Espinosa, Aurelio M. *Romancero de Nuevo México.* Madrid: *Revista de Filología Española-Anejo 58,* 1953. Collection of a wide variety of folksongs popular in New Mexico. Little discussion.

Flores, Laura, and McCaffrey, Mark. "Miguel Méndez: el subjetivismo frente a la historia." *De Colores* 3, no. 4 (1977):46–57. Critical of Méndez's evasion of collective answers to pressing sociohistorical concerns of the Chicano people.

González, Rafael Jesús. "Chicano Poetry/Smoking Mirror." *New Scholar* 6 (1977):127–38. Author comments as an artist who views himself and his fellow poets in the continuous process of perfecting their craft, sharpening the focus of their image, and clarifying their expression.

Hancock, Joel. "The Emergence of Chicano Poetry: A Survey of Sources, Themes, and Techniques." *Arizona Quarterly* 29, no. 1 (Spring 1975):57–73.

Meyer, Doris. "Anonymous Poetry in Spanish-Language New Mexico Newspapers (1880–1900)." *Bilingual Review* 2, no. 3 (September–December 1975):259–75. Discusses examples from late-nineteenth-

century New Mexico newspapers of poetry whose style reflects popular
Spanish verse traditions and whose content and expression reveal some
of the concerns of the New Mexico *hispano* population.

————. "Early Mexican-American Responses to Negative Stereotyping."
New Mexico Historical Review 53, no. 1 (January 1978):75–91. Cites
examples from nineteenth- and early twentieth-century newspapers of
how New Mexico poets combated negative stereotyping by Anglos.

Ortega, Adolfo. "Of Social Politics and Poetry: A Chicano Perspective."
Latin American Literary Review 5, no. 10 (Spring–Summer 1977):32–
41. Author traces the development of contemporary Chicano poetry and
identifies major trends and poets. Concludes that Chicano poets have
neither abandoned the Movement nor limited their poetry to traditional images or to describing social reality.

Ortego, Philip D. "Chicano Poetry: Roots and Writers." *Southwestern
American Literature* 2, no. 1 (Spring 1972):8–24. Stresses the development of a new aesthetic in Chicano poetry based on a glorification of
cultural values and argues that "Chicano poetry is essentially a definition and description of the Chicano people: who are they, what are their
conditions, and what can be predicted for their future" (60).

Lomeli, Francisco A., and Urioste, Donald W. "El concepto del barrio en
tres poetas chicanos: Abelardo, Alurista and Ricardo Sánchez." *De
Colores* 3, no. 4 (1977):22–29. Comprising an element of collective and
individual identity in Chicano poetry, the concept of *barrio* is discussed
in relationship to the work of these three poets. Ortego formulates the
clearest statement on the relationship of cultural characteristics and
values with literature. Central to what Ortego calls the new Chicano
poetics are *chicanismo* and *carnalismo*.

Testa, Daniel. "Alurista: Three Attitudes toward Love in His Poetry."
Revista Chicano-Riqueña 4, no. 1 (Winter 1976):46–55. A sensitive
analysis of the themes of love in the work of this important poet.

Valdés-Fallis, Guadalupe. "Sociolinguistics of Chicano Literature: To-
wards an Analysis of the Role and Function of Language Alternation in
Contemporary Bilingual Poetry." *Point of Contact/Punto de Contacto* 1,
no. 4 (1977):30–39. As title indicates, author focuses on the role and
function of language alternation in bilingual Chicano poetry.

Villanueva, Tino. "Más allá del grito: poesía engagée chicana." *De Colores*
2, no. 2 (1975):27–42. Discusses Chicano poetry within the tradition
of Hispanic *engagée* poetry. Focuses on the distinction between this
poetry and poetry of social protest.

Ybarra-Frausto, Tomás. "The Chicano Movement and the Emergence of
Chicano Poetic Consciousness." *New Scholar* 6 (1977):81–109. Focuses
on the evolution of Chicano poetry within the political context of the

Chicano Movement. Discusses major figures as well as other factors which have contributed to the development of this genre.

D. Prose Fiction

Alarcón, Justo S. "Hacia la nada . . . o la religión en *Pocho.*" *Minority Voices* 1, no. 2 (Fall 1977):17–26. Discusses the role of religion in *Pocho* and how the young protagonist fails to replace religion with positive values.

Brito, Aristeo. "El lenguaje tropológico en *Peregrinos de Aztlán.*" *La Luz* 4, no. 2 (May 1975):42–43. Stresses the way in which the use of tropological language in Miguel Méndez's novel gives unity to a seemingly disorderly presentation of characters and narrative action.

Bruce-Novoa, Juan. "Miguel Méndez: Voices of Silence." *De Colores* 3, no. 4 (1977):63–69. A study of the function of silence in Méndez's work. Author sees the novelist as rescuing the rich Hispanic oral tradition from annihilation in a technologically oriented world.

———. "*Pocho* as Literature." *Aztlán* 7, no. 1 (Spring 1976):65–77. Deals with some fundamental themes in the novel which give it a literary dimension often ignored by critics.

Cantú, Roberto. "Estructura y sentido de lo onírico en *Bless Me, Ultima.*" *Mester* 5, no. 1 (November 1974):27–41. Novel is hailed as a marvel of aesthetic sensibility. Analysis concentrates on the function of dreams in the novel.

Cárdenas de Dwyer, Carlota. "International Literary Metaphor and Ron Arias: An Analysis of *The Road to Tamazunchale.*" *Bilingual Review* 4, no. 3 (September–December 1977):229–33. This study links the novel to important currents in Western literature and focuses on the novelist's portrayal of his characters' inner response to sociohistorical experiences.

Gonzales-Berry, Erlinda. "*Caras viejas y vino nuevo:* Journey through a Disintegrating *Barrio.*" *Latin American Literary Review* 7, no. 14 (Spring–Summer 1979):62–72. Focuses on the novel's structural orientation and correspondence to its basic theme. An excellent critical treatment.

Grajeda, Ralph F. "'. . . *y no se lo tragó la tierra*': Discovery and Appropriation of the Chicano Past." *Hispania* 62, no. 1 (March 1979):71–81. An excellent treatment of the novel's most important themes and techniques. Probably the best critical overview of the work.

Lattin, Vernon E. "The City in Contemporary Chicano Fiction." *Studies in American Fiction* 6, no. 1 (Spring 1978):93–100. Underlying thesis is that Chicano writers are the new romantics in their attitude toward the city viewed antagonistically as a threat to the individual's relation with himself and nature.

————. "The Horror of Darkness. Meaning and Structure in Anaya's *Bless Me, Ultima.*" *Revista Chicano-Riqueña* 6, no. 2 (Spring 1978):50–57. Author discusses the role of the death scenes and the dreams in the protagonist's journey from adolescence to childhood.

Leal, Luis. "Cuatro siglos de prosa aztlanense." *La Palabra* 2, no. 1 (Spring 1980):2–15. An excellent overview of early Chicano prose fiction from the sixteenth through the early twentieth century.

McKenna, Teresa. "Three Novels: An Analysis." *Aztlán* 1, no. 2 (Fall 1970):47–56. An analysis of the structure, styles, and characterization in *Chicano, The Plum Plum Pickers,* and *Tattoo the Wicked Cross.*

Martínez, Eliud. "Ron Arias' *The Road to Tamazunchale*: A Chicano Novel of the New Reality." *Latin American Literary Review* 5, no. 10 (Spring–Summer 1977):51–63. Illustrates the parallels that Martínez believes exist between the Chicano work and recent trends in American, Latin American, and world literature and the arts. He mentions artists as diverse as Carlos Fuentes, Fellini, and Pirandello and artistic trends like surrealism and the new French novel.

Monahan, Sister Helena. "The Chicano Novel: Toward a Definition and Literary Criticism." Ph.D. diss., St. Louis University, 1972. In-depth study of novels by Villarreal, Vásquez, Salas, Rechy, and Barrio.

Ramírez, Arthur. "Estela Portillo: The Dialectic of Oppression and Liberation." *Revista Chicano-Riqueña* 8, no. 3 (Summer 1980):106–14. Focuses on the dialectic embodied in the theme of the oppression of women versus their attempts at achieving liberation. Discusses both Portillo's prose and theatrical work.

Rodríguez, Juan. "Acercamiento a cuatro relatos de '. . . y no se lo tragó la tierra.'" *Mester* 5, no. 1 (November 1974):16–23. Rodríguez sees the work as representing the process of the awakening of the Chicano people, symbolized in the boy-protagonist's self-discovery. As the boy overcomes his superstitious fears of being swallowed up by the earth, so, too, are the Chicano people rejecting their decadent and oppressive religious beliefs which have contributed to their colonial status for decades.

————. "El desarrollo del cuento chicano: del folklore al tenebroso mundo del yo." *Mester* 4, no. 1 (November 1973):25–39. An overview of the major works, figures, and tendencies in the Chicano short story.

————. "The Problematic in Tomás Rivera's '. . . and the earth did not part.'" *Revista Chicano-Requeña* 6, no. 3 (Summer 1978):42–50. Several years after his article in *Mester* (see entry above), Rodríguez reassesses, in part, his earlier conclusions regarding the novel's progressive elements. The critic finds most problematical Rivera's characterization of the Chicanos in the novel (and by extension the Chicano people) as "simple, helpless, backward, timid in the face of oppression. . . ."

Rodriguez Del Pino, Salvador. "La novela chicana de los sententa comentada por sus escritores y críticos." *Bilingual Review* 4, no. 3 (September–December 1977):240–44. A summary of a series of television interviews with Chicano novelists and prominent literary critics on a broad range of topics regarding the novel.

Rogers, Jane. "The Function of the *La Llorona* Motif in Rudolfo Anaya's *Bless Me, Ultima.*" *Latin American Literary Review* 5, no. 10 (Spring–Summer 1977):64–69. Drawing on *The Odyssey* for an apt comparison, Rogers shows how the "weeping woman" motif functions in Anaya's novel on both the mythological and realistic levels, as an integral part of the life of the young protagonist, who, symbolizing both Christ and Odysseus, leaves the security of his home to explore the world of unknown experiences.

Rojas, Guillermo. "La prosa chicana: tres epígonos de la novela mexicana de la revolución." *Cuadernos Americanos* 44 (May–June 1975):198–209. Examines novels by Rivera, Hinojosa, and Méndez which best continue the tradition of the novel of the Mexican Revolution.

Saldívar, Ramón. "A Dialectic of Difference: Toward a Theory of the Chicano Novel." *MELUS* 6, no. 3 (1979):73–92. Examining several important Chicano novels (including ". . . y no se lo tragó la tierra"), Saldívar discovers in them a common "ideology of difference," which emerges from their paradoxical impulse toward revolutionary deconstruction and toward the production of meaning. He concludes that the Chicano novel, which opts for conflict rather than resolution, for difference over similarity, "is thus not so much the *expression* of this ideology [of difference] as it is a *production* of that ideology" (88).

Segade, Gustavo. "*Peregrinos de Aztlán:* Viaje y Laberinto." *De Colores* 3, no. 4 (1977):58–62. Explores Méndez's use of the journey and the labyrinth—two common symbolic systems in world literature, especially the epic—to represent the contemporary labyrinth of the Mexican/American border reality.

Smith, Norman D. "Buffalos and Cockroaches: Acosta's *Siege of Aztlán.*" *Latin American Literary Review* 5, no. 10 (Spring–Summer 1977):86–97. Discusses the protagonist's search for his identity as well as the novelistic techniques that Acosta employs in his two novels.

Tatum, Charles M. "Contemporary Chicano Prose Fiction: A Chronicle of Misery." *Latin American Literary Review* 1, no. 2 (Spring 1973):7–17. A survey of the prose work of several important Chicano writers, with an emphasis on the social dimension in their works.

————. "Contemporary Chicano Prose Fiction: Its Ties to Mexican Literature." *Books Abroad* 49 (Summer 1975):432–38. More contemporary in focus than the article listed above, this one addresses the possible relationship of a single genre, Chicano prose fiction, to Mexican literature. Without attempting to make a case for influences, the author illustrates some similarities between a post-revolutionary Mexican writer and a Chicano counterpart; for example, Juan Rulfo and Tomás Rivera.

————. [Review of] *"Klail City y sus alrededores,* by Rolando Hinojosa." *Latin American Literary Review* 5, no. 10 (Spring–Summer 1977):165–69. A brief study of the novel's techniques and themes as well as some commentary on *Estampas del valle y otras obras.*

————. "The Sexual Underworld of John Rechy." *Minority Voices* 3. no. 1 (Fall 1979):47–52. A general study of homosexuality and alienation in Rechy's novels.

Testa, Daniel. "Extensive/Intensive Dimensionalty in Anaya's *Bless Me, Ultima." Latin American Literary Review* 5, no. 10 (Spring–Summer 1977):70–78. A treatment of the novel's underlying symbolic discourse which gives the work its complexity and artistic excellence.

Valdés-Fallis, Guadalupe. "Metaphysical Anxiety and the Existence of God in Contemporary Chicano Fiction." *Revista Chicano-Requeña* 3, no. 1 (Winter 1975):26–33. This is the most comprehensive study focusing on philosophical themes in Chicano fiction. Valdés-Fallis grapples with the thorny and often controversial question of universality versus social commitment in Chicano literature.

Index